THE SOUTH MEETING HOUSE, BUILT 1772
Bay State Hall, 1854. The Armory, Town Hall, and popularly known as "The Carver Light House."

History
of the
Town of Carver
Massachusetts

HISTORICAL REVIEW
1637 TO 1910

Henry S. Griffith

HERITAGE BOOKS
2011

HERITAGE BOOKS
AN IMPRINT OF HERITAGE BOOKS, INC.

Books, CDs, and more—Worldwide

For our listing of thousands of titles see our website
at
www.HeritageBooks.com

A Facsimile Reprint
Published 2011 by
HERITAGE BOOKS, INC.
Publishing Division
100 Railroad Ave. #104
Westminster, Maryland 21157

Originally published
New Bedford, Mass.
E. Anthony & Sons, Inc., Printers
1913

— Publisher's Notice —
In reprints such as this, it is often not possible to remove blemishes from the original. We feel the contents of this book warrant its reissue despite these blemishes and hope you will agree and read it with pleasure.

International Standard Book Numbers
Paperbound: 978-0-7884-1613-2
Clothbound: 978-0-7884-8766-8

PREFACE

In the course of a conversation about three years ago I was urged to write the history of Carver. It was pointed out that the character of our population is rapidly changing, that among the new residents there are no ties reaching back to Old Colony ancestors, and that should any one undertake to write the story a few years hence there would be no sentiment among the people that would insure its publication. At the present time, too, there are descendants of Carver scattered between the two oceans and these might appreciate such a memento of their New England ancestors. And acting upon the above suggestion much of the data had been gathered when at the annual town meeting in 1912, Frank E. Barrows, Donald McFarlin and myself were delegated to arrange for its publication.

One engaged in historical research appreciates the importance of comprehensive records. Our earliest society records are not complete. Many of them were first kept on loose leaves which later were copied in books, while our ancestors have scarcely left a mark concerning the incidents which so strongly appeal to our fancy. The earlier records were unsigned, in the case of churches they were kept by the ministers, and the 19th century was well under way when the practice of making clerk signed records came into vogue. In some of the records double dating was not invariably practiced, and where I have used single dates during that period the Julian calendar date is to be understood.

Our town records are in a good state of preservation, the older volumes having been preserved by the Emory process. The first books contain vital records copied from the records of Plympton, but generally speaking our vital records begin with the year of the town's incorporation. We have duplicates of the first two volumes of the town records made by Ira Murdock.

The Precinct records in the custody of the Congregationalist Church are not in good condition, and these with the records of the Proprietors of the South Meeting House and the first volume of the Baptist Society records, in consideration of their historical value, should be carefully preserved. Unfortunately the church records of Reverends Campbell and Howland of the first church are missing, and this removes from view the baptisms from 1732 to 1804 (the period of their greatest value) and doubtless other facts that would be of interest. The records of the Proprietors of the Congregationalist Church (1823) and of the Baptist Church (1824) are also missing with whatever of interest they may have contained.

As there was no attempt at a systematic record of vital statistics previous to 1842, the gravestone inscriptions are important and the date of death of some who were not thus honored is lost. The writer, assisted by young friends, copied these inscriptions in 1900, and these transcribed in a book, form a valued record now in the possession of the town. A few mistakes were made in the process of copying, but in view of the fact that the inscriptions are fast becoming indecipherable on some of the older stones, this record will preserve some dates that otherwise might be lost.

The compulsory return of vital statistics was not required until 1850, and to make up for the deficiency the State officials have entered upon a policy that will ultimately put the State Library in possession of copies of the older records and also insure their publication. The writer furnished the State with a copy of the vital records of Carver, and this copy, with additions from the cemetery record above referred to and from private records, has been published, thus relieving this work of anything in the line of genealogy.

In a work of this kind mistakes are easy to make. To take the imperfect records and evolve a complete story without an omission, a repetition or a contradiction requires a mind more proficient in the art of deduction, and with more patience than the writer happens to possess. The historian of a community rich in traditional legends who in the course of his researches becomes acquainted with the social and industrial past, and who is thus in a position to compare the painted picture with the barren field of history, must feel a sense of dissatisfaction with his work. Especially is this true when we attempt to picture the social conditions of the first settlers. We know their experiences as pioneers were replete with dangers and romances, the simple narration of which would make a thrilling story, but when we ask of departed time a revelation of her secrets our question re-echoes across a barren waste.

I fancy I see the smiles of satisfaction—if not of vanity—on the faces of the residents of the first half of the eighteenth century as they review the progress they had made not only in material things, but in the realm of civil and religious liberty. And if we compare that record with that of some of their European contemporaries we may concede their right to boast over their achievements. And when I review the progress made in the Colony from the ascension of William and Mary to the middle of the succeeding century I am forced to hold the opinion that we gained more in the cause of liberty by the English than we did by the American Revolution.

Unfortunately local records are silent regarding the personnel of the Revolutionary Army and the only glimpse we get of the individual records of our patriotic sires is in the more or less conflicting rolls on file in the Archive Department at the State House. These rolls have been classified, indexed and published, and anyone seeking the record of an ancestor is referred to these volumes. In this story I have only sought to give a general idea of what our mother town did in the cause of national independence. My list is so unsatisfactory that I feel like apologizing for it, and the danger of doing an injustice to some enthusiastic patriot impels me to refer to the publication mentioned above as an appeal from my efforts. There was no dividing line between the two Precincts so far as the Revolution is concerned, and it would be an endless genealogical task to make a separate list of the soldiers who resided in the South Precinct, so I have made a list of all who served to the credit of the town of Plympton. In the enthusiastic march to dislodge the enemy from the town of Marshfield, fruitless except as an indication of the unanimous sentiment of the town, those militia men who served under Captains William Atwood and Nathaniel Shaw were mainly from the South Precinct. I suspect the soldier who appears on the rolls as Swanzea Murdock may have been a negro known locally as Swanzea. He was employed by Bartlett Murdock, and with only one name of his own his posterity will excuse him for borrowing that of his employer in such a patriotic cause. The various ways of spelling names as they appear on the rolls is a handicap, and I have followed the modern way of spelling.

At the time this is written there appears no way of obtaining a reliable list of the soldiers who served in the second war with Great Britain, in consequence of which those veterans are denied their place in this story. The State has begun the task of rescuing these names from their tomb in the War Department at Washington, and while the Adjutant General of the State has completed his part the publication will not be made before this work is published.

In my list of volunteers of the Civil War I have included two names who, while residents of the town, did not fill a quota of Carver. Albert T. Shurtleff, the first to enlist, joined a Rhode Island regiment, and Ezra Pearsons enlisted to the credit of the State of Maine.

I express gratitude to the memory of the late Lewis Pratt, who gave me so much from a good memory relating to the old time furnaces; also to the late William T. Davis, an authority on Old Colony history. In my story of the natural conditions of the town I give credit to Miss Helena McFarlin, who furnished me with a list of the birds and wild flowers.

H. S. G.

South Carver, June 19, 1913.

A VIEW OF SAMPSONS POND

CONTENTS

	Page
Natural Conditions	1
Indians	13
The First Speculators	19
A Few Early Laws	31
The First Separation	43
Early Settlers	51
The South Precinct of Plympton	65
Plympton in the Revolution	91
The Congregationalist Church	111
The South Meeting House	121
The Second Separation	135
The Temperance Movement	155
The Baptist Church	163
The Methodist Church	175
The Advent Christian Church	181
The Union Society	185
Furnaces and Foundries	191
The Cranberry Industry	217
Military History	223
Carver in the Rebellion	231
War of 1812–14	241

HISTORY OF CARVER

	Page
Post Offices	243
Small Pox	244
Cemeteries	245
Population	250
Miscellaneous Industries	251
Chronological Events	257
Landmarks	265
Biographical Sketches	271
Precinct Officers	293
Parish Officers	302
Church Members	305
State and County Officers	326
Town Officers	328
Index of Names	341

ILLUSTRATIONS

	Facing Page
The South Meeting House . Frontispiece	
A View of Sampsons Pond	viii
A View of East Head Woods	8
Barretts Pond	16
A Corner on Hemlock Island	24
The Shurtleff Homestead	26
The Sturtevant House	30
Residence of Finney Brothers	32
The Griffith Homestead	40
The Waterman House	48
The Carver Primary Schoolhouse	50
The Wenham Schoolhouse	54
The Popes Point Schoolhouse	58
The Bates Pond Schoolhouse	62
The South Carver Schoolhouse	72
Benjamin W. Robbins	80
The Second Church	88
The Congregational Church	96
Hon. Benjamin Ellis	106
Huit McFarlin	110
Henry Sherman	112

	Facing Page
The Town Hall	120
The North Carver Schoolhouse	122
The High School Building	126
Thomas Hammond, Jr.	136
The Baptist Church	144
The Hammond Homestead	152
The Methodist Church	160
The Methodist Chapel	168
The Advent Christian Church	176
The Union Church	178
Lewis Pratt, Jr.	182
The Charlotte Furnace Building	186
Hon. Peleg McFarlin	190
Hon. Jesse Murdock	200
Eben D. Shaw	208
Federal Screen House	210
Section of Federal Village	214
A Section of the Wankinco Bog	218
Albert T. Shurtleff	222
Capt. William S. McFarlin	224
Maj. Thomas B. Griffith	232
The Soldiers Monument	234
Thomas Southworth	238
Lakenham Cemetery	248

ILLUSTRATIONS

	Facing Page
Harrison G. Cole	256
George P. Bowers	264
Horatio A. Lucas	272
A Section of East Head Game Preserve	274
Andrew Griffith	278
William Savery	280
Mrs. Rosa A. Cole	288
Dea. Thomas Cobb	296
John Maxim, Jr.	304
Mrs. Priscilla Jane Barrows	312
Ellis H. Cornish, M. D.	320

History of Carver

HISTORY OF CARVER

NATURAL CONDITIONS

The town of Carver, comprising about twenty-four thousand acres, is located midway between tidewater in Plymouth and tidewater in Wareham. The centre of the town would fall near 41 degrees 52 minutes north latitude while a meridian 70¾ degrees west from Greenwich would intersect the parallel near the centre of the town. The Weweantic river separates a short section in the southwest from Middleboro, the Wankinco about the same distance of the southeastern border from Plymouth, otherwise the town has no natural boundaries. Generally speaking the town is bounded on the north by Plympton, on the east by Kingston and Plymouth, on the south by Plymouth and Wareham, and on the west by Wareham and Middleboro.

The northern and southern sections are rolling interspersed with ponds and swamps with the central section mainly level. Several thousand acres in the southeastern section is made up of barren hills, sterile except for scattering scrub oaks and pines and occasional fertile spots. The conditions surrounding the swamps are peculiarly adapted to cranberry culture, and the upland, worthless in a commercial sense, is noted for its scenic beauty. The most desirable land for agricultural purposes is in the north section where the earliest settlements were made.

While the town is generally noted for its sandy soil, there are marks of a glacial drift and occasional spots of rich deposits. Stretching across the central section in a southeasterly course a windrow of boulders separates the better soil of the north from the sandy soil of the south. The widest deviation in this windrow is in the territory from Sampson's pond to Cedar brook, which is made up of bowlders. One extension which has acquired the sobriquet of The Ridge protrudes from the main drift in a southerly direction and separates the pond from the large cedar swamp which appears to be in the same depression. Tillson's brook, which unites the cedar swamp with the pond, makes its connection around the southerly end of the ridge.

Three streams, dignified in local history by the name of rivers, form the basis of the town's drainage system, viz.: The Winatuxet, the Weweantic and the Wankinquoah. Lakenham brook, running northerly from its source in Lakenham pond, in its junction with Mahutchett brook, gives rise to the Winatuxet. This river is also fed by Annasnapet brook, which flows westerly across the north end of the town. In turn this brook is swelled by two smaller streams, Huntinghouse brook and another to the east, both running northerly and emptying their contents into Annasnapet brook.

The Weweantic rising at Swan Hold and flowing across the town in a southwesterly course, with its great tributary, the Crane brook, drains the larger half of the town. Wenham brook, which flows from Wenham pond southerly; Horseneck brook, flowing from the Centre swamp easterly; Causeway brook, flowing from a swamp on the Wenham road southerly; Beaver Dam brook, flowing from Beaver Dam pond westerly; Cedar brook, running westerly from the cedar swamp; two brooks flowing out of New Meadows westerly; a blind brook flowing westerly from No-Bottom pond, and Atwood brook, flowing southwesterly from Bates' pond, all add to the majesty of the Weweantic.

With the exception of East Head, West Head and the swamps on the Wareham-Carver town line, the Crane brook drains the territory south of the cedar swamp, including the southerly section of the swamp itself. This stream flows from Federal ponds southwesterly, pouring its accumulated waters into the Weweantic just before it leaves the town. Dunham's pond sends its surplus water down the Crane brook either directly through a short brook that connects its easterly shore, or indirectly through Tillson's brook, which flows from the cedar swamp southwesterly into Sampson's pond. This pond also receives water from the New Meadows country through a brook that crosses Rochester road east of Union church, and sends its surplus to the Crane brook through its southerly outlet, Sampson's brook.

Cedar pond and Clear pond are closely related and connect with Crane brook through the westerly outlet, more or less blind, that makes through the swamp southwesterly. Indian brook, rising in Indian swamp and running southerly, fed itself by a brook running from near the southwesterly point of Sampson's pond, adds to the waters of the Crane brook.

East Head brook, running from East Head and West Head brook, running from White springs, give rise to the Wankinquoah, which drains the swamps in that region and empties its waters in Tihonet pond. The swamps in the extreme southerly section of the town also drain into Tihonet pond through Mosquito brook. Rose brook has its source in these swamps, but drains but a small part of them.

Cooper's, John's, Triangle, Gould's Bottom and Barrett's ponds have no outlets.

The large area of the town, sparsely populated, with numerous ponds, streams and jungles, unite to make the territory a favored breeding ground of the fish, animals and birds that thrive in this latitude.

Fish formed a staple article of food for the earlier settlers and in the days of the first residents the industry developed three fish weirs. Sampson's and Doty's ponds were breeding places for herrings until their egress and ingress was closed by the development of manufacturing along the Weweantic river. These ponds were also stocked with white perch, a valued food fish until the species became land locked, since which it has so far degenerated as to become nearly worthless. During the latter half of the 19th century some of the ponds were stocked with black bass and that species has become the most valuable for food. The list of fresh water fish that have always thrived would include pickerel, red perch, shiners, white fish, roaches, hornpouts and brook trout.

Deer, the largest of our wild animals, find favorable conditions. Through persistent hunting they were exterminated in the latter half of the 19th century but under the protection of the law they regained a foot hold and the opening days of the 20th century found them so numerous as to be actually depredatious.

The first settlers found beavers and wolves in abundance. The former were highly prized for commercial reasons and quickly exterminated while war was declared on the latter also for well known reasons and they too disappeared. Foxes and skunks have ever been regarded with suspicion and while they have never had the protection of the law they still thrive. Being valued for their furs there is a double motive for destroying them and the persistency in which they hold their own is creditable to their cunning. Other animals which are valued for their furs, but which appear to be disappearing are otters, minks, raccoons, muskrats and weasels.

The woods once teemed with hare and rabbits, but these are liable to be extinct. The destruction of their breeding places in the process of cranberry bog construction is the main cause of the extermination of this game, with increasing population, forest fires and persistent hunting as contributing factors. Gray squirrels, red squirrels, and chipmunks are undiminished.

The first settlers declared war on crows, crow blackbirds and red birds (brown thrashers) in the interests of their corn fields, but in spite of these inconveniences the birds are with us yet and as we get better acquainted with them we rejoice that they have not been exterminated.

Following is a list of the birds of the town:

Land Birds

American cross bills
Blue birds
Blue jays
Bobolinks
Brown creepers
Brown thrashers
Cat birds
Cedar waxwings
Chats
Chebecs
Chewinks (tohee)
Chickadees
Chimney swifts
Cow birds
Crows
Cuckoos
Doves
Gold finches (yellow birds)
Golden crowned kinglets
Grackles (purple and bronze)
Hawks
Humming birds
Indigo birds
Juncos
King birds
King fishers
Martins
Maryland yellowthroat
Meadow larks
Night Hawks
Nut hatches (red breasted and white breasted)
Orioles
Ospreys
Ovenbirds
Owls
Pewees
Phebe birds
Purple finches (linnets)
Quails
Rails
Red winged blackbirds

Redstarts
Robins
Rose breasted grosbecks
Ruffed grouse
Sand pipers
Scarlet tanagers
Shrikes (butcher birds)
Snow buntings
Sparrows
Swallows
Thrushes
Vieros
Warblers (myrtle, chestnut sided, etc.)
Whip-poor-wills
Woodpeckers
Wrens

Waders

Bitterns
Plovers
Blue herons
Snipe
Yellow legs

Water Birds

Black ducks
Grebes
Loons
Mallard ducks
Wood ducks

Being located on the line between Labrador and the South, and having ample resting and feeding places in the lakes, we are annually visited by migrating birds. When a storm is approaching from the northeast myriads of gulls retreat inland and our lakes are made lively by these playful habitants of the deep. The list of birds which we can claim only as transient visitors in addition to gulls and terns, would include:

Blue wing teal
Brant
Coots
Cormorants (shags)
Gadwalls (gray duck)
Geese
Golden eye (whistlers)
Green wing teal
Mergansers
Pintail
Red head ducks
Shelldrakes
South Southerlys (Old Squaws)
Spoonbills
Widgeon

Crows, blue jays, juncos, meadow larks, quails, ruffed grouse, chickadees, woodpeckers, bald eagles, tree sparrows and occasional robins are year around birds.

The town is noted for its growth of lumber, soft pine, cedar and oak being staple products down to the 20th century, and it is evident this growth must have been gigantic before its settlement. In digging ditches in the process of bog construction charcoal has been found imbedded three feet below the surface, indicating the growth of timber and also the prevalence of forest fires in pre-historic times. In point of commercial value the oak takes third place being preceded only by white pine and cedar. South Meadow cedar swamp comprising about one thousand acres; Doty's swamp, New Meadows swamp and other smaller patches were dense with a virgin growth in memory of those now living, while many acres of original growth of white pine has been cut in the memory of the present generation. The early records mention large whitewood trees, but this species, if it has prevailed in the past, has become extinct. The following species have been and are now thriving:

White pine, cedar, oaks, pitch pine, maples, hemlock, white birch, black birch, hornbeam, poplar, cherry, locust, sassafras, elm, willow and beech.

The attractions of nature are perpetual. No snow so deep that the pines and cedars do not wave their green branches above it; no winter so bleak as to hide the beauties of the holly, the laurels and winterberries. The scrub-oak hills of

A VIEW OF EAST HEAD WOODS
Burned Country

NATURAL CONDITIONS

sand are famous for trailing arbutus that appears even before the snow has left the valleys, and in no clime or soil do the water lilies, sabbatias, goldenrods and asters reach a more perfect state of development. In the season the swamps are fragrant with the blossoms of the honeysuckle and sweet pepper bush, and the variegated autumn leaves clothe the driveways and hills with indescribable beauty.

That this town has its share of the decorations that give inspiration to country scenery, the following list, still incomplete, may testify:

White

Alder (smooth)
Arrowhead (sagittaria)
Arrow woods
Asters
Baneberry
Bayberry
Bearberry (mountain cranberry)
Beech plum
Black alder (winterberry)
Blackberry
Black huckleberry
Blueberry
Bunchberry
Button bush
Cat brier
Checkerberry (wintergreen)
Choke berry
Cinquefoil
Clover
Creeping snowberry
Dangleberry
Dodder
Elderberry
Evening lychris
False Solomon's seal
False spikenard
Floating heart
Gall of the earth
Gold thread
Goldenrod
Holly
Indian pipe
Inkberry
Lady's tobacco
Lady's tresses
Leather leaf
Mayweed
Meadow rue
Meadow sweet
Mountain holly

Mountain laurel
Night flowering catch fly
Ox-eyed daisy
Partridge vine
Pearl everlasting
Plantain
Queen Anne's lace
Rattlesnake plantain
Rattlesnake root
Shad bush (wild pear)
Shinleaf
Snapwood
Spotted wintergreen
Star flower
Swamp honeysuckle (azalia)
Swamp huckleberry
Sweet everlasting
Sweet fern
Sweet gale
Sweet pepper bush
Thoroughwort
Trillium (painted)
Turtle head
Viburnum
Virgin's bower
Water cress
Water lily
White fringed orchis
White violet
Wild lily of the valley
Wild sarsaparilla
Wild strawberry
Wind flower (anemone)
Wintergreen (pipsissiwa)
Withwood
Yarrow

Yellow

Bellwort
Black eyed Susan
Butter and Eggs
Buttercup
Cinquefoil
Common St. John's wort
Cynthia (dwarf dandelion)
Dandelion
Fall Dandelion
Evening primrose
Gerardia
Golden aster
Golden ragwort
Goldenrod
Hawk weed
Hedge hyssop
Horned bladderwort
Indian cucumberroot
Jewel weed
Loose strife
Marsh marigold
Moth mullein
Mullein
Mustard
Poverty grass
Purslane
Stick tight
Sundrop
Tansy

NATURAL CONDITIONS 11

Toad flax
Wild indigo
Wild parsnip
Wild sunflower
Wild yellow wood sorrel
 (oxalis)

Witch hazel
Yellow clover
Yellow eyed grass
Yellow pond lily
Yellow Star grass

Pink

Amphibeous knot weed
Arbutus
Arethusia
Bouncing Bet
Burdock
Bush clover
Calopogon
Clover
Common milkweed
Cranberry
Dogbane
Fireweed
Hog peanut
Joe-pye-weed
Knotweed (polyganella)
Lions heart
Marsh St. Johnswort
Meadow Beauty
Milkwort

Moccasin flower
Motherwort
Musk Mallow
Coreopsis
Fleabane
Pogonia
Purple geradia
Rhodora
Round leaved mallow
Sabbatia (sea pink)
Sheep laurel
Steeple bush
Sundew
Sweet briar rose
Swamp loose strife
Tick trefoil
Wild rose
Yarrow

Blue or Purple

Aster
Bird-foot violet
Blue curls
Blue eyed grass
Bluets
Blue flag (Iris)

Blue toad flax
Blue Vervain (verbena)
Catnip
Common speedwell
Cow vetch
Common violet

Gill-over-the-ground
Indian tobacco
Iron weed
Lobelia (water)
Lupine
Mad dog's skull cap
Meadow violet
Pennyroyal

Peppermint
Pickerel weed
Robin's plantain
Self heal
Sheep's bit
Spiderwort
Thistle
Venus' looking glass

Red

Cardinal flower
Pitcher plant

Wood lily

Green or Greenish White

Cow wheat
Dock
Grape (wild)
Horse radish
Poison sumach
Weeds:
  Carpet weed
  Chick weed
  Ground cherry
  Goosefoot
  Pig weed
  Pin weed

Poison ivy
Staghorn
Virginia creeper (woodbine)
Pipewort
Sandwort
Trumble weed
Velvet weed
Wild pepper grass

Miscellaneous

Butterfly weed
Cypress spurge
Cat-tail
Ground nut
Hoary pea
Jack-in-the-pulpit
Lousewort

Liveforever
Rabbits foot clover
Scouring rush
Sweet flag
Skunk cabbage
South Sea water bubble
Trumpet honeysuckle

INDIANS

Unfortunately our main source of knowledge of our predecessors on this soil is founded on tradition, which is often a libelous story, for the human mind is not apt to minimize an event that struck terror to its infant conceptions. No voice of the Pawtuxets comes down to us in literature, none of their architecture stands as a monument to their art, yet we have many silent reminders of their handiwork. A walk around the shores of our lakes, or across some newly plowed field, is frequently rewarded by some arrow head, pestle or war club upturned from its resting place. Thousands of these mementos are scattered through our homes and too often perhaps not fully appreciated for these are the only tokens that link our civilization with the lives of the children of nature that once inhabited this region.

And when we read of the cruelties of the Indians it is well to remember that this is the white man's story. The red man is silent. And lest we be unduly impressed with our own case we may recall that in 1698 the white man placed a bounty of fifty pounds on the scalp of an adult Indian and ten pounds on the scalp of a child under ten. Five years later the sport of hunting and scalping children was abolished, while the practice of capturing them alive and selling them as slaves was substituted. Thus was the process of exterminating an inferior race turned to a source of profit to its superiors.

There were no Indians permanently located in the limits of the future town of Carver in 1620 or thereafter although roving bands strolled through the region occasionally. This rendered settlements hazardous and one Ephraim Tinkham who had squatted near Lakenham in 1650 was warned that unless he returned within the danger line he could expect no protection from the Colony.

After the close of King Philip's war Indians who settled here, with certain exceptions, enjoyed the rights conferred upon the whites, and their rights were looked after by Commissioners appointed by the Governor. In 1702-03 the town of Plymouth voted a grant of land to Samuel Sonnett, an Indian, and his wife, Dorothy. This land, forming the basis of the Indian lands in Carver, was located on the southerly side of Sampson's pond, and bounds and measurements not being definite, it must have included considerably more than the area named, for it took in all the land between the Casey swamp and the pond, and extended from the Indian lot, so-called, to Sampson's brook. The bounds were more definitely established two years later by Surveyor William Shurtleff. The only incumbrance was the general law providing that land of Indians should not be sold without a permit from the General Court. Under the conditions of the vote the grantee and his heirs were guaranteed the right to fish in the ponds and streams and to gather tar and turpentine on the common lands.

The Seipets appear in town a few years later, possibly marrying into the Sonnett family. Bartlett Murdock, who had inherited the farm on the east side of the pond, employed one of these Seipet boys, who seems to have been endowed with the traditional cunning of his race. Among the anecdotes that illustrate the character of the boy is one that concerns the time when the South Meeting house was erected. The building had been framed and raised, when Murdock was horrified one early morning on beholding his Indian boy climbing carelessly over the skeleton. Ascending to the plate by the ladder, he walked up one of the outside rafters, thence the entire length of the ridge-pole, and down another rafter to the plate, from which he skipped nimbly to the ground. On another occasion young Seipet was sent out on an early morning to bring in a yoke of oxen for the day's work. His return was not expected promptly, for cattle ran at large and often strayed a long ways from the clearing; but not returning late in the afternoon, Murdock became alarmed and started out on horseback to learn the fate of his trusted employee. After covering a long distance he met Seipet returning with his cattle and with a good excuse for his tardiness. He had traced the oxen as far as Cranebrook pond, a distance of five miles, and as the ground was crossed and counter-crossed by cattle tracks, the master asked how he had followed the track, for in Murdock's eye there was no difference between the tracks of his own oxen and those of his neighbors. Seipet expressed surprise at the ignorance of his employer, as he replied: "You think Seipet not know his own ox tracks?"

In 1780 this land was owned solely by the Seipets, and the Plymouth County Commissioners were authorized to sell as much of it as was necessary to pay the debts and give a comfortable support to Desire Seipet in her old age. The sale, effected in 1783, transferred a large part of the tract, and that on which the village of South Carver now stands, to Lieut. Thomas Drew. In 1810 Launa Seipet, also an aged woman, resided on the reservation. By special act of the General Court she was placed in the care of the Selectmen of Carver, and for her support another section of the Sonnett land was sold to Benjamin Ellis. This sale included what was left of the Indian land north of Bodfish Bridge road. It would appear that she was the last survivor of the family, and residing with her were two daughters, Betsey and Hannah. Betsey married, but died childless. Hannah married Augustus Casey, with whom she lived on the old clearing, where were born and reared Frank, Thomas, William, John, Joseph Young, Augustus Green, Hannah (married Turner), Betsey (married Phillips), and Sarah (married Jackson). Joseph and Thomas enlisted and saw service in the navy in the Civil war.

For the aid of some of the Casey heirs other tracts have been sold from the Sonnett land, until

BARRETTS POND
From the Turner Field

about forty acres remain, and that now known as "The Casey Place."

On the name our predecessors gave this region we can only speculate, for students and interpreters of Indian language differ. By one it is given as Warkinguag; by another as Mahootset.

While we have a few Indian monuments in the way of landmarks, their meaning is veiled in mystery, and our efforts towards an interpretation of them leaves us still unrewarded regarding the individual experiences of the red men who tilled these grounds before us. Weweantic is interpreted as a wandering stream; Winatuxett, the new found meadows; Quitiquas, the island place; Annasnapet, the small shell brook; Swan Hold, possibly a corruption of Sowhanohke, meaning the South land; Polypody, a place of brakes; Mahutchett, the place on the trail.

There are also many other names suggestive of history or mythology. King Philip's spring comes down to us with a bloody pedigree; the Pokanet field sings the fame of Pokanet, who prospered as the slave of the Shurtleffs, and whose camp was near the river in the field that now bears his name; Wigwam swamp; Indian burying ground; Indian brook, and Sampson's pond are suggestive names.

THE FIRST SPECULATORS

To comprehend the ground work of our present structure it is necessary to go back to the beginning and note through what various processes our ancestors came into possession of their land. The authority of the body that granted it is not in question, and who owned it previous to the white man's assumption has no place in the calculation. And so in our own language our history begins in the year 1620.

The first land system of the Colonists consisted in parceling out the land at the opening of the season, but this method so soon gave rise to dissatisfaction that in 1624 permanent grants began to be made, and as the Colony grew the home-seekers began to branch out into the wilderness. While the town of Plymouth was never formally incorporated, its corporate life dates from 1636, and the region now within the limits of the town of Carver, being in the jurisdiction of the Pilgrim town, all land grants of this territory were made by the town of Plymouth.

Connecting the Indian village of Pawtuxet with Agawam and Nemasket were the two trails, Agawam path and Nemasket path. The former leading over barren hills offered no attractions to the home-seekers, but the latter leading through fertile valleys, over running brooks and waving meadows, early caught the eye of the hardy souls that were crowded out of the settlement. Beginning in 1637 and ending with the incorporation of the town of Plympton, all of the land now in Plympton and Carver was granted by the mother town.

The marsh meadows were the chief attraction, and many of the grants were of the meadows alone, the grantees holding their residences in Plymouth. These grants were located at South Meadows,* Doty's meadows, Six-Mile brook, Mahutchett, Swan Hold, Beaver Dam brook, and Crane brook. By the end of the period several settlements had been made.

The first to take the Nemasket path was John Derby, who in 1637 took up a claim of sixty acres at Mounts hill, near the little lake that later became known as Derby pond. The following year he was joined by Thurston Clark, Edward Doty and George Moore, while Stephen Hopkins went still further into the woods and took a grant at Six-Mile brook. It is probable that this grant of Doty's was the first grant of land within the municipal limits of Carver, although the grant of one hundred and fifty acres in 1637-38 to John Jenney on either side of the brook was the germ of this town in the woods. By the terms of this

---

*The term South Meadows originally included all of the meadow land on the Weweantic river from Swan Holt to Rochester, the lower meadows being referred to as the Lower South Meadows. The name was afterwards applied to the village of Centre Carver, which was known by no other name up to the time of the Civil war.

THE FIRST SPECULATORS

grant it was constituted a farm within the jurisdiction of Plymouth and to be known as Lakenham.

The bounds of Plymouth were not definitely located until after the end of this period. A court order of 1640 adjusting the bounds between Plymouth and Sandwich provided that "the bounds should extend so far up into the woodland as to include the South Meadows towards Agawam, lately discovered, and the convenient upland thereto." For many years the western bounds were in dispute, and various conferences with the Proprietors of South Purchase were necessary before the dividing line was definitely established.

Nor were the individual grants definitely located and described. The records are evidence of the fact that many of the grants included a much larger area than their terms would indicate, and also of the frequent disputes among individual grantees over ranges. In the latter part of the period town surveyors were annually elected, who were kept busy making surveys of earlier grants and placing their surveys on record.

It would be difficult to resurvey some of these grants from the recorded descriptions. The heap of stones and the red oak tree have long since passed from the stage, but out of these humble beginnings has grown our more exact method, and petty disputes, though not unknown, are not as frequent as of old.

The main grants before the year 1640, in addition to those previously mentioned, were to John

Pratt, at Wenham; Bridget Fuller, at Doty's; John Barnes, at Six-Mile brook (including upland); John Dunham, at Swan Hold (including upland); Richard Sparrow and John Atwood, at Lakenham; and Goodman Watson, George Bonum and Andrew Ring, at South Meadows.

During the succeeding forty years grants of various dimensions were made along the South Meadow river to Andrew Ring, Abraham Jackson, Jonathan Shaw, William Nelson, George Bonum, Ephraim Tinkham, Lieut. Morton, William Harlow, Nathaniel Morton, Hugh Cole, Joseph Bartlett, John Cole, Daniel Dunham, John Fflallowel, Samuel Doty, John Lucas, John Jourdan, John Waterman, John Barrows, Nathaniel Wood, William Ring, Jonathan Barnes, Benony Lucas, Samuel Harlow, Richard Cooper, Ephraim Tillson, Thomas Pope and George Watson; at Lakenham to John Rickard, James Cole, Jonathan Shaw, Robert Ransom, George Watson, Daniel Ramsden and Benejah Pratt; at Doty's to Thomas Lettuce, John Rickard, Gyles Rickard, Jr., and John Pratt; at Mahutchett to Ephraim Tillson, William Haskins and Peter Risse; at John's pond to Samuel Savery; at Beaver Dam brook to George Watson; and at Wenham to John Dunham.

By the dawn of the 18th century the pioneers had a well established system of farms; grants were enlarged to take in nearly all of the upland, and the tide of population set in.

Before 1705 grants at Swan Hold were made to Joseph Dunham, John Pratt, Nathaniel Dunham, Micager Dunham, Benejah Pratt, Jeduthen Robbins, Eleazer Pratt, Joseph Pratt, Joseph Dunham, Sr., and Abial Shurtleff. These grantees were also given authority to construct a dam for flowing their meadows. Small tracts were granted at Popes Point to Joseph Churchill, George Morton and Edmund Tillson, while land formerly of George Watson was better described for the benefit of his grandson, Jonathan Shaw. Land that had been granted to Abraham Jackson, William Harlow and George Morton in New Meadows in 1698 was also more definitely described.

As these years mark the end of the individual grants by the town of Plymouth, and the grantees had reached the point where they would break away from the parent town of the Old Colony, it is well to note how their destinies were swayed by two important events of the first century. The first settlers of Plymouth were kept within a limited area on account of marauding bands of Indians, but after the spirit of the natives had been broken by the disastrous ending of King Philip's war, the drawback from that source was ended. And a few years later when the dethronement of James II. disposed of their twin enemy, Sir Edmond Andros, the Colonists rapidly increased under their new charter, meeting-houses sprung up in the forests, and New England entered enthusiastically upon its remarkable career. It is also well to remember in considering these twin enemies of the early colonists, that the white man and the red man broke even.

The indivadual grants, mostly of which have been named, with two general grants made before Plympton was incorporated, left the new town without any common land in its jurisdiction. The proprietors of the cedar swamp, as also the proprietors of the rest of the common land, henceforth had jurisdiction in the division of these lands. A large portion of this common tract was located in the future town of Carver, consisting of the cedar swamp and the land south of it as far west as the easterly shore of Sampson's pond. It included about one-fourth of the modern town's area.

At a town meeting in Plymouth in 1701-02 an ordinance was passed dividing the cedar swamp,* and Jacob Thompson was chosen surveyor to make the division with John Bradford and Samuel Sturtevant as assistants. Under the provisions of the ordinance every freeholder was to have a share; every male child born in the town who had reached the age of twenty-one and who resided in town one-half of a share; any resident who succeeded an original proprietor, one share, unless said proprietor left a son; children to inherit a share if the father was entitled to one; but under no conditions should anyone hold more than one share. Non-residents, except children as above noted, were prohibited from holding

---

*This vote included all of the cedar swamp in the town of Plymouth, which at that time embraced the future towns of Plympton, Halifax and Carver. Only the South Meadow and Doty swamps were in the future Carver, which accounts for the omission of Great Lots 19, 20 and 21 in this story.

A CORNER ON HEMLOCK ISLAND

shares unless being the owner of at least one hundred acres of tillage land occupied by a tenant.

As this tract had so long been utilized as common property, this vote to end the custom provoked a contest that could not be avoided by a town vote. Committees were named to watch poachers; any proprietor convicted of cutting cedars pending the division forfeited his claim; and any poacher not being a proprietor was to pay a fine of twenty shillings for each tree. While the plan looked well on paper, the surveyor was in a sea of constant commotion. Some lots were better located than others; some had a superior growth; every proprietor had a choice; and it was several years before the division was made among the proprietors, while the disputes had not ended two centuries later.

Under the Thompson plan the swamp was divided into eighteen Great Lots, and these Great Lots subdivided in the process of division among the proprietors. Great Lots were intended to contain forty acres each, but they were not symmetrical in shape. Some began at a common point and extended in long triangles across the swamp; some were generally rectangular, and others cannot be described in geometrical terms. It would seem to a modern engineer that the swamp could have been divided with more regularity, but the ragged general form of the tract without including upland presented a problem that taxed the civil engineering of the times.

There was still a greater disparity in the shape and size of the subdivisions. It is apparent that the surveyor placed a broad interpretation on the terms of his instructions and undertook to equalize the disparity in values by varying the size and form of the lots.

In 1828 Sylvanus Bourne resurveyed the swamp and pointed out inconsistencies in the Thompson plan, and filed a plan of his own. Modern surveyors consult both plans as a basis of surveys.

Doty's Cedar Swamp, situate in the Northerly section of the town, also came under the general grant, although independent of the large swamp. This was known as Great Lot No. 22 in the division. The original owners were John Gray, John Holmes, Samuel Rickard and Josiah Rickard.

At a town meeting in Plymouth, February 9, 1701-02, the following ordinance was adopted:

"That every freeholder That hath ben soe for six years last past That hath not had 30 ackers of land Granted to them by the Inhabitants of the Town within 20 years last past shall have 30 acrees of land laid forth to them out of the Commons belonging to sd Town (by the persons hereafter Named that are the Towns Committy or Trustees to act in ye Affare) or soe much land as to Make it up 30 acrees with what they have already had Granted to them sience sd Tirme of years & its further voted That all Town born Children now Inhabitants in sd Town that have been Rated towards defray publick Charg in sd Town for 14 years last past shall have 30 acres

THE SHURTLEFF HOMSTEAD

Birthplace of a numerous Family, and standing on the Farm that has stood in the Shurtleff Name for more than Two Centuries

apece of land laid out to them out of sd Town Comons as abovesd & that None shall Take up aney Meadow ground or sedor swamps by vertue of this Grant and it further voted that every man May take up his share abovesd as ner to his own land as may be: and noe man shall take up sd land agnst an other mans Land until the owner of sd land doth Refuseth it & if two men doe pitch on one pece of land the Committy have hereby power to determine whose it shall be."

The Committee chosen at the meeting to effect the division was composed of Capt. John Bradford, Capt. James Warren, Left. Shurtlef, Left. Nath; Southworth, Insign: Nath: Morton and Samuel Sturtivant.

Before the town committee had progressed far with the division, the town of Plympton was incorporated and the common lands located in the two towns passed to the control of the Proprietors, two hundred and one, who organized by the choice of a clerk and adopted the style of The Proprietors of Plymouth and Plympton Commons. Thomas Faunce was the first clerk, and those who served in that position before the Proprietors' work was finished in 1790 were Samuel Bartlett, John Cotton and Rossiter Cotton.

At a general meeting of the proprietors, Capt. Warren, Benjamin Warren, Lieut. Shurtleff and Samuel Lucas were chosen as surveyors to make the division. The tract was located in the Eastern section of the present town of Carver and the Southern section of Plymouth. Under the plan of operations as devised by the surveyors it was first divided into ten Great Lots, and these subdivided. The first Great Lot was cut up into 21 small parcels, the second into 22, the third into 22, the fourth into 21, the fifth into 20, the sixth into 20, the seventh into 19, the eighth into 18, the ninth into 18, and the tenth into 20. These total 201 parcels to be divided among the proprietors.

The next step in the division was to assign the freeholders to the several Great Lots. This was no small task, as each proprietor had a choice of position. And after the Great Lots had been assigned to the individual owners the question of alloting the parcels to the individuals was taken up for solution, and another perplexing problem faced the surveyors. The proprietors of each Great Lot held meetings by themselves to draw for their parcels. The subdivisions were numbered and each proprietor drew a number which in theory was to be the number of his lot. The drawings were not altogether satisfactory, and time was extended for the proprietors to trade, and it was upwards of eighty years before the work of the proprietors was finished.

The first Great line was described as follows: "Beginning at two pine trees marked numbered 1-2 standing at ye going over between ye Great West pond and a little pond at ye head of it rainging East South East 180 rods from two pine trees marked with a heap of stones between them at Cobb hill by South Meadow path and from the trees first mentioned the line extendeth South 15 Westerly by a rainge of trees to a maple tree marked numbered 1-2 standing at Pratts meadow and from thence the same course to ye town line thence beginning at the trees first numbered the line extends North 15 Easterly so far as to take in all the common land belonging to the Proprietors and all ye common lands lying to the westward of sd line to belong to ye first lot there being twenty one shares in the lot.''

This was the line between the first and second Great Lots, the first lot comprising all of the common land west of the line. The western line of the first great lot was naturally irregular according to the ranges of former grants. The previous grants bordering the first lot on the west were those at South Meadows, George Barrows, Sampson's pond, and the land of Samuel Sonnett. The final owners of the first division of the first great lot were Samuel Lucas, Caleb Loring, Elisha Bradford, Thomas Holmes, William Harlow, John Andros, Benj. Eaton, Sr., Mr. John Rickard, Eleazer Pratt, Nathaniel Harlow, Nathaniel Jackson, John Pratt, Mecager Dunham, John Jackson, Nathaniel Dunham, Joshua Ransom, Elkaneth Cushman, John Carnes, John Bryant, Left. William Shurtleff and Mr. John Murdock.

The second lot fell to (?), Isaac King, Joseph King, Ephraim Cole, Ebenezer Eaton, Samuel Bryant, John Sturtevant, Samuel Rickard, Joseph Bradford, Nathaniel Howland, Joshua Pratt's children, Giles Rickard, John Curtice, Elisha Cobb, John Doty, Richard Everson, Adam Write, John Wood, James Cole, Daniel Dunham, George Barrows and Samuel Wing.

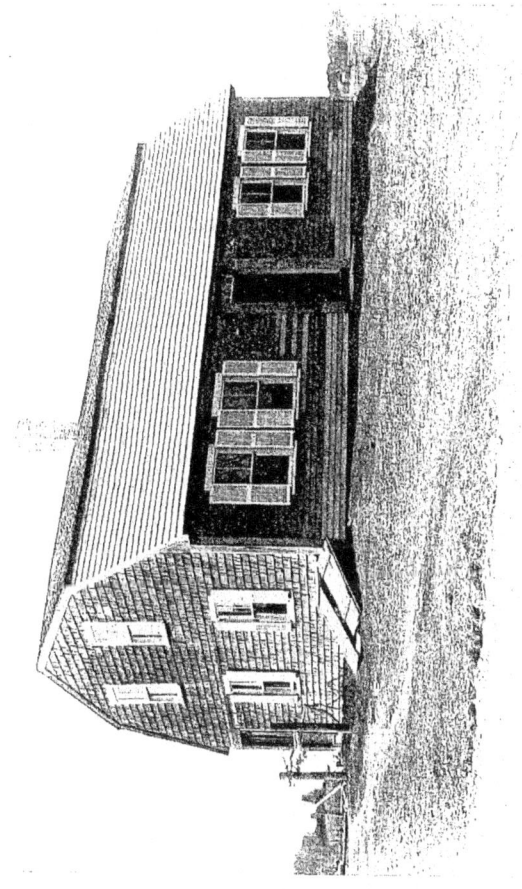

THE STURTEVANT HOUSE
Built Before the Revolution.

A FEW EARLY LAWS

It is not the purpose of this work to deal in general history, but there are some timbers in the general structure so closely related to local development that a brief review is justifiable.

Our starting point in civil government was in the compact signed on board of the Mayflower in Provincetown harbor. In the wave of enthusiasm in which the Pilgrims left their native country they made no calculation on the cost of the venture, but before landing they adjudged it prudent to make an agreement as a safeguard against a clashing of authority that might jeopardize the peace of the Colony, and on the wisdom of such a course their posterity has recorded the verdict "they builded better than they knew." And in our own day these words may be accepted as the basis of all just governments: "In ye name of God amen. We whose names are under-written, the loyall subjects of our dread soveraigne Lord, King James, by ye grace of God, of Great Britaine, Franc, Ireland king, defender of ye faith, &c., haveing undertaken, for ye glorie of God and advancemente of ye Christian faith, and honor of our king and countrie, a voyage to plant ye first colonie in ye Northerne parts of Virginia, doe by these presents solemnly and mutualy in ye presence of God, and one of another, covenant and combine our selves togeather into a civill body politick, for our better ordering and preservation and furtherance of ye ends aforesaid; and by virtue hereof to enact, constitute, and frame such just and equall laws, ordinances, acts, constitutions, and officers, from time to time, as shall be thought most meete and convenient for ye generall good of ye colonie, unto which we promise all due submission and obedience." Such was the constitution of the Plymouth Colony, and on this basis was made the laws that governed our ancestors until the union of the colonies in 1690. The leading town officers under the compact were selectmen or townsmen, a town clerk, constables, raters, jurymen, tithingmen and surveyors.

Much of the land of the future towns of Plympton and Carver was granted under the Old Colony although but little of it was occupied. A few scattering farms dotted the tract, and respectable clusters of residences appear at Colchester, Lakenham and Wenham, but the residents were all freeholders of the old town whence they journeyed on town meeting days, holidays, court days and sabbaths. It is not probable that any thought of establishing a new town had its inception before the union.

The charter of William and Mary was granted as a basis for the government of the united New England colonies, and as this charter was the foundation for all laws preceding the constitution of the United States, it is a document worthy of consideration.

In considering the charter no comparison should be made with modern theories, but in comparison

RESIDENCE OF FINNEY BROTHERS
Standing on First Land cultivated by White Men in Carver

A FEW EARLY LAWS 33

with contemporary governments it will be found to be liberal. And when we notice that liberty of conscience was guaranteed to all sects except Papists, we may compare it with the chronological edicts of Louis XIV.; and perhaps our judgment would be tempered by recalling that the charter was granted by a king and queen who had just ascended the throne through a revolution and the passions engendered had not abated. Even at that moment the exiled Stuart was intriguing to worm his way back to the throne from which he had been ejected by the uprising of his subjects.

Under this instrument, the executive authority was vested in a Governor and a Lieutenant Governor appointed by the crown, advised and assisted by twenty-eight councillors or assistants.

The law making power was vested in the Governor and Council, and two representatives from each town elected by the property holding freeholders. To this legislative body was given the name of the Great and General Court, and after its organization it was vested with authority for the annual election of the twenty-eight councillors, also of regulating the number of representatives to which each County, Town or place should be entitled.

Sheriffs, provost marshals, Justices of the Peace, Judges of Oyer and Terminer, were appointed by the Governor by and with the consent of the Council; probate matters, including the appointment of executors and administrators, were left with the Governor and Council. The acts of incorporation of towns and parishes under preceding governments, with certain limitations, were confirmed, and the adoption of laws governing local affairs rested with the General Court.

Appeals could be had from the judgments of the courts, and also from the decrees of the Governor, to the crown. The Governor held the power of proroguing the General Court at any time, and the Court could not legally adjourn for more than two days at a time, without his consent. The crown held the veto power over both the Governor and the General Court.

The authority of the Governor to prorogue the General Court, and the veto power held by the crown, were the cause of no little clashing of authority in after years, but under the charter the colonies developed rapidly, both in numbers and prerogatives, and when they reached 'the point of abolishing the veto power the tie that held them to the mother country was represented by a brittle cord. And even after the rebellious colonies had won the right to legislate for themselves, unhampered by any veto power from across the sea, they founded their liberties in the forms, regulations and theories that had grown up under the charter.

The democratic theory of permitting each locality to control its domestic affairs was recognized by the charter and the adoption of laws regulating local affairs was the subject of the constant consideration of the General Court. The recognition of this theory eventually led to the Revolution, for as each colony added to its prerogatives it became jealous of outside interfer-

A FEW EARLY LAWS 35

ence, and bound together by this theory, they combated for the principle in war.

In November, 1692, before providing for town governments, the General Court made provision for ministers and school masters, making it compulsory upon towns to provide themselves with "an able, learned orthodox minister of good conversation to dispense the word of God to them," also a school master to "teach children and youth to read and write," both to be supported by a town tax. The same month the New England town meeting was confirmed, each town being required to hold an annual town meeting in the month of March for the election of town officers and the transaction of town affairs. The necessary officers consisted of a board of three, five, seven or nine selectmen or townsmen, a town clerk, constables, surveyors of highways, tithingmen, fence viewers, clerk of the market, and a sealer of leather. The Selectmen served as overseers of the poor unless a separate board was chosen, also as assessors. Their warrant was committed to a constable and required him to collect and pay to the Selectmen or their agent.

In order to be eligible for a place on the Board of Selectmen the candidate must "be able and discreet, of good conversation," and a freeholder must have property to the amount of twenty pounds to entitle him to vote. The duty of a clerk of the market required him to visit, at least once a week, the bakeshops to guard against the selling of short weight loaves. The price of wheat was regulated by the Selectmen, and the size of the loaf accordingly. The sealer or searcher of leather was a busy officer under compulsion to inspect and seal all leather tanned in his jurisdiction.

Towns were authorized to make by-laws regulating their affairs and subject to the approval of the court in quarter sessions; they must perambulate their town lines once in three years; Selectmen must see that there were no loafers in town, and if any child or other person was found misspending his time he must be sent to the House of Correction there to receive ten lashes on the bare back; the Selectmen were vested with authority to "bind out" minors; and anyone enjoying the hospitality of the town three months unquestioned, obtained a settlement. In the case of an undesirable citizen the constable ordered the person out of town, and in the event of a refusal to move, the person was taken by force to the place of last abode.

Every male resident between the age of sixteen and sixty, with certain exceptions was forced into the militia, and under statute compulsion to attend all musters and exercises of his company. All persons liable were subject to being called to duty in times of danger and they were expected to have their equipment ready at all times. The equipment which every one liable to military duty was under compulsion to provide for himself, consisted of a firelock musket with the barrel not less than three and one-half feet in length, a snapsack, a colar with twelve bandeleers or cartouch box, one pound of good powder, twenty bullets, twelve flints, a sword or cutlass and a worm and priming wire.

Regimental musters were required once in three years, and company musters four days in each year, while the Captain of a company must canvass twice a year to see that the regulations were complied with. Towns must keep their military stores based upon one barrel of powder, two hundred pounds of bullets and three hundred flints for each sixteen persons in town subject to military duty.

A system of alarm for calling out the militia in times of sudden danger: three guns called out the militia and a penalty awaited anyone who neglected to report promptly at the training green when the alarm was sounded. As a safeguard against oppression no Captain should quarter a soldier or seaman on a private resident without the resident's consent under penalty; and the militia could not be sent out of the Colony without their consent, or the consent of the General Court.

The lower court was called the Court of Common Pleas, and made up of at least three of the Justice of the Peace for the County. The next higher court consisting of all of the Justices of the Peace for the County, was known as the Court of Quarter Sessions, or Sessions of the Peace. Appeals from these courts were to the Superior Court of Judicature with jurisdiction over all the province and made up of one Chief Justice and four associate Justices appointed by the Governor and Council.

The reckless method of granting and staking out land—perhaps mainly through the unscientific method of surveys—called for legislation. The first act for the quieting of possessions provided that the possession dating previous to October 19, 1652, and not questioned before May 20, 1662, should be sufficient title; while three years unquestioned possession from October 1, 1692, should constitute a sufficient warranty. An exception clause gave infants, persons non compos mentis, and those in prison or captivity three years extra in which to prove a claim; while persons beyond the seas had seven years of grace. The privy council objected to this act for the reasons that the rights of the crown were not protected and further that the time of three years was insufficient. To meet these objections, the act was amended saving the rights of the crown and requiring unquestioned possession from October 1, 1692, to October 1, 1704, necessary to guarantee possession to the holder or those claiming under him.

Statutes were enacted in 1692 and 1693.

Establishing and guaranteeing trial by jury.

Establishing weights and measures.

Requiring intentions of marriage to be posted in some conspicuous place at least two weeks before the event.

Establishing habeas corpus proceedings.

Establishing 6 per cent. as the legal rate, contracts calling for a larger rate to be void.

Establishing post office rules.

Establishing systems of highway improvements.

A FEW EARLY LAWS

Thanksgiving custom reaffirmed.

Hogs running at large to be yoked from April 1st to October 15th, and ringed all the year.

Sheep not to run at large unaccompanied by a shepherd.

No strong liquor to be sold or given an Indian.

Idiots and lunatics must be cared for by the Selectmen.

In these same years:

There were thirteen crimes punishable by death.

Laws against witchcraft were adopted.

The exportation of raw hides was forbidden.

The cord of marketable wood must be cut in four feet lengths, and when piled must be eight feet long and four feet high. If a delivery did not come up to these regulations, the injured party must sue, and in case of conviction the wood was forfeited, one-half to the complainant and one-half for the use of the town's poor.

The penalty for one offence compelled the convicted party to sit upon the gallows with a rope tied around the neck and the other end thrown over the gallows. On the march from the gallows to the jail, he should be given not less than forty lashes, and forever after he must wear the letter A two inches in length cut from cloth of a different color than the clothing either on an arm, the back or some conspicuous place about the person. Conviction of a neglect in wearing the letter was punishable with fifteen lashes.

Inn holders were licensed, and regulations governing them adopted:

Lodgings and a supply of refreshments must be constantly on hand.

An apprentice, servant or negro should not be entertained without an order from his master.

No one should be permitted to remain in the inn above one hour, except travellers.

No one should be permitted to drink to excess.

No one admitted Sundays except travellers.

For any conviction, one-half of the fine went to the informant, and one-half to the use of the Town's poor.

Inn holders were required to furnish bonds with sureties for the keeping of the regulations.

And as a further guarantee Selectmen were burdened with the duty of seeing that Tythingmen were annually elected and qualified. The duty of the Tythingman was to inspect the taverns and inform on all violations of the laws; also to inform on all idlers, disorderly persons, profane swearers, Sabbath breakers and law breakers in general. The legal badge adopted for the Tythingman was a black staff two feet in length with a three inch brass tip on one end.

Anyone convicted of receiving stolen goods from an Indian, was to restore the goods to the rightful owner with an equal amount in value of specie, or if the goods had been disposed of, double the value in specie.

This brief resume covers only the starting of legislation under the charter, and from these beginnings was built up and perfected, by repeals, amendments and additions, the social system that was in vogue when the Colonies banded themselves together for the purpose of moving the veto power from London to some point on the American con-

THE GRIFFITH HOMESTEAD
Built Before the Revolution. Standing in the Family Name Upwards of One Hundred and Fifty Years

tinent. If some of these statutes seem unaccountable to us, perhaps if we compare these laws of the pioneers, with some of the legislation which we propose to meet modern conditions, and with two centuries of experience and education to our debit, the comparison, after all may not be very damaging to the first dreamers in the world of civil liberty. James I. was on the throne of Great Britain when the Pilgrims sailed and the following monarchs reigned during our colonial life, the year named being the time they ascended the throne:

    1625   Charles I.
    1648   The Commonwealth, or Oliver Cromwell.
    1660   Charles II.
    1685   James II.
    1689   William and Mary.
    1694   William III.
    1702   Anne.
    1714   George I.
    1727   George II.
    1760   George III.

THE FIRST SEPARATION

Isaac Cushman, grand son of Robert the Pilgrim, was Plympton's god-father. Thomas, son of Robert and father of Isaac, had long been the noted Ruling Elder of the Pilgrim church when he died in 1691, and Isaac was slated as his successor.

To be a Ruling Elder in the Plymouth church was only the second ambition of Isaac Cushman—perhaps the third—*and he kicked over the slate. Residing in the west end of the town where two groups of settlements had begun to flourish, Colchester and Lakenham, Cushman's heart was with his neighbors and eight miles from the old church had begotten notions in their heads that the proper step under the circumstances would be to have a church of their own and to have their neighbor and friend for a minister. Such was the dream that laid the foundation for the "upper society."

But there were obstacles to overcome before the new society could legally have the minister of its choice: there were dead branches to lop off

---

*In addition to the call of Isaac Cushman to settle over the new church, he was wanted as successor to Rev. Mr. Fuller of the First Church of Middleboro. But the bond of sympathy between him and the residents of the new society could not be broken by the more tempting offers from the larger parishes.

before the tree would relinquish the sprig. Chief among these was the church rule, that a man must serve the church as Ruling Elder before he could be ordained as a minister. Isaac had never served in such a capacity, but he declined the offer and began his ministry over the new society without an ordination. Of course this meant three years of agitation in church circles, but Cushman continued to preach until the church receded and gave him the regular ordination in October, 1698. The Precinct was incorporated in November, 1695. The fact that Cushman continued in that capacity as long as his health would permit, and that he was pensioned by his grateful people in his last days, is sufficient evidence of his head and heart.

Thus called together in the duties and services of the church, the fellow workers in the woods soon conceived the idea of a separate town and in less than twelve years the town of Plympton was born. The new Precinct included Lakenham, but not South Meadows, but when Plympton was incorporated the new town extended over all of the territory covered by the future town of Carver.

The following comprise the voters of Plympton for 1708-09:

Group A*

Isaac Cushman
Thomas Cushman
Dea. John Waterman
Ensign Elkanah Cushman
Frances Cook
Lieut. John Bryant

---

*Group A includes the residents of Plympton, and group B those of the future town of Carver. The division may not be strictly accurate, but it is fairly correct.

THE FIRST SEPARATION

Jonathan Bryant
John Everson
Richardson Everson
Benjamin Eaton
John Bryant
John Bryant
James Bryant
Peter West
Samuel Bryant
Joseph Phinney
James Bearce
Samuel Sturtevant
Robert Waterman

Benjamin Curtice
David Bosworth
Nehemiah Sturtevant
Samuel Sturtevant, Jr.
Ebenezer Standish
William Sturtevant
Joseph King
Peter Thompson
Job Simmons
Isaac King
William Churchill
Isaac Cushman, Jr.
George Sampson

Group B

Lieut. William Shurtleff
Edmund Weston
Joseph King, Jr.
John Wright
Adam Wright
Isaac Sampson
Benjamin Soule
Nathaniel Harlow
Samuel Fuller
Dea. John Rickard
Eleazur Rickard
Josiah Rickard
John Pratt
Jeduthen Robbins
Jabez Eddy
Henry Rickard
Edmund Tillson

John Doten
Robert Ransom
Samuel Waterman
Ephraim Tillson
John Tillson
Jonathan Shaw
Benoni Shaw
John Cole
John Carver
George Bonum
Benoni Lucas
John Barrows
Dea. Nathaniel Wood
Eleazer King
Thomas Shurtleff
Abial Shurtleff
Caleb Loring

Regardless of the provisions of its charter, the new town stepped immediately into the enjoyment of the immunities and the sufferance of the responsibilities of a pioneer settlement. Expecting to eke their subsistence from the soil, they immediately declared war on crows and blackbirds, and every householder must either produce two of the former or six of the latter between March 15th and June 15th under penalty of having two shillings added to their tax bills. There was hustling among the householders to get the quota of ebony birds, for coy as the crow is, he was easier to get in those early days than two shilling bits.

Hogs enjoyed the freedom of the town, provided they were ringed and yoked according to law, and hogreaves were annually chosen to see that the law was complied with.

To guarantee the abstinence from work and play on the Sabbath, tythingmen were also chosen and sworn to the faithful discharge of their duties. The Sunday morning beats of these officials, armed with the badge of their authority, rendered it injudicious for anyone to trifle with the law. The tythingman was not a popular officer, and the position not generally desired. The records show that these officers seldom succeeded themselves.

Not the least of the town's perplexing problems concerned wildcats, deer, and undesirable citizens. The former, because so depredatious between 1720 and 1740 that the war against them was encouraged by a town bounty. Sportsmen spurred on perhaps by the necessities of the table, were such destroyers of deer that the question was

THE FIRST SEPARATION 47

taken up by the town and the law invoked for their protection.

Undesirable citizens were warned out of town according to law. In 1711 the Selectmen exercised their jurisdiction for the first time, when the board issued its warrant to John Coal, requiring him to warn Marcy Donham to depart said town. The nature of Marcy's offence does not appear, but she evidently did not meet with the approval of the town fathers.

The town in compliance with the statutes, started its school system in 1708 through an ordnance instructing the Selectmen to employ a school master. This was the limit of the town's duties in the matter, and after the master had been employed, the place for holding the school was left with its patrons. Many of the young obtained their education in their own homes from books provided by themselves, while the master was present as a guide and guest.

Human nature was the same in those days as we find it in the dawn of the twentieth century, but methods of controlling it have changed. Young people were obliged to attend church Sundays under penalty of a poke from the tythingman, but once in the Meeting House they were young folks still and the town occasionally found it necessary to choose a committee to occupy seats among them in church and watch their conduct, to insure the minister an undisturbed opportunity.

But, the question that furnished the voters with their constant agitation, was the continual efforts to divide the town. The town of Plympton was not well established as a municipality when an unrest manifested itself, and the new town may be said to have been ushered into existence with a sectional line as a birth mark. The Meeting House was the heart of the town, and at the outset there were freeholders with so remote a residence that they never felt the pulse. From the Plympton meeting house to the Wareham line, is upwards of twelve miles, and with the travelling facilities of the times even the South Precinct found it advisable at times to exempt the residents of the Tihonet region from the rates on condition that the exempted pay their taxes to the Wareham authorities.

Lakenham, and more especially South Meadows, early started an agitation for the division of the town, that was not ended until the division came three-quarters of a century later. These movements were resisted at first and when they could no longer be held back, a compromise was effected by the incorporation of the South Precinct. Still the agitation continued, and time after time, the town voted against "setting the Precinct off as a separate town." In the spirit of compromise many town rights were conferred upon the rebellious Precinct, and when the town was born it stepped among its sisters well trained in its duties.

There appears no striking evil over which the Precinct complained, and it is probable that the residents of Lakenham stood with the old town against division. But the South Precinct embraced the larger part of the territory of Plympton and naturally, the South Precinct enjoyed the

THE WATERMAN HOUSE AT SNAPPIT
Built Before the Revolution

larger per cent of the increase in population. And as every new settler was in the remote section, every new settler added one to the forces of discontent, hence the inevitable could only be postponed.

THE CARVER PRIMARY SCHOOL HOUSE

EARLY SETTLERS

It is easy to see, why the struggling farmers of Plymouth placed such a high valuation on the fresh meadows, in the days before the cultivation of fine top, clover and timothy; equally as plain why the luxurious meadows found in the limits of the future town of Carver, should receive the name of the South Meadows. In the earliest colonization of this region, the grants of land were made and the first settlers located in relation to these meadows. Thus, in our earliest history, we find our pioneers at South Meadows, Lakenham (adjacent to Winatuxett Meadows), Mahutchett Meadows, Cranebrook Meadows, Doty's Meadows, Fresh Meadows and New Meadows.

There were large landowners—promoters in the true sense—among the early settlers. The Shaws, Ransoms, Watsons and Coles at Lakenham; the Cobbs at Mahutchett; the Rickards and Watermans at Snappit; the Dunhams and Pratts at Wenham; the Shurtleffs, Lucases and Tillsons at South Meadows; the Barrows and Murdocks around Sampson's pond, and the Atwoods at Fresh Meadows.

The dangers and privations that always follow the pioneers of a new country, gave romance to the lives of our first settlers. The unsanitary state of the country made up of hills and undrained swamps, and the exposures on account of insufficient housing, rendered them susceptible to disease, while their distance from the doctors of the settlements left them to battle for themselves.

The first houses were located in the valleys, with the barns from one hundred to three hundred yards away according to drainage. The houses were thus located, in order to be near water and for a protection against the elements during the Winter months.

These houses were built under disadvantages and consequently of the simplest design. While lumber was in abundance, the means of turning it to boards were lacking. Furniture, cooking utensils, farm implements and wearing apparel must be mostly of the home made order, while communication with the settlement at Plymouth and with neighbors, was carried on through Indian trails, which in later years were adopted as the highways and improved. And when we consider the situation of even the most favored ones, we must admire the faith and hardihood of a race that suffered and braved so much to make the world what it is.

In the struggle to sustain themselves from the land, they faced natural enemies that baffled their wits and developed their sporting instincts. Crows, blackbirds and red birds dug their corn after it had been planted, while wolves, foxes, wild cats and other carnivorous animals skulked after their fowl. For more than a century, bounties were paid for the heads of crows, blackbirds and red birds, while wolves and wild cats were exterminated in this manner. Beaver were plentiful in the earliest days, but they were exterminated on account of the value of their furs. But while birds and animals diminished the means of subsistence, there were counter advantages of no little consideration. The ponds teemed with fish, Sampson's, Doty's and probably Clear being breeding grounds for herring, and this was a large item on their bill of fare. The woods were full of deer, rabbits and edible birds and this went far towards supplying the farmers with meat. The only species that diminished under free hunting and trapping were deer, and laws to protect them were early enacted. Such in brief were the conditions that confronted the farmer settlers in the year 1700.

But a wonderful advance was on the slate for the new century, little foreseen by the lonely farmers who witnessed its dawn and, perhaps, not fully appreciated by their descendants who, having won their independence, battled with its vexatious problems in the century's closing twilight. Still wonderful as we now behold it was the century that transformed our community from a few scattered farmers, living upon their crops and warring on blackbirds, to a town of social and industrial enthusiasm. Saw mills and grist mills, two meeting houses, three iron manufactories, forges, acres of tillage lands, taverns, school houses, stage lines, a new precinct and a new town, were the local achievements, while in the larger field, we were transformed from a group of struggling colonies sleeping on their arms in constant fear of Indian massacres and trembling for the next move of the monarch three thousand miles away, to a nation of independent people with full faith in their ability to sustain their rights. And while we contemplate the glory of their achievements, it is inspiring to review the pleasures and hardships of those lives devoted to the cause of human progress.

Essential to the building of better homes, and to the wants of a people who must live from their land, were saw mills and grist mills, and to the establishment of these the early settlers devoted their energies.

These mills might seem slow in the eyes of the fast operators of today, but like their builders, they did their work. Their construction was simple. A dam to hold a pond for the power was the first essential. A low building open on one side, with a long, low extension into which projected the long log as the saw worked its way through, was located on declining ground in order for the better handling of the heavy logs. Most of the machinery was of wood, and the long saw shot up and down at every revolution of the water wheel, hence the name—The Up and Down mill. Most of these mills were company enterprises, the owners dividing the time when each should operate it in lieu of the modern method of dividing the profits. Grist mills were located on the same dam, and forges for doing iron work became a necessity in every community and they, too, were located near the mills.

In the winter months, these mills became the centres of activity and society for the male

THE WENHAM SCHOOL HOUSE

EARLY SETTLERS

population. Even the millers were not rushed, and many stories could be told while the saw was plowing its way slowly but surely along and the manufacture of boards was a pleasure and a process that often entertained the farmer's wife and children.

On a Winter day when the snow precluded any other duty, the farmer shouldered his bag of grain and started for the mill. He carried no orders to hurry back, for his wife attended to the milking, while the boys had been trained to do their part. There appeared to be no reason why he could not properly loaf around the mills and forge all day, picking up bits of news and gossip for the amusement of his family when he returned. And many were the debates around the mills on questions that related to their farms, their church, their neighborhood, or their rights so nobly conferred upon them by the charter of good King William. Practical jokes had their place in the exercises of the day, and whenever an extra large log must be rolled down upon the carriage, there were plenty of spare hands to give a lift just for the fun of it. And when night ended the fun around the mill, the farmer could shoulder his bag of flour—minus the toll—and wade home through the snow in the light of the rising moon. If the mill happened to be too far away, the horse could be utilized as a means of transportation.

Think you, after such a vigorous day with little or no food, did the supper steaming on the crane or simmering in the coals, tempt the farmer to exclaim that he lived in the best days the world ever knew? Yet a few years later what an advance in the facilities that catered to the wants of the people, for in this better day the housewife could burn a roaring fire for an hour in a large brick oven, rake out the ashes, insert her pot of beans, rye bread, pumpkin pies and fowl, and then while her cooking was going on she could go about her other work, stopping occasionally we may be sure to take a peek through the little aperture in the oven, to see her pies and beans gradually assuming their famous brown.

The girls made their own dolls and doll's clothing, and no little pleasure was found in learning to do the duties that fell to the lot of women. The boys were free to hunt and trap the game. They made their own boats and fishing poles, their cross bows, carts, sleds and cornstalk fiddles, and they told stories at night in the light of the open fire, while their older brothers and sisters gathered in the larger houses and taverns for social events, where the village fiddler sawed into immortal song the old "kitchen spree."

Another item of hallowed memory in the society of the times clustered around the swing. Every hamlet had its village swing located in some clump of gigantic trees, where on holidays and in the long summer twilights, the young gathered for social joys and there has always been a suspicion that Cupid had a perch in the branches of the same old trees.

Of course there were disadvantages in those days, little inconveniences that in souls of fun and courage, only served to develop a rugged char-

EARLY SETTLERS

acter. To get out of bed in an old farm house when the thermometer outside hovered around zero, go shivering down to the kitchen to find that the high wind had completely extinguished the fire, called into action no little sand and self-reliance, for an extinct fire could not easily be rekindled. While the others remained in bed, one of the older boys must don his boots, still stiff and cold from the baptism of the preceding day, and in the face of the biting wind wade across the fields through snow that buried the fences, to borrow fire from a neighbor. And then to get the coals back through the gale with life enough in them to start a blaze, was no small test on the boy's ingenuity. Such in part was the training of the boys who left their beds in darkness to dig the trenches at Bunker Hill.

While Edward Doty*, the hot tempered passenger of the Mayflower, may have been the first to till the soil of Carver, there is not satisfactory evidence that he resided on his possessions, and to Jonathan Shaw falls the honor of being the first permanent resident of the territory embraced in the present municipal limits of the town. Shaw had a house at Lakenham as early as 1660, and John Pratt, who had a residence south of Doty's pond in 1675, was a close second. The exact site of these houses may not go unquestioned, but there

---

*Edward Doty's farm was the land now owned and occupied by Finney Brothers. Thus the names was given to Doty's cedar swamp and Doty's pond, which later acquired the name of Wenham pond.

are reasons for stating that Shaw's house stood on the site of the present Sturtevant house south of the Green. The present house was built as early as 1750 (possibly earlier), and a tradition says it was the third house built on that site. The Pratt house probably stood on the site of the present residence of Allerton L. Shurtleff.

Early neighbors of Shaw and Pratt were John Dunham at Wenham, Benony Lucas at South Meadows and John Benson at Fresh Meadows. At that time the main traveled road from Plymouth to Middleboro, led through Annasnapet and Parting Ways, this road being referred to by old residents as "the old way" as late as the last of the last century. The road through Darby was in use, however, at the same time. Shaw's residence stood about midway between Plymouth and Middleboro, Mahutchett was a mile to the southwest, Popes Point two miles to the south and South Meadows three miles to the southeast.

Among those who joined the Lakenham settlement by the year 1700 or soon after were the Bonums, Watsons, Kings, Robbins, Watermans, Rickards, Wrights and Ransoms. There was a boom in the settlement of this region at the time through the division of the common lands. The Shaws and Watsons held possessions in the west section where their descendants settled. Watson held land on Rocky Meadow brook, and Thomas Pope owning a grant at the junction of this brook with South Meadow river, gave the name of Popes Point to the land, which later became the local name of the village that grew up around the furnace.

THE POPES POINT SCHOOL HOUSE

EARLY SETTLERS

The Rickards and Watermans located at Annasnapet; the Ransoms owned the large tract between the Doty farm and Lakenham brook; and the Pratts and Crookers the tract between Plymouth street and Wenham road.

While the earlier settlers of Lakenham patronized the mills at Plympton, the settlers of this region soon had such facilities of their own and mills were in operation at Lakenham, South Meadows and probably Wenham. The industrial activities of the people were confined to agricultural pursuits until the decade 1730-40, when the Popes Point furnace was established and a remarkable impetus given to the social and industrial life of this region. The building of the first iron furnace, the first meeting house and the establishment of the first three school districts, marks this decade as a memorable one in the development of the settlement.

The Shermans joined the Precinct before the Revolution, purchasing a large tract from the Ransoms. John Sherman conducted a tavern on the site of the residence of James S. McKay*.

Fresh Meadows was a thriving village before the Revolution. Fifty years after Plymouth Rock, there was a bridge across the river near where the wide bridge is now located known as Benson's bridge. The Benson property must

---

*The business of the tavern was moved in 1815 to the John Shaw house, near the Green, now owned by Mrs. Horace C. Robbins. In this tavern was located Sherman hall; where public meetings, balls, etc., were held. It was a lively center, especially on muster days, when the militia made it its headquarters.

have included much of the land between the Wareham road and the river, the original homestead being a short distance back from the N. S. Cushing farm, where the spot is now located by straggling remnants of apple trees. The burying ground was on a hill easterly from the Cushing house, which is now marked by a lone headstone, the rest having been carried away by boys.

The first saw mill was established early in the 18th century, about one-half mile above the present mill and where the rudiments of the dam may still be seen. A few years afterwards, the old mill was deserted and the dam built upon its present site.

Joshua Benson was a thrifty inn keeper, whose tavern stood on the hill opposite the old mill. From the eminent position of the tavern, one could look over the mill and up the Plymouth road and the enterprising proprietor who may be presumed to have had a stock of Jamaica rum on hand, must have looked up this road with a business eye, as the well-to-do merchants journeyed between Plymouth and New Bedford. On a dusty day in summer, how refreshing to man and beast must have been a halt at the gay old tavern; and when the cold blasts of winter chilled the travellers through and through, how inviting must have been the red logs that burned on the hearth and the stock in trade of the genial proprietor.

On the dam beyond the mill looking from the tavern, was located the grist mill and the forge. With these thriving industries and with a gay and contented population, Fresh Meadows is a pleasant dream. The swamps in that region were prolific with huckleberries which the residents turned to good account, the men, women and children gathering them for the markets of Plymouth and New Bedford. Coming to meet the stage from all directions, the point where they gathered at the junction of the Charlotte Furnace road with Rochester road, came to be known as Huckleberry Corner. Nathaniel Atwood occupied his old homestead later known as the Bates Place on the west side of Bates* pond; Eli Thomas and Ephraim Griffith tilled their farms up the Popes Point road; Joel Shurtleff and Caleb Atwood farmed their clearings up the Rochester road; William Washburn lived on his farm opposite the M. E. Church of later times, Deacon Asaph Washburn established his home beyond the river near Benson's bridge.

Reckoned from the standpoint of continued influence, George Barrows and John Murdock were the pioneers of South Carver. Through marital connections Caleb Cushman, (whose wife was a daughter of George Barrows), established the Cushman farm about 1740; and later the Saverys were settled in the village through the Barrows girls. The Barrows property skirted the west shore of the pond and John Murdock held the claim to the land on the east side. The pond itself was lightly regarded, except for the fish it yielded and the grassy coves for their hay giving and pasturage qualities. Grassy Island was also used

---

*Bates' pond was called Atwood's pond at that time.

as a pasture, being approached through a slough from the west shore. The old Barrows' homestead stood at the junction of Mayflower road with Rochester road; the Murdock homestead was the farm on the east side of the pond, later known as the Israel Thomas farm; the Tillson farm was located about midway between Rochester road and Meadows road, in what is now known as New Meadows; and it is probable that the main highway at that time passed the Tillson house, the Silas Shaw house, the Barrows house and the Murdock house and so on to the fishery at the outlet of the pond. Rochester road as we travel it, was laid out in 1698, but it is probable that the main travel south was on the east side of the pond, and the old roads leading to Halfway ponds and Agawam, show signs of having once been main travelled roads.

The success of Popes Point furnace, had fired the heart of Bartlett Murdock and through his agitation, operations towards the establishment of Charlotte Furnace were begun in 1760. The meadows south of the pond were dyked creating Furnace pond and flowing the coves and Grassy Island, for which annual damages were paid.

There were but few residents south of the pond at that time. The Seipets living on the Indian farm, hunted and tilled the land on which the village of South Carver stands; Bartlett Murdock moved further south and laid the foundation for the Island Farm; David Shurtleff lived on his farm which proved to be his monument, going thereafter by the name of The David Place; the Cush-

THE BATES POND SCHOOL HOUSE
Originally stood East of the McFarlin Homestead

EARLY SETTLERS

mans were clearing their land; the Dunhams were farming up the Plymouth road and laying the foundation for Dunhamtown; the Bumpusses, Maxims and possibly others were scattered between the pond and Tihonet. At the same time the Barrows family was settling the north side of the pond, and Martin Grady* was located in the woods in the direction of Wankinco. But the establishment of Charlotte Furnace laid the foundation for the village of South Carver, which went merrily on after the Revolution.

---

*Martin Grady's house and farm was the one later owned by Thomas Shaw, near Half-way house so called. Grady's pond thus acquired its name.

THE SOUTH PRECINCT OF PLYMPTON

The western precinct of Plymouth, incorporated in 1698, included the hamlets of Colchester and Lakenham. The main settlements were clustered around Colchester brook and even Lakenham was only two miles away, South Meadows not being covered by the new society. But when Plympton was incorporated a few years later, it embraced all of the territory now included in the Town of Carver.

When the Plympton meeting house was built, it was located fairly in the centre of its supporters. When the settlers spread out over the South lands clearing farms in that large tract stretching towards Agawam and Rochester the meeting house was left far to one side, and in less than forty years from the incorporation of the New Society an agitation for still another meeting house began to manifest itself based upon the same logic that induced the Western society to withdraw from the Plymouth church.

As this territory to the South grew in numbers and influence various compromises were offered to discourage the new meeting house proposition. In 1716 one fourth of the schoolmaster's time was spent at Lakenham and one fourth at South Meadows; and in 1731 the South was granted 20 pounds towards preaching in that vicinity the ensuing Winter. But the agitation grew — natural conditions favored it — while the breach between the old society and the embryo society gradually widened. Nothing stood in the way of an outbreak but the opportunity and this came when the town of Plympton voted salaries to two ministers. The venerable Cushman had worked his way into the affections of his people and no hints of dismissal are visible. But he was too old for active service. To control the situation the town voted him a small salary while the regular salary was voted Rev. Jonathan Parker recently ordained. And this furnished the mutineers with their opportunity.

At a special town meeting in May 1730, a protest against voting salaries to two ministers in one meeting house signed by 49 of the Southrons was filed with the moderator. Again at a meeting in November a stronger protest with 54 signatures was entered but the old society refused to yield. This protest shows a trace of the prevailing feeling: "We have done our duty in times past in supporting the minister here settled............ we look upon the circumstances of the case of Mr. Parker's call not agreeable to Scripture rule or the practice of Churches." The protest concludes with the statement that several of the subscribers have petitioned the Selectmen for a town meeting to "set us off either as a town or precinct."

The first impulse of the Southrons was for either a town or a precinct but the contest developed a bitterness that rendered a compromise improbable. The old society was rigidly opposed to either at first, but as the breach between the sections widened, the North found it advisable to look with favor upon a separate precinct with a view to prevent the division of the town. The General Court accepted the petition which was promptly committeed and the old society went to work. At a special town meeting in June, 1732, a committee consisting of David Bosworth, Samuel Bradford and Joseph Thomas was instructed to establish the line setting off the proposed South Precinct; and a committee composed of Capt. Caleb Loring, Samuel Sturtevant and Joseph Thomas was sent to the General Court then in session to answer the petition of the South end people.

In September the committee to whom had been referred the petition visited Plympton, perambulated the proposed dividing line, and heard all interested parties. The committeemen undoubtedly took a judicial view of the situation and their judgment was tempered with mercy. They decided upon a separate precinct and as the new precinct would take away one third of the ratable estates it should pay one third of Mr. Cushman's salary while he lived. Upon their own request the families of Edmund Tillson, Isaac Nye, Elisha Witton, Eleazer Cushman, Eleazer Rickard and Ephraim Tillson were to remain with the old society. The division line was practically the Plympton-Carver town line although several unimportant changes have been made. The act incorporating the Precinct passed its final stage November 16, 1732.

Six of the freeholders of the new precinct immediately petitioned John Murdock of Plymouth, one of his Majesty's Justices of the Peace, for a precinct meeting and the warrant addressed to Barnabas Shurtleff one of the petitioners summoned the new society in legal meeting Monday, December 18, 1732. At this meeting Barnabas Shurtleff was chosen Moderator, Joseph Lucas Clerk, and Capt. Barnabas Shurtleff, Richard Dwelly and Samuel Lucas, Precinct committee. At an adjourned meeting January 8, 1732, Capt. Shurtleff, John Murdock and Joseph Lucas were chosen Assessors, and Jabez Nye, Collector. Eighty pounds were raised for the support of the minister and Mrs. Mary Shaw was authorized to entertain the ministerial candidates at the expense of the Precinct.

The bitterness engendered by the conflict between the old and new precincts manifested itself for several years after the separation. At this first legal meeting of the new society it was voted not to pay the assessment against them for the salary of "Mr. Jonathan Parker." It was held by the debaters that they had agreed to pay one third of Mr. Cushman's salary but not that of Mr. Parker. The old society had the legal end of the argument as the assessment was due before the South Precinct was incorporated but there was a chip on the shoulder of the young society. Plympton appealed to the courts while the South Precinct voted to stand by their constable in resisting the assessment and Capt. Barnabas Shurtleff was chosen to assist in the defence.

SOUTH PRECINCT OF PLYMPTON

The precinct was unfortunate in its first ministry. Not only was there constant turmoil with the common town but the relations between pastor and people were not pleasant. Which party was in the right does not appear at this day but it is probable that there was a lack of compromise on both sides that always leads to misunderstanding. The first salary was to be 80 pounds with an honorable support ever after so long as the minister remained with the society. In the first candidate's answer to the call he said "an honorable support for myself and family should God give me one." This was indefinite and the freeholders debated. Should they bind themselves to support the minister's family as long as it lived? The candidate explained that he meant to be understood as saying as long as he remained their pastor and with this explanation the doubters were satisfied. They did not stop to consider what a world of varied construction was wrapped up in that innocent clause "an honorable support" and before they could get a separation from the first minister this question must be sifted by the courts.

At the adjourned meeting Benoni Shaw, John Witton and Samuel Jackson were constituted a committee to procure preachers until the Precinct was ready to give a call. In less than a month— February 15th — the voters were ready and the first call was given Rev. Othniel Campbell.

The ordination of a minister was an event of great import in that generation and the ceremonies attending the ordination of Rev. Mr.

Campbell gave birth to the first general holiday of the South Precinct, June 2, 1733. Committees were appointed to entertain the ministers and other invited guests while ministers from Rochester, Plymouth, Kingston, Middleboro, Taunton, Raynham and Plympton lent the dignity of their presence. Samuel Shaw entertained the ministers and their horses at the expense of the Precinct.

Mr. Campbell's first salary was 80 pounds and this was gradually increased until in 1741 it had reached the highest limit — 160 pounds. In addition to the salary he was sometimes granted extra remuneration whenever any unusual event occurred. In 1742 the salary was dropped to 40 pounds lawful money with an additional gift of five pounds "in consideration of the rise in things the past year." This sudden fall in the salary has no bearing on the relations between pastor and people but is entirely due to the general financial disarrangements of the Province.

March 1, 1742-43 the Precinct voted to postpone action on the minister's salary and the following September 40 pounds were raised for "supplying the pulpit." There was trouble between preacher and people and this was the outcome. At a church meeting December 6, Rev. Mr. Campbell was dismissed. A Precinct meeting was summoned December 26 to see if the Precinct would concur in the action of the church. Each faction pulled the political string with an artistic hand; great excitement prevailed throughout the Precinct; and expectations of a sensation filled the meeting house on the day of the public meeting.

Capt. Barnabas Shurtleff was chosen moderator and in calling the meeting to order he enquired to know if anyone had anything to say against the warrant. There being no response to this challenge he added: "Here is a paper put in by James Shaw and others directed to no person, no meeting nor no date and therefore the moderator will take no notice of it."

The main question was then put, that is to see if the Precinct would concur in the action of the church in dismissing Rev. Mr. Campbell. In the eagerness of both factions to win many voted who were not legally entitled to that privilege and the moderator refused to count the hands. In this predicament he ordered the house divided, those favoring concurrence in the women's seats and those opposed in the men's seats, and the women's seats containing the majority of the freeholders he declared for concurrence. Joseph Bridgham, Elisha Lucas, Abel Crocker, John Shaw, Samuel Shaw and Samuel Jackson were named as a committee to procure a new minister.

In the passions of the contest the Precinct voted not to pay the charges of the Council of Churches but wisely reconsidered the action the following January when the necessary appropriation was made and Ensign Nathaniel Atwood instructed to act with the treasurer in adjusting the dispute with Rev. Mr. Campbell. But the breach between Mr. Campbell and the Precinct authorities was too wide to be bridged by local hands and the minister appealed to the courts. Capt. Barnabas Shurtleff and Joseph Bridgham were selected to represent the Precinct at the May session of the "Peace" "or at any other court he may rest his case." Mr. Campbell lost his case in the lower court and appealed to the Superior Court of Assizes which entered his appeal and continued it much to the chagrin of the anti-Campbell faction.

The case was thoroughly discussed in the Precinct and the antis expressed their minds freely over what appeared to them the injustice in the assumption of jurisdiction by the Superior Court. A special Precinct meeting was called when Atwood and Bridgham were instructed to appeal to the Great and General Court for "help and relief from the burden and difficulty we labor under" as a result of allowing this case to go beyond the general sessions of the peace. Mr. Campbell won a judgment but the Precinct refused to submit and the matter was continued until 1748 when a second appeal was made to the General Court for assistance in settling with Mr. Campbell and "to compel him to give up the church records." Nothing resulted from this move and in 1751 the committee had reached an agreement with their ex-minister by allowing him 10 pounds in addition to the court's allowance. This agreement was subsequently ratified by the Precinct and the matter was closed.

After the dismissal of Rev. Mr. Campbell there was no settled minister in the Precinct until the ordination of John Howland. In April, 1745, the church voted a call to Lemuel Briant to which the Precinct concurred the following month with a salary of 46 pounds and 5s. A committee was

THE SOUTH CARVER SCHOOL HOUSE

named to acquaint Mr. Briant of the proceedings and the meeting adjourned one month. At the adjourned meeting a settlement was voted Mr. Briant and there he drops from the records. The following January John Howland was called by the church, the Precinct concurred February 8th with a salary of £46 1s the first year and an "honorable support thereafter." Perhaps we can see in Mr. Howland's answer something of the character of this truly remarkable man.

To ye Chh. and Congregation in ye South part of Plympton, Gentlemen—In as much as God in his Providence has been pleased to Prosper My Poore Labors among you as to Incline your Souls to Give Me a Call to ye Worke of ye Gospel Ministry among you and after Given Thanks to God for —— ye hearts of ye People Towards men and having maturely Considered on ye Proposition I Do Accept of your Call Expecting such a Maintenance as ye Gospel allows to Those that Waite att ye Alter, that Accepting of ye Salery as Voted with your finding of me my Wood Praying that the Grate Sherard wold —— the little Vine which he hath Planted and be Mindful of his Little Flock and build you up into Spiritual House and Restore unto it its former Peace —— and Unity, that brotherly love may not only continue but increase, that all strife envy and evil worke may be put away, that we may be so Blessed and Prospered that he that soweth and he that Reapeth may be one. Desiring a remembrance in your prayer that I may make full proof of my Ministry and so take

Heed to myself and doctrine so that after I have Preached to others I myself may not be cast away. I rest yours in all sincere Love and Respect.

Plympton, June 21, 1746.

John Howland.

Mr. Howland had preached to the people at intervals since the retirement of Rev. Mr. Campbell but his salary did not begin until July 14, 1746, and that date may be properly named as the beginning of his ministry.

There was a wide variation in his salary during his ministry owing to the financial fluctuations of the country. The second year it was increased to £185; the third year to £286; the fourth year dropped to £200; and in 1750 it was dropped to £40, one half of which was to be in supplies. From that period to the Revolutionary disturbances it ranged around £65. In 1778 he was voted £64, but at a special Precinct meeting he was voted an additional £128. In 1779 his salary was £400 and the year following it jumped to the princely figure of £1800. In 1781 it dropped to £75 in silver. In this varying credit of the country the Precinct became bewildered to such an extent that in 1782 it voted to petition the General Court for instructions and advice respecting the support of the minister. The same year the Precinct voted in despair to give the Collector one silver dollar "in the room of thirty paper ones."

This alarming inflation of prices was not the only obstacle in the path of the peace of the Precinct. The Baptists were on the increase and with their increasing strength swelled the murmurs of discontent with the rates; while the South Meadow people who had built a meeting house in the Southern part of the Precinct were in a constant state of rebellion. There had been so much friction with these malcontents that the Precinct voted to petition the General Court for authority to let the people south of the South Meadow river decide for themselves whether they would belong to the old church.

Rev. John Howland saw the Precinct develop to its zenith and enter its decline. He saw his country pass through trying ordeals; the government overthrown by revolution; the powers of the Precinct melting away one by one; yet through all of these vicissitudes he seems never to have lost his supreme faith.

In 1794 John Bennett of Rochester, dissatisfied with the doctrine preached in his church, petitioned to become a member of the South Precinct of Plympton by virtue of a small tract of marsh meadow owned by him within the limits of the Precinct. In 1799 John Samson, Isaac Shaw, Isaac Mann, Jr., John Bryant, Joshua Perkins and Elkanah Shaw, petitioned the General Court to set them within the jurisdiction of the First Precinct of Middleboro. These mutineers resided in the Rocky Meadow district and their petition was opposed. The committee authorized to act for the Precinct was instructed to settle with the petitioners, provided it could come to an agreement by sacrificing Samson and Shaw.

During the last quarter of the eighteenth century, opposition to the rates developed strength rapidly. The Revolution, the Constitution and the incorporation of the town of Carver gave strength to newer methods of church government and the old regime, recognizing the strength of the opposition, made frequent abatements. While the Precinct was not legally dead until 1833, the dawn of the 19th century saw its surrender to public sentiment for its power had waned, its Assessors powerless and its rate bills optional with the tax payer. Annual remittances of the taxes against the Baptists and the South Meadow people were made and amounts raised to cover the deficiency. Not infrequently the Precinct voted to assess those who would volunteer to pay the assessment and so the custom of supporting the minister by voluntary subscriptions came in robed in the raiment of the old order. In 1806 for the first time, the Precinct voted to pass the contribution box after services every Sunday evening.

Through all of these vicissitudes is stamped the greatness of Rev. John Howland. When his people were blessed with abundance he shared in their blessings; when they were pinched by poverty or shaken by financial disturbances he shared in their misfortunes. To carry his people through hard years, he volunteered to take a reduced salary or to accept a part of it in "corn, rye, or any other provisions which he might want and which his people could spare." Thus for sixty years he stood as a bulwark of faith in prosperity and in adversity, and in the dissensions among his people his voice seems to have been for peace and his sincerity never questioned. Perhaps it was one of his rewards to give up his life before the actual dismemberment of his church.

And now arose the question of selecting a successor to the venerable Howland. Calls were voted Lothrop Thompson, Daniel Thomas and Gaines Conant but they all ended in failure. In January, 1807, Rev. John Shaw accepted a call and became the third settled minister of the Precinct. He was ordained October 7 by the following Council: Rev. Samuel Niles and Deacon Jacob Pool, Abington; Rev. Joseph Barker and Deacon Perez Thomas, Middleboro; Rev. Noble Everett and Capt. Jeremiah Bumpus, Wareham; Rev. Adoniram Judson and Maj. Benjamin Warren, Plymouth; Rev. Jonathan Strong and Deacon William Linfield, Randolph; Rev. James Kendall and Benjamin Whiting, Plymouth; Rev. Abel Richmond and Deacon Jacob Thompson, Halifax; Rev. Asa Mead and Deacon David Edson, Bridgewater.

With the ministry of Shaw began the dissolution of the Precinct, although attempts were periodically made to prolong its life. At regular and special meetings the question of holding portions of the services in the South Meeting house, and later in the Central Meeting house furnished a bone of contention for half a century. While the troubles of the Precinct were carried into town meetings the town as a whole remained impartial and the last days of the Precinct and the first days of the Parish were marked by a succession of struggles, compromises and defeats for those who heroically strove to maintain the old regime.

In 1808 the minister was instructed to preach one-third of the time in the South Meeting house, and a committee named to see where the centre of the town would fall. Such attempts to establish one church in town were moves of the insurgents and opposed by the old guard. The year following the mutineers stayed at home on election day, while the Precinct without opposition voted that every ratable man be taxed and the collector was instructed to "try and see what he can collect." At this meeting it was voted to put out the collection of taxes in the South part of the Precinct to the lowest bidder, but there was no bid. The next move was to elect Jesse Murdock collector at a commission of 20 cents per pound, but Murdock declined the offer, and another committee was named to find someone who would serve the Precinct as Collector. This committee reported its inability of finding anyone who would accept the position and the meeting adjourned. At a meeting in November following Maj. Nehemiah Cobb, an uncompromising leader of the old church, volunteered to collect the taxes against these rebellious Southrons, but he was not successful and the following January the rates against forty-eight men who had paid towards the support of the Baptist minister were remitted by a margin of five votes and against a written protest signed by 28 of the old guard.

In 1811 James Vaughan and Thomas Hammond, a committee to consult in matters pertaining to taxation and to make proposals to the Baptists, reported that they were unable to find a committee of the new society that was willing to confer, and the following year the Precinct voted to circulate a subscription paper to see how much could be pledged for the salary of the minister, Rev. Mr. Shaw having consented to remain another year for what volunteer subscriptions could be obtained. In 1813 the birth of the donation party occurred, when by vote the day after Thanksgiving was set apart as a day when anyone so disposed could meet at the residence of the minister with their own choice by way of contribution.

In 1816 the standing committee was instructed to meet a committee of the Southern society to apportion the money raised for preaching and also to "persuade those of the Baptist denomination to take proper measures to be set off or to be taxed by the Precinct."

In 1824 the Centre meeting house having been erected, the Precinct voted that all persons south of the Plains have preaching in their own meeting house in proportion to what they subscribed for the support of the minister. Undaunted by numberless defeats, a new committee was chosen to circulate a paper for the purpose of seeing how many would volunteer to pay their taxes. But revolutions do not run backwards, and the old method of supporting the pulpit by compulsory taxation was dead forever. Recognizing finally in 1825 that further efforts to revive the ancient regime were useless, a special meeting was called in July, which voted to pass subscription papers for the support of preaching in the North and Central churches. This plan worked so satisfactorily that the next year the South was taken into the plan, and Jabez Sherman for the North, Capt. Lothrop Barrows for the Centre, and Deacon Asaph Washburn for the South were named as a soliciting committee to raise funds for the support of preaching in their respective churches. The annual meeting for 1827 was held in the Central building, and the two societies united for that year.

As it is true that the Precinct was dead long before it was abolished by legislative enactment, it is also true that the Parish was in existence before it was formally adopted as a custom. The old died and the new was born in a common twilight, when the ideal of the fathers blended in the ideal of the sons. The last Precinct meeting was held October 18, 1830, and the first Parish meeting March 28, 1831.

There were radicals and conservatives in that conflict. The conservatives held relentlessly to the old way, the radicals as stoutly for a change. Between these extremes there appears a strong faction whose purpose was to hold the Precinct together in one strong compact and in whose minds sectarianism held a secondary place. This faction fought and compromised against a division of the church, but the Fates were against them.

BENJAMIN W. ROBBINS
From a Photograph taken in 1882

SOUTH PRECINCT OF PLYMPTON

At a period corresponding with the demise of the Precinct the South disappeared as a disturbing factor. Methodism had its birth in that end of the town about 1828, and those unconverted to the doctrine of Wesley were left to shift for themselves. This faction controlled the South Meeting house, but it lacked the soul to give it life, and save occasional efforts there was no organized church work until the Union society was organized in 1853.

But for another quarter century after the passing of the Precinct the union under the Parish between the North and Central societies continued. Both societies had the use of church buildings, both were positive forces in the community, both were ambitious to keep their houses open for public worship, but each was too poor financially to stand alone.

This policy of union, desirable as it seemed to many, in the development of sectarian matters at that age, was unnatural. The tendency of the age was against it, and gradually we see the societies drifting apart.

No language can present this cleavage in a more eloquent manner than that presented by the Parish votes. With a few notable exceptions the Parish meetings were held in the North meeting house, and the old society leaders disliked to yield to the extent of holding any of the services in the Central building, however much policy may have pointed out the wisdom of such a course. And yielding to this demand for a while one-third of the services were held at the Centre; then one-third during nine months of the year; then one-third for six months of the year; then one meeting in every seventh; then one-third for five months of the year. In 1853 nine services were held in the Central building, and in 1854, the year that witnessed the end of the union it was voted to hold one-sixth of the services in the Centre church provided that society would pay for them. Thus ended the union of the two societies and long before the Parish was abolished it had relinquished all claims to the outlying districts, confining its jurisdiction to the northern end of the town with a section of Middleboro, and came to be known as the church and society of North Carver.

There were practical reasons why the Parish should remain intact and when the societies parted the question of supporting a minister became a serious problem for both. At times there was no settled minister over the old society and its meeting house had become so poor that it was the main fact that led to the resignation of Rev. Stillman Pratt. From this time to the end of the career of the Parish its annual meetings were stereotyped affairs — simply the election of officers and a vote to leave the affairs of the Parish in the hands of the Standing Committee. There were years when no Parish meetings were held the management of its former duties having been assumed by the church. Thus the Parish, like its predecessor the Precinct, yielded by force of circumstances to newer methods of church government. From 1896 to 1903 there was no Parish

SOUTH PRECINCT OF PLYMPTON 83

meeting, and in 1903 a meeting was called for the purpose of deeding the church building, Parish meadow and woodlot to the church, and in 1907 the final act — a vote to abolish the Parish.

The material body of the Precinct was similar to that of our modern town. A moderator was chosen to preside at the meeting and its adjournments, and the annual meeting was held in March. At the beginning of the meeting an auditing committee was chosen to examine the account of the treasurer, and as the account was brief the auditors finished their duty and reported before a new treasurer was chosen.

A standing committee, annually elected, was the executive arm of the Precinct, bearing the relation to its affairs that a board of Selectmen holds in the affairs of a town.

Assessors were annually chosen who assessed the poles and estates for the support of the church. The Baptist church was the first to attack the work of the assessors holding it unfair to tax one for the support of a doctrine foreign to his belief. In the latter days of the Precinct it was voted to apply to the courts for authority for the assessors to enforce their decrees, an authority they already held but which had become obsolete through public sentiment.

The position of a collector was an undesirable one and not until 1764 did one of these publicans succeed himself. So unpopular was this official as sentiments changed, that frequent special meetings were necessary to fill the vacancy caused by the declination of the elected officer, and twice at least the Precinct voted to prosecute its collector for declining to qualify. Consider Chase seems to have been imbued with peculiar taste or qualifications for this position, and he was several times accepted after endeavoring to fasten the duties on some other candidate.

The years 1743 and 1744, no assessments having been made, there was no work for a collector, and this situation occurred frequently in later years. Sometimes as a matter of precedent, or law, a collector was chosen and the Precinct voted that in the event of any work falling to him he "should be honorably rewarded." The compensation of this official varied. Sometimes he was agreed with for a stated amount; sometimes he was voted a commission; sometimes the collections were put up at auction; and once at least the Collector volunteered to do the work for what he could collect from people who resided outside of the Precinct and once also he was paid by subscription among the wealthier residents of the Precinct.

The most serious situation confronting a Collector arose in consequence of the inflation attending the Revolutionary finances. The Collector was held responsible for his collections, and after making his collections to find that his money was almost worthless he was in a sea of trouble. To help him out of this dilemma the Precinct voted to fix the ratio with which he could exchange his paper for silver. One Collector who found his receipts heavily loaded with counterfeits, was released on the ground that he "took it ignorantly."

Frequently, beginning in 1781 when the authority of the Precinct had begun to wane through the persistent mutiny of the South Meadow people, two Collectors were chosen, one for the North and one for the South. To fill the latter position was a difficult undertaking, for that section of the Precinct was solidly opposed to the rates, and it was necessary at times to vote to sustain the Collector in the event of a law-suit following his attempt, before any one would accept.

Beginning with 1734-35 an agent was annually chosen "to keep the key to the meeting house and see that it was swept." In 1765 this agent was called the sexton, but the 19th century was well under way before this official became permanently known under that designation.

The critic of the twentieth century does not appreciate the importance of the Meeting house of the seventeenth century. The residents were scattered farmers without newspapers, telephones or railroads, and with no communication through the mails. Even horses and carriages were not in common use, roads were rustic and blind, and the travelling was necessarily slow. The custom of meeting at the taverns had not developed and the family really lived in a world by itself unmindful of the wishes or circumstances of its neighbors. It can readily be understood how, under such conditions, the Meeting house should be regarded as the first essential of civil government, the centre where the isolated people could meet to learn of each others sorrows and joys, and to transact business of a common concern. And the sermon, for there was no reading matter available and few could read even if they had the books, and thus to the common people the Bible and the sermon furnished the only message between people and people. Hence the erection of a Meeting house was essential before a community could be robed in the rights, immunities and powers of a civil body.

In the early days of the 18th century the residents of the South section of the town of Plympton felt the necessity of one of these Meeting houses and in 1731 the initial papers were drawn. The building was to be located on the hill north of the burying ground and the subscriptions, one third in money and two thirds in specie, were payable to Richard Dwelley and Isaac Waterman. The temple was erected according to plan between October, 1731, and December, 1732.

The location of the Meeting house was a bone of contention from the start. While there appears to have been no dissatisfaction over the original site the rapid growth of the Southern section of the new Precinct early gave rise to discontent which became the subject of agitation for upwards of a century. In 1767 a serious attempt was made to move the building to a lot near the Cross Paths, the South Meadow people contending that the Meeting house should be near the centre of population, and as their polling strength approached that of the defenders of the old site they proved a factor to be reckoned with. The question came to an issue at a Precinct meeting in the year above mentioned when a motion to move the building was defeated, but by such a narrow margin that it did not end the agitation. At the same meeting it was voted to enlarge the building and plans were adopted to carry the ordinance into effect.

The South Meadow people refused to abide by this verdict and they caused a special meeting to be called to act upon reconsideration. Some went so far as to demand a division of the Precinct. While they lacked the strength to force a reconsideration they alarmed the old guard who, fearing a weak committee rescinded all previous orders and voted with a sweep "to take affairs in their own hands," and in this drastic manner the old building was enlarged, but against the loud protests of the Southrons.

The South Meadow people were so persistent in the matter that the friends of the Precinct decided it the part of wisdom to bring some pressure to bear that would end the agitation. Accordingly at a meeting in 1769 it was voted to leave the whole question to a disinterested committee composed of Capt. Josiah Snell of Bridgewater, Col. John Thomas of Kingston and Thomas Mayhew, Esq., of Plymouth. The Arbitration Board thus constituted visited the Precinct, viewed the situation, heard all persons interested, and in September rendered its report. The report counselled unity but decided that the Cross Paths was not a proper place for a Meeting house. This report silenced the agitation for a while but it did not remove the cause and the same question came up two generations later in its old virile form.

This temple stood for nearly a century and until it became in a condition unfit for public uses, while the financial condition of the Precinct coupled with the old dissatisfaction over the question of a location interposed serious barriers in the way of the erection of a new building.

The extreme South enders had erected a building of their own, but as the Precinct had refused to use it according to the wishes of the Proprietors, these residents added their strength to that of the South Meadow people in the fight for the location of a new Precinct Meeting house.

Rev. John Shaw may be considered as the last of the ministers of the old regime and after he surrendered his charge the Precinct rapidly decayed. A serious attempt beginning in 1816 and ending in 1821, was made to get the fragments together but to no purpose. The line of cleavage between the two societies was too marked and to add to the perplexities of the situation the Congregationalists were hopelessly divided on the question of location.

In 1816 the Precinct voted to demolish the old structure and build anew on the same site. This was the olive branch held out by the old guard who really favored a site near the Green, but by way of a compromise this plan was suggested only to be rejected by the South Meadow people. Two weeks later all previous orders were reconsidered and a committee consisting of Ensign Barnabas Lucas, Capt. Joshua Cole and Nathan Cobb named to make an estimate of a new building. In January following all votes were again reconsidered

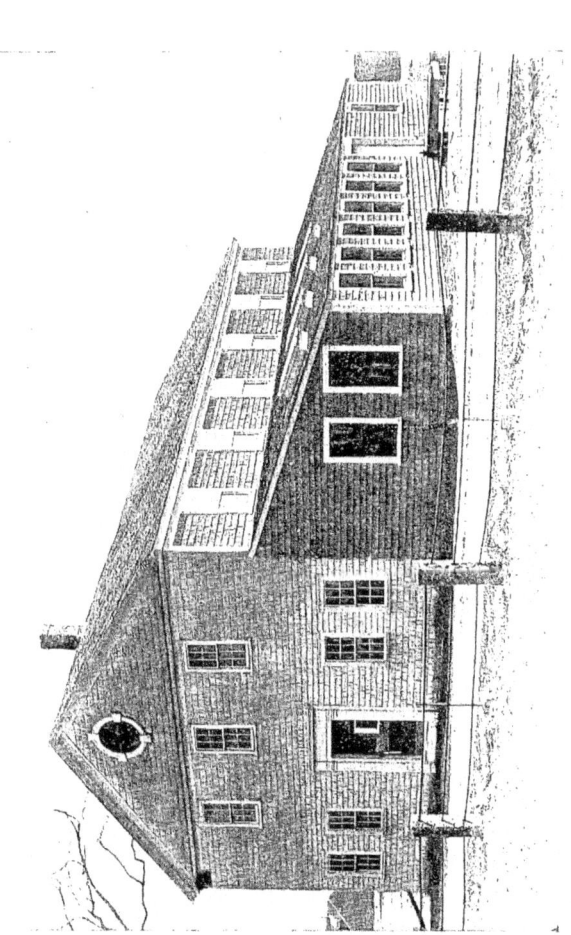

THE SECOND CHURCH, BUILT 1823

After 1860 King Philip's Hall; Lower Floor used by Chandler Brothers as Shoe Shop. Later remodeled for Screen House with Upper Story divided into Lodging Rooms for Employees

and the Precinct began anew by voting an assessment of one hundred and fifty dollars on the pew holders for the purpose of repairing the building. This action did not meet with success as the assessment was not collectable in those degenerate days of the Precinct. The friends of the Precinct gave up the struggle at this point and rested until 1819 when they voted to build a new Meeting house near the Green provided some one would contribute the lot, and in 1820 they voted unconditionally to build a new Meeting house in the North end of the Precinct. While the vote appears on the Precinct records it was not strictly speaking a Precinct move, and no serious effort was made to hold the Precinct to the contract. The South and Centre had retired from the compact forever and when the building was built it was financed by the Proprietors of the North Meeting house. The question of a location was not settled and no sooner had the plan started than the Congregationalists of the Centre united with the Baptists to build the Central Meeting house. This union between the two sects for the erection of the temple resulted in its common use for nearly fifty years or until the plan of its construction died a natural death through the death or neglect of the Proprietors.

PLYMPTON IN THE REVOLUTION

In common with other Old Colony towns with one notable exception Plympton entered seriously into the problems that led to the Revolution. Not the least of the obstacles in the way of the execution of its work was the financial straits in which the town found itself, and however heartily she may have desired to play her part in the great struggle she was hampered by circumstances beyond her control. But hers was no isolated case for it is a well known fact that the problem of financing the country through a seven years' destructive war transcended every other problem. The soldiers were ready but the means were lacking.

However, unless the cause went by default, the town must assist in caring for her soldiers, caring for their families, and providing its quota of beef and other necessities called for by orders of the Continental Congress. No sooner did the storm break than the country's money and credit vanished. Attempts to supply the deficiency by issuing paper met the fate expected for there was no permanent government and the fiat of the Continental Congress died when the congress adjourned. What wonder that the continental currency, with its cable cut, soared away into a bodyless myth? And how natural for people to use the term in measuring items of no conceivable value. So far did the currency soar that in one year the town of Plympton voted seventy-eight thousand pounds for war purposes, and for all practical purposes the appropriation may as well have been seventy-eight millions, for however easily the appropriation may have been made and the paper collected it was forever worthless. Committees were appointed to fix the ratio between the new and old "emitions" and hard money. Sixty to one was easily written and proposed — not so easily sustained when one of the quantities compared was in hiding and the other uncontrollable. The Committees might as well have attempted to fix a ratio of velocity between Plymouth Rock and the East wind, and we may smile as we speculate on the feverish debates in town meeting upon the question of accepting the Committee's report, with a vote of non concurrence. And so while we appreciate the sacrifices of the soldiers at the front we should not forget the sacrifices of those who stayed at home.

The townspeople shared the sentiment against the Stamp Act and assisted in the agitation for its repeal. Its representative in the General Court for 1765 was instructed to act with the representatives from Boston, believing that what Boston desired, Plympton should desire, and having full faith in the patriotism and judgment of the Boston leaders. The town voted promptly against paying anything from the Province treasury for damages sustained in the disturbances against the Stamp Act, while the matter of erecting a monument in honor of the services of Pitt in securing the repeal of the obnoxious law it was content to leave at the discretion of the General Court.

Following the repeal of that law tariff taxes became the storm centre of the town's revolutionary spirit. Here again the Boston leaders were entrusted when it was voted unanimously to concur with the representatives from the town of Boston in the matter of boycotting certain imports and of promoting manufacturing in the Colony. In 1768 Capt. John Bradford was chosen as the town's representative to a convention in Faneuil hall "to take under consideration the dangerous situation we apprehend this Province is in." Gov. Bernard had dissolved the General Court at a time when the Colonists were apprehensive of an attack from the French, and fearful of the loss, through British usurpation, of their civil and religious liberties.

In July, 1774, Capt. George Bryant, William Ripley, Dea. Samuel Lucas, Capt. Seth Cushing, Dea. Thomas Savery, Benjamin Shurtleff and Joseph Perkins were named as a committee to consider the alarming state of public affairs and report at a later meeting. This report indicates the seriousness with which the committee viewed the situation and their resolution to meet it firmly. The report says:

"In the first place we recommend unto all to be deeply humble before God under a deep sense of the many aggravated sins which abound in the land in this day of our calamity which is the fundamental cause of all the calamities that we feel or fear and repent and turn to God with our whole hearts. Then we may humbly hope that God will graciously be pleased to return unto us and appear for our deliverance and save us from the distress we are now laboring under and prevent larger calamities coming upon us.

We also recommend that the town by no means to be concerned in purchasing or consuming any goods imported from Great Britain after the first day of October next and until our grievances are removed, and with regard to entering into any combination respecting purchasing goods imported from Great Briton we humbly conceive it would be very improper to act anything of that nature until the result of Congress shall be made public and upon the report thereof we advise the town to be very active in pursuing the most regular method in order to promote the good of the public and the flourishing state of the same.''

The above committee with the addition of David Megone, James Harlow, John Bridgham, John Shaw, Isaiah Cushman and Isaac Churchill were continued to act upon the report of the Continental Congress.

The struggle was on in earnest now and there shall be no turning back until we are freed from British power. Seriously and carefully but firmly the town stood by the provisions of the Congress and the proposals of the patriot leaders for furthering these ends. Families and friends must be separated, brothers may strike at each other from opposing sides in the bloody conflict, for in the dark hour of war more emphatically than at any other time is fulfilled the saying of the prophets: "Ye cannot serve God and mammon." The out and out Tories departed and their lands were seized and rented for the benefit of the town treasury.

Another considerable faction with Tory learnings that could not go to the extent of forsaking property and associations whose voice was always on the side of regularity and who constantly scanned the cloudy horizon for the star of peace that would compromise the differences between crown and subject. When in 1775 the town voted to pay the Province tax to Henry Gardner of Stow instead of to the Province Treasurer these conservatives called a special town meeting to act upon reconsideration. It is admitted that these conservatives had regularity on their side but the town had cast its lot in the vortex of revolution where precedent and regularity are abolished and by a large majority it refused to reconsider its revolutionary action.

In that tempestuous year of 1774, Plympton's representative in the General Court was instructed to "do nothing that is inconsistent with our charter rights and privileges," but in case the Governor should adjourn the Court to Boston said representative must refuse to attend, unless the Governor would first remove the British soldiers from the town. Deacon Samuel Lucas was chosen as the town's representative to a Provincial congress at Concord.

Early in 1776 a committee of six was named to solicit for the poor of Boston and Charlestown, and Capt. Seth Cushing was chosen representative to the General Court to be holden in Watertown. The following Committee of Safety, Correspondence and Refraction was chosen by the town: Thomas Savery, Thomas Loring, Jr., Isaiah Cushman, Eleazer Crocker, Joshua Perkins and Benjamin Ward. And in these stirring pre-revolutionary days, the town of Plympton discounted the Continental Congress by forty-two days, declaring for independence at a town meeting May 23d when, according to the records of the town clerk, "voted unanimously independence of Great Briton," and caused the Selectmen to take a special oath to take a full account of the number of the inhabitants of this town agreeable to the order of the Continental Congress.

In the last years of the war the town had to exert itself to fill its quotas, and the calls were provided in town meetings. Years of hardships, financial discouragements and uncertainties, had made enlisting hazardous, but the town found a way to hold its own and its quotas were always provided for. It is fair to state that the total enlistments, including re-enlistments from the town during the war equalled one-third of the population. The olive branch was never held out to the Tories. In 1783 it was voted "not to receive any of the Refugees which had fled to the enemy for protection into this town," and to emphasize the vote it was voted to hire out their lands and turn the rentals into the town treasury.

THE CONGREGATIONAL CHURCH
Built 1859

PLYMPTON IN THE REVOLUTION

The town sent two representatives to the convention that framed the Constitution of 1780. The representatives made their report, but the records are silent as to any final action. It is probable that there was difference of opinion as to the merits of the instrument which was compromised by delay. In 1780 the following committees were chosen to report at a subsequent town meeting, work and places of service of the various soldiers who had served in the revolutionary army from Plympton:

For Capt. Sampson's company: Isaiah Cushman, Isaac Churchill, Sylvanus Bartlett.

For Capt. Harlow's company: Timothy Ripley, Dr. Dean, Benjamin Cushman.

For Capt. Shaw's company: Nehemiah Cobb, Eleazer Crocker, Deacon Lucas.

For Capt. Hammond's company: Joseph Barrows, Benjamin Ward.

It is known that these committees performed the work assigned them and made a full report to the town. The report was not recorded nor does it appear that it was formally adopted. Such a paper would have been of great assistance in the matter of securing pensions for the veterans, and from the historical standpoint the loss is irreparable. Why the paper was not recorded may be a matter of conjecture, but upon this point Lewis Bradford* speaks plainly, using the word "embezzled" to express his indignation.

---

*Lewis Bradford was town clerk of Plympton from 1812 to 1851. His records are replete with historical sketches, genealogical items, and explanations, making the town records of Plympton unique and instructive from the historical standpoint.

Marshfield was the one point in the Old Colony where Tory sentiment predominated, and had the fortunes of war elected that the initial battle of the Revolution should be fought among these hills, it is evident the Red Coats would have met with a reception even more vehement than they experienced on Lexington green. When the report that a detachment had been sent from Boston to reinforce the Crown sympathizers in the neighboring town spread, the military spirit of the Old Colony awoke and there was consequently much excitement in this region, and on the very day that the patriots of Concord and Lexington were "firing the shot heard 'round the world," nearly two hundred fellow patriots of Plympton were hurrying across the country to fire a similar shot in Marshfield. So large a force marching out of so sparsely settled a community reads more like a crusade than a military uprising, and in so unanimous a cause the farmer's wives and daughters must have watched the proceedings with intense interest.

There are obstacles in the way of obtaining a complete and reliable list of the soldiers that fought in that war for the credit of Plympton and a more or less indefinite list must necessarily follow. The town records are silent in the matter, and there is danger of mistakes from both sides of the reckoning in making up the list from the pay rolls on file. The fact that a roll was sworn to in Plympton, may not be prima facie evidence that the soldiers were invariably Plympton sol-

PLYMPTON IN THE REVOLUTION

diers, and on the contrary the town may have had soldiers whose names are lost in the unsystematic methods of recording. Often a name appears on the rolls many times and it is not always easy to determine whether it is a repetition of the same person, or a record of two or more soldiers by the same name.

Companies were raised in Plymouth County and it is fair to assume, that these embraced Plympton soldiers. In justification of this, many names appear on these unidentified rolls—names that sound familiar—but with nothing to identify them they must be omitted from the list.

There were Plympton* men in at least five military companies at the breaking out of hostilities, and these companies after the march to Marshfield, were reorganized and continued in the militia during the war. The army was often recruited from the ranks of the militia, detachments, and sometimes the whole company being detached to reinforce the Continental army

---

*Deborah Sampson, while not in the service to the credit of her native town for well-known reasons, has earned a place in Plympton's story of the Revolution. She was born Dec. 17, 1760, a descendant of Governor Bradford, Myles Standish and John Alden. In the latter years of the war, dressed in male attire, she enlisted at Bellingham for the credit of the town of Uxbridge under the name of Robert Shurtleff. She was severely wounded, in 1782, but succeeded in hiding her identity; but, being stricken the following year with a fever, she was sent to a hospital in Philadelphia, where her physician discovered her sex and caused her discharge. By a special provision her name was added to the pension list, and after her death the pension went to her husband, Benjamin Gannett, as a "soldier's widow." She was specially honored by the state and nation.

temporarily, to be returned to the ranks of the militia after the crisis had passed.

The following commissioned officers were in the service at various times during the Revolutionary conflict:

Capt. William Atwood: Marched with his company to Marshfield.

Capt. John Bradford: Marched with his company to Marshfield; continued in the militia as Captain in 1775 and 1776, serving as Continental agent.

Capt. John Bridgham: Marched with his company to Marshfield; Captain in the militia in 1775, and in Capt. Cotton's company in Rhode Island in 1778.

Capt. George Hammond: Private in Capt. Shaw's company at Marshfield; commissioned as Captain of the militia in 1776 and serving until 1778.

Capt. Thomas Samson: Sergt. in Capt. Bradford's company at Marshfield; ensign in the militia in 1775; Captain of a company of militia 1776; marched with his company to Bristol, R. I., on an alarm December, 1776; went on a secret expedition against Newport, R. I., September-October, 1777; Captain in the militia 1778; in command of a company in Rhode Island in 1781 three days.

Capt. Nathaniel Shaw: Marched with his company to Marshfield; in the militia 1776; marched with his company to Bristol, R. I., on an alarm December, 1776; also Captain in the militia 1778.

PLYMPTON IN THE REVOLUTION 101

Lieut. Elijah Bisbee, Jr.: Sergt. in Capt. Loring's company at Marshfield; Lieutenant in Capt. Ebenezer Washburn's company in Rhode Island 1776; in command of Capt. James Harlow's company at Bristol, R. I., 1777; at Castle Island 1778.

Lieut. Nehemiah Cobb: Lieutenant in Capt. Bridgham's company at Marshfield; Lieutenant in militia 1775 to 1780; in detachment to reinforce Continental army in Rhode Island in 1780 three months.

Lieut. Joseph Cole: Private in Capt. Shaw's company at Marshfield; commissioned Lieutenant 1776; Second Lieutenant with Lieut. Frances Shurtleff at Bristol; in Capt. Sampson's company secret expedition against Newport; Second Lieutenant, Capt. Ebenezer Washburn's company 1778.

Lieut. Joshua Loring: Sergeant and ensign 1776-77-78; commissioned Lieutenant May 1779; in Capt. Jacob Haskins' company 1779-80.

Lieut. Joshua Perkins: Sergeant in Capt. Shaw's company at Marshfield; commissioned Lieutenant 1776, Capt. George Hammond's company; in command of a detachment from the company that was sent to Bristol, R. I. on an alarm in March 1777; Lieutenant in Capt. Hammond's company in 1778; also in Capt. Calvin Partridge's company stationed at Dorchester Heights 1778.

Lieut. Zephaniah Perkins: Lieutenant in Capt. Thomas Samson's company in 1776; also Lieutenant in same company at Bristol, 1776 and 1778.

Lieut. John Shaw: Sergeant in Capt. Atwood's company at Marshfield; Second Lieutenant in Capt. George Hammond's company 1776; Second Lieutenant in Capt. Shaw's company at Bristol 1776, and in Capt. Hammond's company 1778.

Lieut. Frances Shurtleff: Lieutenant in Capt. Shaw's company 1776; in command of a detachment that was sent to Bristol, R. I. on an alarm, December, 1776; Lieutenant in Capt. Shaw's company 1778.

Lieut. Silas Sturtevant: Second Lieutenant in Capt. Thomas Samson's company, commissioned 1778; Lieutenant in Capt. Samson's company in Rhode Island 1781.

Lieut. Job Weston: Sergeant, Capt. Loring's company Marshfield; Second Lieutenant, Capt. James Harlow's company 1776; commissioned 1776, Second Lieutenant of Capt. James Harlow's company commanded by Lieut. Elijah Bisbee, Jr., Bristol 1776; Third Lieutenant, Capt. Samson's company secret expedition against Newport; Second Lieutenant, Capt. James Harlow's company 1778; Lieutenant, Capt. Jesse Sturtevant's company detached from militia to reinforce Continental army three months in Rhode Island 1780.

Those whose service was limited to the march to Marshfield:

Capt. William Atwood
Sergt. Joseph Atwood
Nathaniel Atwood
2nd Lieut. Joseph Barrows
Corp. Simmons Barrows
Jonathan Barrows
Benjamin Benson

Salathiel Bumpus
Rowland Hammond
Bartlett Murdock
Thomas Muxam
Gideon Perkins
Robert Sturtevant

Capt. Thomas Loring
Ensign Ignatius Loring
Sergt. James Churchill
James Bishop, Jr.
Nathaniel Bonney, Jr.
Ebenezer Bonney
Noah Bosworth
Winslow Bradford
Ephraim Bryant
Joseph Bryant
Joshua Bryant
Isaac Churchill, Jr.
Isaac Churchill, 3d
John Churchill
Nathaniel Churchill
Elkanah Cushman, Jr.
Isaiah Cushman, Jr.
Samuel Cushman
Thomas Cushman
Abner Hall
Thomas Harlow
Job Holmes
Job Holmes, Jr.
Joshua Loring
Josiah Perkins, Jr.
Luke Perkins
Nathaniel Pratt, Jr.
Jonathan Rickard
Nathaniel Rider
Joseph Ripley
Josiah Ripley
Timothy Ripley, Jr.
Henry Samson
Noah Sturtevant
Zadok Weston
Elisha Whitten, Jr.
Adam Wright
Benjamin Wright

(In Capt. Bradford's company).

Corp. Issacher Bisbee
Sylvanus Bartlett
Nathaniel Churchill
Stephen Churchill
Heman Crocker
Isaac Cushman
Joel Ellis

(In Capt. Bridgham's company).

Sergt. Bartlett Murdock
Ephraim Griffith
Simeon Holmes
Joseph Lucas
Daniel Pratt
Eleazer Robbins
John Shaw
David Wood

(In Capt. Shaw's company).

Sergt. Eleazer Crocker
Sergt. Elisha Lucas
Corp. Eleazer Rickard, Jr.
Drummer Isaiah Tillson
Caleb Atwood
John Atwood
James Doten
Sylvanus Dunham

Daniel Faunce
Nehemiah Lucas
John Rickard
Benjamin Shaw
Benjamin Shaw, Jr.
Jonathan Shaw

John Shurtleff
Edward Stevens, Jr.
John Stevens
Daniel Vaughan, Jr.
Joseph Vaughan
David Wood

Those whose service was limited to the detachment under Lieut. Frances Shurtleff to Bristol, R. I., in December, 1776:

Sergt. Consider Chase
Sergt. Timothy Cobb

Nehemiah Cobb
David Ransom, Jr.

Those whose service was limited to Capt. Thomas Samson's company that marched to Bristol, R. I., in 1776:

Drum. Shadrach Standish
John Bradford
John Churchill

Isaac Loring
James Magoon
Asaph Soule

Those whose service was limited to the march to Bristol, R. I., under Lieut. Elijah Bisbee, Jr., in 1777:

Sergt. Joel Ellis, Jr.
Joshua Loring
Corp. Nathaniel Sherman

Elisha Whitton
Joseph Wright
Samuel Wright, 2nd

Those whose service was limited to the detachment under Lieut. Joshua Perkins, which went to Bristol, R. I., in 1777:

Sergt. Joseph Barrows
Corp. Simeon Barrows

Ellis Griffith
Bartlett Murdock

Those whose services was limited to Capt. Samson's secret expedition against Newport in 1777:

Isaac Bisbee
Jonathan Barrows

Samuel Bradford
Benjamin Ransom

Those whose service was limited to Capt. Samson's three days expedition to Rhode Island in 1781:

Levi Atwood
William Cobb
Edmund Cole, Jr.
Benjamin Bosworth
Consider Briant
Caleb Churchill
Samuel Fuller
Ichabod Hatch
William Harlow
Joshua Palmer
Josiah Parrish
Calvin Perkins
Ebenezer Ransom, Jr.
Frances Ripley
Asa Soule
Zephaniah Soule
Caleb Sturtevant
Eliphalet Waterman

Those at Marshfield and other services in the militia:

Caleb Atwood
Abner Barrows
William Barrows
Abner Bisbee, Corp.
George Bisbee, Corp.
Issacher Bisbee, Corp.
John Bisbee
Noah Bisbee
James Bishop
Samuel Bonney
Simeon Bonney
Perez Bradford
Gideon Bradford, Jr.
John Bridgham, Jr., Sergt.
Benjamin Bryant, Corp.
Levi Bryant, Fifer
Zenas Bryant, Drummer
Benjamin Cobb, Corp.
Jonathan Cobb
Nathan Cobb
Samuel Cobb
John Chamberlain, Corp.
Daniel Churchill, Jr.
Ebenezer Churchill
Elias Churchill
John Churchill
Joshua Churchill
William Churchill
Joseph Crocker, Corp.
Benjamin Cushman
Jacob Cushman
Josiah Cushman
Zachariah Cushman
Amaziah Doten
John Dunham
Silas Dunham
Freeman Ellis, Sergt.
Stephen Ellis
Nathaniel Fuller
John Fuller

106 HISTORY OF CARVER

Barnabas Harlow, Corp.
Nathaniel Harlow
Ebenezer Lobdell, Corp.
Caleb Loring
Ignatius Loring, Jr., Fifer
Ezekiel Loring, 2nd Lieut.
Elijah Lucas
Samuel Lucas
John Muxam
Joseph Perkins
Josiah Perkins
Ebenezer Ransom
Elijah Ransom
Joseph Ransom
Isaac Rickard
Lemuel Rickard
Theodore Rickard
Isaiah Ripley
Samuel Ripley, Corp.
Peleg Samson
Zabdial Samson
Ambrose Shaw
Caesar Smith
Ebenezer Soule, Corp.
Zachariah Standish
Lemuel Stevens
William Stevens
Cornelius Sturtevant, Ser.
Frances Sturtevant, Corp.
Isaiah Thomas
Ichabod Tillson, Drummer
John Tillson
Benj. Ward, 2nd Lieut.
Jabez Weston
Isaac Wright
Joseph Wright
Joseph Wright
Levi Wright
Samuel Wright

Those who served at Marshfield and later in the Continental army:

William Cobb
Ebenezer Dunham
Simeon Dunham
Issacher Fuller
Lazarus Harlow
Barnabas Lucas
Elijah McFarlin
Daniel Soule
Silas Sturtevant
William Sturtevant
Peter Thayer
Benjamin Tubbs
John Washburn

Those who served at Marshfield and in Capt. Samson's secret expedition against Newport:

Josiah Chandler
Ebenezer Cushman
Gideon Samson
Edward Stevens
Jacob Wright

HON. BENJAMIN ELLIS

Those who served at Marshfield and with Lieut. Joshua Perkins at Bristol:

Andrew Barrows
Peleg Barrows, Corp.
James Murdock, Lieut.
Jabez Muxam

Abial Shurtleff
Joshua Totman
William Washburn, Sergt.

Those who served at Marshfield and with Lieut. Frances Shurtleff at Bristol:

Hezekiah Cole
Isaac Shaw Lucas
John Lucas
Eleazer Robbins

Thomas Savery
Benjamin Shurtleff, Jr.
Daniel Vaughan
Samuel Vaughan, Sergt.

Those who served in the militia and later in the Continental army:

Asa Barrows
Barnabas Cobb
Roland Cobb
Ephraim Cole*
Joseph Chamberlain
Joshua Churchill
Stephen Churchill
Thomas Doten
Thomas Doty
Noah Fuller
Benjamin Fuller

Eleazer Holmes
Jonathan Holmes
George Harlow
John King
Isaac Lucas
Ezra Perry
Ephraim Pratt
Ebenezer Standish, Corp.
Moses Standish
Asa Sturtevant
Isaac Tinkham

---

*Ephraim Cole, Joseph Chamberlain, Thomas Doty, John King, Barnabas Lucas, Benjamin Lucas, Elijah Rickard, William Sturtevant and William Whiting are known to have been in camp at Valley Forge. Cole, and possibly others, died there.

HISTORY OF CARVER

Those who served in the militia for varying periods; some probably served in detachments that reinforced the Continental army at critical times:

Ichabod Atwood
Stephen Atwood
Ephraim Barrows
Malachi Barrows
Carver Barrows
Moses Barrows
John Bartlett
Jephtha Benson
Calvin Bradford
William Bradford
Daniel Bumpus
David Bumpus
Seth Bump
Benjamin Briant, Corp.
Joshua Briant
Nathan Briant
Samuel Bridgham
Gersham Cole
Zebedee Chandler
David Churchill
Ebenezer Churchill
Elias Churchill
Joseph Churchill
John Churchill, Sergt.
Timothy Churchill
Benjamin Crocker
Isaiah Cushman
William Cushman
Seth Doten
Asa Dunham
Israel Dunham
Robert Harlow
Ezekiel Johnson
Seth Johnson
Isaac Lobdel
Simeon Loring
Abijah Lucas
Asahel Lyon
Joseph McFarlin
William Morrison
Ephraim Morse
Steven Raymond
Elijah Richards, Corp.
Abner Rickard
Eleazer Rickard
Eleazer Ripley
David Shurtleff
Gideon Shurtleff
Ephraim Soule
James Soule
Sylvanus Stevens
Nehemiah Sturtevant
Ephraim Tinkham
Joseph Whitten
Joseph Wright
Joshua Wright
Zadok Wright

PLYMPTON IN THE REVOLUTION

Those who served at Marshfield, in the militia, and in the Continental army:

John Barnes
Benjamin Blossom
Jacob Bryant
Caleb Cushman
Elijah Dunham
Abner Harlow
Asa Hooper
Samuel Lucas, 3d
Noah Pratt
William Ripley

Those whose service was limited to the Continental army who served for periods of various lengths:

John Appling
Benjamin Barrows
Malachi Barrows
John Bates
Elnathan Benson
Reuben Bisbee
Isaac Bonney
James Bonney
Oliver Bradford
Sylvanus Brimhall
Ford Bryant
Luther Bryant
Luther Bryant
Patrick Bryant, Sergt.
Samuel Bryant
Joseph Chamberlain
Stephen Churchill
Andrew Cushman
Isaiah Cushman
Thomas Cushman, Jr., Corp.
Zebedee Cushman
James Dunham, Jr.
Noah Eaton
William Gardner
Ellis Griffith
Ferdinand Hall, Drum major
Elijah Harlow (died)
James Harlow
William Harlow
Eleazer Holmes
Jonathan Holmes, Corp.
Barnabas Jackson
Jacob Loring
Benjamin Lucas
Consider Lucas
Elisha Lucas
Ephraim Lucas
Zebedee Lyon
David McFarlin (died)
Elijah McFarlin
John Morris (died)
Elisha Morton
Pero Murder* (negro)

---

*Discharged by General Washington for meritorious service.

Edward Murdock
Jesse Murdock
Swanzey Murdock
Prince Newport (negro)
Ebenezer Perkins
John Perkins
Josiah Perkins
Consider Pratt
Benjamin Pratt
Nathaniel Pratt
Elijah Rickard
Frances Ripley
Jacob Loring Ruggles
William Sampson
Ichabod Shurtleff
Peleg Standish

Caleb Stetson
David Sturtevant
Frances Sturtevant, Jr.
John Taylor (died)
Isaac Thayer
Joseph Tinkham
Robert Waterman
Samuel West
William Whiting
Isaac Whitten
William Whitten
Ebenezer Wright
Edmund Wright
Joseph Wright
Joseph Wright
Nathan Wright

HUIT McFARLIN

THE CONGREGATIONALIST CHURCH

The history of this society to the close of the ministry of Rev. John Howland, is identical with the history of the Precinct. The last years of the Howland ministry marked the beginning of the dissolution of the Precinct and from that period societies and sects began to multiply.

After the death of that remarkable man who had watched over the society from 1744 to 1805, the church faced the problem of choosing his successor and that at a time when it was weakened by dissensions. After trying in vain to reach a settlement with Lothrop Thompson and Gaines Conant, John Shaw was ordained October 7, 1807, and became the third ordained minister of the church. The new pastor was destined to pass through a trying ordeal which should tax his resources, involve him in debt, and at the same time bring out the tact and compromising spirit that mark him as a worthy successor to John Howland. Financial troubles at length compelled him to resign and at a Council in 1815, he was formally dismissed. There was still a tender feeling between pastor and people and he left the charge with a hearty recommendation from the church.

Doctrinal disputes had appeared with the inception of baptism in the Precinct a quarter century previous to the ministry of Shaw. For a time the dominating spirits of the church kept a ruling hand on the situation, but as the devotees of the new faith increased in numbers, the cleavage became more marked, and only the diplomatic powers of Howland kept up the semblance of union. And these disputes came as a legacy to Howland's successor, and to break out anew and to ultimately divide the Precinct after Shaw left the ministry.

There was a desire on the part of the majority to see the union continued, and this desire was shared by the Baptists. But there were doctrinal reasons which stood in the way of a lasting union. An early attempt was made to avert disintegration by the abrogation of the 12th article of faith* whenever a Baptist was admitted to the church membership. An amendment reserving the right to convince the new member of the error of his ways by argument pacified the radicals, and probably a more effective way of keeping alive the embers of discord could not have been devised. This article was the rock on which the societies split. Benjamin Shurtleff, a leading member of the old society, petitioned his church to expunge the article from its creed, but after a long hearing the petition was turned down and Shurtleff had no alternative but to withdraw and join the Baptist society.

For twelve years after Shaw left the ministry of the old society, and Cummings the ministry of the new society, there was no ordained pastor over

---

*The 12th Article of faith related to infant baptism.

HENRY SHERMAN

CONGREGATIONALIST CHURCH 113

either. Church meetings were regularly held and each society manœuvred for itself, but the meetings were so lightly attended that the leaders became alarmed and their united efforts fanned the memorable revival of 1823. Rev. Luther Wright was stationed over the societies and September 14th was set apart as a day when all of the communicants should go forward and acknowledge their sins. Accordingly at the appointed time, the church was filled and when the invitation was given all left their seats and standing in the aisles, assented to a long confession read by the minister.

This signal for an awakening was followed through the following winter by protracted meetings, at which numerous ministers lent their assistance and many conversions were made. At least two days of fasting, humiliation and prayer were observed, Christmas, 1823, and February 5th, 1824. A committee was appointed to look after delinquents, with special instructions to learn why the residents of the South had habitually absented themselves from the house of worship. As a result of this revival twenty-eight joined the church. And now arose the subject of apportioning the time of services between the two societies. At a meeting in the North school house, Deacon Thomas Hammond, whose residence was near the Central Temple and who was a Proprietor of that building, argued for services in both buildings, but no vote was taken.

At a subsequent meeting, it was decided to hold one-third of the services in the Central building, but the ultras rallied, reconsidered, and voted to join with the Precinct and engage a minister to preach all of the time in the Temple near the Green and to petition the Domestic Missionary Society for assistance. But so weak was the old society financially, and so alarmingly were the signs of incohesiveness, that the conservatives appealed to outside ministers for advice. In response to this appeal a committee of ministers investigated the conditions and advised committees from the different sections of the town to get together, select a Board of Reconciliation, and pledge each other to stand by the decision. The old society, acting upon this advice, named a committee to confer with a like committee of the Baptist society. Under the proposed terms of reconciliation, the Council was to revise the articles of faith and establish plans and places of holding public services. The two committees went about their duties with enthusiasm, but the Baptists were unyielding on one point, and that point happened to be the one obstacle in the way of union. They were willing to commit the matter of time and place for holding public services, but on the question of infant baptism they had nothing to arbitrate. It is apparent that both societies were suspicious, for when the orthodox committee reported to its sponsors, naming the Council, its report was rejected and a new committee appointed to name the personnel of the proposed Council.

The arbitration board as finally agreed upon, was composed of Rev. Abel Richmond of Halifax, Rev. Oliver Cobb of Rochester, Rev. Richard S. Storrs of Braintree, Rev. Sylvester Holmes of

New Bedford and Rev. Frederick Freeman of Plymouth. The Council convened and gave the town its best efforts, but the cleavage over the 12th article could not be bridged and the dream of one church in town did not come true. Thus, while the societies could not formally unite, they travelled peacefully together for a while listening to the same discourse, worshipping in the same meeting house, while each proceeded to build stronger its sectarian walls.

The Baptists were not the only heretics the old society was called upon to combat. Methodism appeared about 1830 and two years later, Phebe Shurtleff asked for her dismissal in order to join the Reformed Methodist Society. A committee was chosen to convince her of the error of her ways, but the committee proved powerless, Miss Shurtleff was immovable, and there was no alternative but to vote her dismissal.

Still another and more alarming epidemic broke out in 1835, when Louisa L. T. Chase was converted to the views of Emanuel Swedenborg. This was regarded as a serious matter, and Deacon Nathan Cobb, Ebenezer Cobb and Levi Vaughan were delegated to handle the case with power to call on ministers of other towns for advice and assistance. After laboring in vain to convince Mrs. Chase of her mistake, the committee called Rev. Elijah Dexter of Plympton and Rev. Emerson Paine of Middleboro in consultation. A special church meeting was called and after considering the case, the heretic was excommunicated.

In 1841, several members of the church entered the ranks of the Millerites and in consequence were excommunicated. Again in 1853, Thomas Cushman filed accusations against Mary Fuller, charging her with false and erroneous doctrines. After a hearing, at which it was shown that she had rejected one of the articles of faith and been converted to the doctrine of Universalism, she was expelled.

It will be noted, that the period extending from 1830 to 1850 was prolific with heresy and the result was the final separation of the church in Carver. Methodism had gained a foothold in the South; Baptism held the Centre; Advents and Universalists had laid the foundation for a following and even Spiritualism had claimed its own. And worn out by seventy-five years of incessant fighting for unity, the old society relinquished its claims contemporaneously with the agitation for a new church building at the North end of the parish and under the ministry of Rev. Stillman Pratt, the First Church of Carver entered upon its modern career.

Following the custom of churches in the earlier days, this society kept a watchful eye over the moral welfare of its members. At times the committee on discipline had a crowded docket and frequent meetings were necessary to relieve the docket. In most cases the defendant confessed and was immediately restored to good standing. Many were the chastisements for unchristian conduct, but little of a serious nature appears to have been charged against the communicants. Petty cases which another generation would appeal to the courts were taken up by the church, and again and again small disputes were adjusted to the satisfaction of all parties without recourse to the civil tribunal.

John Maxim, Jr., proved a most stubborn defendant on doctrinal grounds. Complaint having been filed against him "for disorderly walk inasmuch as he had, as it appeared, rejected the leading articles of faith to which he had assented when he became a member of the church, and had not attended public worship in the church, or communed with them for a number of years." Though a messenger was despatched to notify Maxim of the indictment, he refused to appear for trial and regarding the case as hopeless he was excommunicated.

The case of the eccentric but brilliant James Savery* was the most noted of the church trials of this society. Charged with "unchristian walk and conversation, particularly in absenting himself from the house of worship, traveling here and there on the Lord's Day, unchristian feeling and conversation towards those of his brethren who had labored to redeem him," he became the topic for discussion throughout the Precinct.

Previous steps had been taken to redeem him, both on the part of the brethren and the church, when it was decided to take the third gospel step

---

*While a man of sterling character, James Savery was so eccentric as to antagonize the conventionality of common folks. With Albert Shurtleff he shocked the thoughtless people of the town, by voting for abolition long before the rank and file could see anything objectional in chattel slavery.

and he was suspended until such time as he should make Christian satisfaction. After five years of rebellion he went forward, confessed his misdemeanors and was restored to fellowship. Again he came before the disciplinarians when, in 1823, a committee was named to labor with him in regard to making a disturbance in the choir, and failing to come to an agreement, Nathan Cobb was detailed to call on him and respectfully request him not to sing in such a manner as to interrupt the singers. The following year he faced trial on an indictment of four counts as follows filed by Bennett Cobb:

Cutting wood on the Lord's Day.
Disturbing the choir by irregular manners.
Casting reflections upon the singers.
Disturbing the religious services of the young.

After a patient hearing during which the defendant was unyielding, Savery the eccentric, was excommunicated. Still belligerent he continued the contest, until his case went up on appeal to a Council of Ministers. In this Council he was overruled, the church proceedings covering the trial were adjudged regular, and in 1831 he made a full confession and was restored to fellowship in the church.

Rev. Stillman Pratt was the first installed minister over the society after Rev. Plummer Chase, and he was destined to make the most lasting impression of the pastors who followed Rev. John Shaw. During the larger part of the intervening time, ministers had been supplied by the committees with no settled pastor much of the time.

Chase seems to have been a strong character, whose influence was exerted on both the religious and civil affairs of the community. He was installed in 1828 and remained with the society seven years. Reverends Luther Wright, Paul Jewett and Jonathan King held brief sway.

Rev. Stillman Pratt was ordained August 2d, 1851, by the largest Council that met in the parish, presided over by the veteran, Israel W. Putnam of Middleboro. This ministry may be considered the dividing line between the two societies, although the friendly feeling continued, resulting in occasional joint services in the Central Temple. Pratt was engaged with the understanding that he should reside at the North end of the parish and devote all of his time to the society at the Green. Thus this ministry may be called the beginning of the local history of the Congregationalist Church Society.

The first year of the new ministry was eminently successful, although at the cost of the health of the pastor. One-third of his time was devoted to a Boston periodical, from which source he derived one-third of his income. But the inconvenience of getting to and from the city, compelled him to give up that part of his labor and his second year was devoted solely to the society. Mr. Pratt resigned in 1854.

His successor, Rev. Nathaniel Coggswell, remained over the society until 1857. The main feature of this ministry, was the preliminary steps towards the erection of a new church edifice which, however, was not realized until two years later.

MINISTERS

Rev. Othniel Campbell (ord.)	1732—1744
Rev. John Howland (ord.)	1746—1805
Rev. John Shaw (ord.)	1806—1815
Rev. Luther Wright	1823—1824
Rev. Nathaniel Barker	1825—1826
Rev. Seth Chapin	1827
Rev. Plummer Chase (ord.)	1828—1835
Rev. Paul Jewett	1836—1838
Rev. Jonathan King	1839—1841
Rev. E. W. Robinson	1846
Rev. E. Gay	1847
Rev. Stillman Pratt (ord.)	1851—1854
Rev. Nathaniel Coggswell	1855—1857
Rev. W. C. Whitcomb	1858
Rev. ———— Greenwood	1859
Rev. John Moore	1860
Rev. Henry L. Chase (ord.)	1864—1867
Rev. H. P. Leonard	1868
Rev. W. W. Livingston (ord.)	1873—1878
Rev. H. P. Leonard	1880—1881
Rev. Charles F. Goldsmith	1883—1884
Rev. Nehemiah Lincoln	1888—1891
Rev. Oscar F. Stetson (ord.)	1902—1909
Rev. James J. G. Tarr	1911—

TOWN HALL, TOWN OFFICES AND LIBRARY
Built 1886

THE SOUTH MEETING HOUSE

The South Precinct of Plympton covered a much larger area than that embraced by the old society, with the principal settlements in the extreme North, and the new society was not destined long to travel without dissensions. As the farmers spread out over the Southlands, the cast-iron custom of going to church soon led to discontent on the part of those who resided at a distance from the house of worship, and in less than forty years from the raising of the church building at Lakenham, appeared an agitation for still another temple in the Southern section of the Precinct.

A subscription paper was in circulation in 1772, and at a meeting of the subscribers that year Joshua Benson, John Shaw, Bartlett Murdock, Benjamin Ward, and Joseph Barrows were named as a building committee. The hill north of the residence of Peleg Barrows was selected as the site, and to guard against extortion the following prices for labor and materials were established by vote of the subscribers: Carpenters 3s, 3f per day; narrow axe men 2s, 4d, 3f; teaming 6s, 8d; oak timber 4s, 4d, per ton; merchantable boards 1L, 17s, 4d; one and one-fourth inch boards 21L, 6s, 8d, per ton. The size of the building was to be

42 by 37 and Benjamin Ward* was authorized to raise it and finish the outside.

The following year, the subscribers assumed the style of Proprietors, and voted to build the building by pews, the amount subscribed to be adjusted with the amount bid for the pew. Fifty men were appointed to raise the structure and by way of a guarantee, the Proprietors voted to purchase two barrels of rum and to furnish it in sufficient quantities to both workmen and spectators. By October, 1774, the building was so far completed that the first legal meeting was held within its walls, at which John Shaw was chosen moderator and Joseph Bridgham vendue-master. Nearly all of the subscribers became Proprietors by virtue of bidding in a pew and they, with their successors, were the owners of the meeting house.

A two-story building of massive oak frame formed the material body of the Temple. The pulpit was on the east side with the main entrance from the west. The pews were of the style of the times, painted white with mahogany trimmings, while a huge sounding board assisted the minister in reaching the ears of the auditors.

As soon as the building was fitted for public meetings, began a half century struggle between the South Meadow folks and the rulers of the Precinct. In July, 1775, a special meeting was called to see if the Precinct would vote to instruct

---

*At this celebrated "raising" Benjamin Ward performed a feat that has been handed down in folklore. After the frame was raised, he startled the spectators by shouldering his broad axe and ascending the ladder he walked the plate from corner to corner.

THE NORTH CARVER SCHOOL HOUSE

Rev. John Howland to hold a part of the weekly services in the South meeting house. The proposition was defeated by a vote of 26 to 20, whereupon another meeting was called to act upon reconsideration and this also was defeated by the narrow margin of 21 to 20. So persistent were the agitators, that in October the minister was instructed to preach one-fourth of the time in the new meeting house. This was only a temporary move and at the next March meeting, the Precinct voted to raise ten pounds by taxation "to help the sufferers at the South end to preaching." A similar grant was made the following three years, then came the Revolutionary period with sixty-two pounds in 1779 and two hundred sixty-two pounds in 1780.

About this time the war against the rates developed and further appropriations may be regarded in the nature of compromises, but as in numerous historic parallels they served only to fan the embers of discontent.

In 1785 no appropriation for preaching was granted, but in lieu of it ten pounds was raised for the purpose of abating the taxes of those who resided most remote from the regular meeting house, while it was further voted to indemnify the Collector should he be put to unnecessary expense in collecting the taxes south of the river. The year following, Barzilla Besse, Peter Shurtleff and Jabez Muxom, who resided towards Tihonet were exempted provided they paid taxes in Wareham, and the Precinct voted to support preaching in the new meeting house in proportion to taxes paid into the treasury by residents south of the river.

In 1788 preaching one-fourth of the time was granted the South, but the spirit of another age was spreading and liberal as these concessions may appear, the Precinct had to redeem its promise to protect its Collector and before the year ended, it was flatly voted to have no preaching outside of the regular meeting house.

The mutineers stood firm and in 1792 the rates against the following were abated: John Shaw, Bartlett Murdock, Simeon Holmes, Roland Hammond, Capt. Ward, Joseph Atwood, Bartlett Murdock, Jr., John Shaw, Jr., Ichabod Tillson, Carver Barrows, Benjamin White, Ebenezer Dunham, Crispus Shaw, Samuel Atwood, Gideon Perkins, John Atwood, Ephraim Griffith, Ephraim Griffith, Jr., George Hammond, Benjamin Tubbs, Frances Bent and Jonathan Shaw. This may be considered the end of the serious attempt of the Precinct to tax the people south of the river. While the form continued nearly forty years, the assessments were optional with the tax-payer, the clause "provided it can be collected" was added to the assessments, while the amounts annually raised to replace the taxes that could not be collected, was an admission that the old regime had passed away. And before the dawn of the 19th century, the Precinct having given up the struggle, and the town voting a year later not to support the minister by a town tax, the Proprietors were left with a free hand. No theology appears to have disturbed their dreams, but their meeting house was there, and the congregation—let him preach who would. Thus the Baptists found a forum and still later when the church had been divided and sub-divided, bolder heretics found a hearing in this Temple. Aside from the problem of public services, the Proprietors passed through a stormy career—forever wrestling with the matter of repairs. The first fifteen years saw the physical structure stand the test, while all efforts were centred in an attempt to consecrate the Temple to public worship, but as the builders passed and their work began to decay, the troubles of the sons multiplied. As a matter of fact, the building was never finished according to original plans for while agents were periodically appointed to collect arrearages and sell pews for the purpose of raising funds with which to finish the meeting house, the ledger accounts bear witness to the obstacles that beset the workers. To accomplish this end, merchandise of any description was acceptable and iron ware was gladly hailed as legal tender.

In 1792 a rally was made, which continued through two decades. An heroic effort was made to raise funds by placing new pews on the market, but there were already pews enough to meet the demand. Ichabod Benson and Nathaniel Atwood were persistent dunners, but they barely succeeded in collecting enough from back assessments to make imperative repairs. Thus after a fruitless effort to place their meeting house on a more satisfactory footing, the Proprietors lost heart and they were ready to listen to proposals that would have been spurned by their fathers.

In the preceding forty years momentous changes had transpired, chief among them so far as this story is concerned the Colonies had developed into a nation and the Precinct into a town. The area of the new town was dotted with settlements, the church was divided, thrifty furnaces were in operation at Popes Point, Federal and Charlotte around which clustered happy villages, and the theory that there should be a more united work on the part of the young town than could be expected with so many struggling societies gained ground. In 1820 a meeting of the Proprietors was called on petition of Benjamin Ellis et. al., to see if said Proprietors would vote to tear down their meeting house and build one in the centre of the town. The meeting assembled, the question debated with that seriousness its importance deserved, when it was decided by a vote of 10 to 7 to surrender the Temple and rebuild near the Centre provided the North would do the same. This was a safe proposition for the seven remonstrants, for the North was strongly orthodox, the Centre Baptist with no taste for union meeting houses at that time, and so the dream of one church in town passed.

No alternative was left the Proprietors but to rally again. Ben Ellis, Jesse Murdock, Ira Murdock, John Savery, Nelson Barrows and Huit McFarlin—men of nerve and muscle and finance—resided around the old meeting house and rather than see it go down in ruins, they would infuse new life into its creaking joints. A meeting was called, regular set of officers elected, assessment

THE HIGH SCHOOL BUILDING

voted, the Collector patted on the back, and Jesse Murdock, John Bent and Eli Atwood named as the committee to put the building in good repair. The result was a complete remodeling of the inside, necessary repairs on the outside, paint, doorsteps, window springs, and on a wave of enthusiasm the old Temple started on its last career and its decline, so far as that generation was concerned.

Thus passed two more decades and the mortal drift had shifted to 1840. Most of the bodies of the old Proprietors had been carried into their meeting house and from there tenderly through the valley to the Western hill, while their descendants faced the old problem of repairs.

On petition to John Savery, Esq., a meeting of the Proprietors was called to assume the time worn burden. The meeting assembled, Joseph Barrows, clerk, John Bent, second, Treasurer, John Savery, Israel Thomas and Ben Ellis repair committee, and for lack of material said repair committee was clothed with the authority of Assessors, and the meeting adjourned. After two more adjournments a quorum was mustered, an assessment made, the Treasurer instructed to proceed with his duty with all possible speed and the meeting adjourned without day. It was a race with death and the Proprietors lost. The assessment was not made, the Treasurer did not report for—had they not adjourned without day?

But there was yet a career of glory for the old meeting house. Conditions had changed, men had moved, ideals had grown, there were rugged heirs of the Patriarchs in the world and while night dropped its curtain on the old, the dawn of a new career broke upon the old Temple.

In 1854 a meeting was called and a committee composed of Benjamin F. Leonard, Salmon F. Jenkins, Rufus C. Freeman and John F. Shaw instructed to remodel the meeting house. No repairs this time, no setting of glass or patching of roof or building of "more seats under the woman's stairs," but a revolution. In place of the auditorium, a dance hall; in place of the pulpit, a Moderator's cage; in place of the forum of peace, a magazine of war. And so out of the centre of preachings and funerals grew the centre of mirth, of political gatherings and preparations for civil strife. Thus the meeting house of 1772 gave way to Bay State hall and town house of 1854.

While the outward form of the building was unchanged the inside was completely remodeled. The pulpit and gallery were removed and a second floor laid. On the upper floor a stairway, hallway and two spacious ante-rooms took up the north end, while a large hall occupied the remainder of the space. The large oak braces gave the room a lordly air, while the martial spirit was roused by a row of glittering muskets that stood in their racks across the south end of the hall.

About three-fourths of the lower floor on the south side was fitted as an auditorium for town and other public uses. On the east side a boarded enclosure about ten feet square, was set apart for the use of the Moderator and Town Clerk, with an aperture in front through which was protruded the ballot box. If the Moderator happened to be of short statute, his head could barely be seen above the board fence, while the "heeler" who lurked around to see whether the voter who approached to deposit his ballot in the protruding box, voted the white or the buff ballot was amply protected by that same oxide red. In the northwest corner was enclosed the Selectmen's office with its long old table, its library of public documents and its cabinet holding the standard of weights and measures. In the northeast corner was located the powder house—a room set apart for muskets, canteens, uniforms and general munitions of war.

These halls, both upper and lower, were the center of many stirring meetings. Not infrequently one political party would be using one for a rally meeting at the same time the other hall was being occupied by the opposing party devotees. During the days of Civil war, these halls were the centre of activity. Here meetings were held to stir the patriotism of the young; here through many a stormy meeting the town voters wrestled with the knotty problems of war. Here the optimist and pessimist, the thoughtless and the serious, met to don the straps and start for the front, and here was the last meeting place of many of the boys, who went away with visions of glory and returned only in the memories of the friends at home.

For twenty-five years following the close of the Civil war, this building continued in its career of mirth and glory. Town meetings, political meetings, dances, temperance societies and various public usages kept the old spirit alive.

Not alone the residents of Carver, but the young of surrounding towns availed themselves of its spacious rooms and far and near it came justly by the name of The Carver Light-House. And why not? For standing on the highest eminence between bay and bay the light streaming from its windows could be seen from every approach—and it stands too on the highest eminence between our fathers and us.

A meeting house built on the pew-holders plan, sooner or later drifts into the fog. While enthusiasm lasts the owners are listed, but when enthusiasm lags, proprietors die, and heirs lack interest to register their claims, and the responsibility of ownership falls into neglect.

This meeting house did not escape the common lot. For the first twenty years of its life, it was in appreciative hands, then came changes in ownership to be followed by a decade of uncertainty. Again in 1825 the legal heirs were hunted up and listed, but only for a brief reign, when they should again disintegrate to meet no more. A feeble attempt was made in 1840 to rouse the dying order, but only the final gasp, for rapidly after that effort the ownership and care drifted away together, leaving to unidentified descendants the reconstruction of the ancient edifice. Among the proprietors of the first forty years were many Baptists, who were prominently identified with the Carver society. Following is a list of the Pro-

SOUTH MEETING HOUSE

prietors, with the year in which they came into ownership:

Original: Peleg Barrows, John Muxom, Joseph Barrows, Joshua Benson, Jr., Frances Sturtevant, John Shaw, Bartlett Murdock, Ephraim and Benjamin Ward, William Morison, Salathiel Bumpus and William Washburn, Ephraim Griffith and Joseph Atwood, Seth Barrows, James Murdock, Elkanah Lucas, John Bridgham, Bartlett Murdock, Bartlett Murdock, Jr., Obadiah Lyon, Joshua Benson, John Atwood and Simmons Barrows, Samuel Lucas and Huit McFarlin, Nathaniel Atwood, Jr., and Lieut. Caleb Atwood. (Pew No. 7 does not appear to have been sold, and pews numbers 25 and 26 were not sold until 1792, and No. 27 in 1825). In 1782, Thomas Muxom. In 1792, Lieut. Ichabod Benson, Benjamin White and Capt. Elisha Murdock, Robert Shurtleff, Ephraim Griffith and Joseph Atwood, and Samuel Atwood. In 1794, Ebenezer Shurtleff. In 1805, Benjamin Ellis, Ensign Gideon Shurtleff, Ichabod Tillson, and Rowland Hammond. In 1816, Thomas Shurtleff, Eli and Jonathan Atwood, George and Thomas Barrows and Benjamin Ellis. In 1825, John Bent, 2nd.

Proprietors through gallery pews built in 1792. Original: Rowland Leonard and Co., Elezur Lewis, Peleg Barrows, Jr., Ebenezer Dunham, Jr., Eli Atwood, Capt. Benjamin Ward, Carver Barrows, and John Shaw. In 1793, Peter Shurtleff. In 1794, Lieut. Ichabod Benson, (2 pews), Samuel Dunham, John Bumpus, Benjamin Wrightington and Elisha Murdock. In 1816, Zadock Wright and Elisha Murdock.

In 1825, Proprietors were listed as follows: John Bent, 2nd, Peleg Barrows, Peleg Savery, Thomas Shurtleff, John Muxom, Jonathan Atwood, Benjamin Ellis, Alvan Shaw, Thomas Tillson, Capt. Samuel Shaw, Asaph Atwood, Ira Murdock, James Ellis, James Shurtleff, Asaph Washburn, Obed Griffith, Wilson Griffith, Ellis Griffith, Silvanus Griffith, Stephen Tillson, John Tillson, Luther Tillson, Capt. Elisha Murdock, Elisha Murdock, Jr., Lydia Hall, Israel Thomas, Nelson Barrows, Joseph Barrows, Luther Atwood, Jesse Murdock, Silvanus Shaw, Perez Shaw, Silas Shaw, John Bent, Joseph King, Jonathan King, Huit McFarlin, Nathaniel Shurtleff, 2nd, John Savery, Stephen Griffith, Capt. Eli Atwood, Stephen Cushman, Zoath Wright, James Wright, John Bumpus and Benjamin Wrightington.

Proprietors previous to 1825, whose ownership is of uncertain dates: Thomas Hammond, Benjamin Hammond, Lot Shurtleff, Nathaniel Standish, Gen. Ephraim Ward, Col. Benjamin Ward, Joseph Ellis, Joshua Atwood, Perez Washburn, Luther Atwood, Crispus Shaw, Ichabod Dunham and Joseph Robbins.

There is record of twenty-eight pews on the ground floor and twenty in the gallery. Those on the ground floor were numbered up to 26, numbers 27 and 28 being designated as "the seats where the east door entered" and built in 1825. Most of the gallery pews were built in 1792, although a few were added in later years.

In 1841 a legal auction was held to sell pews for the purpose of raising funds for making repairs. At that time pews, or fractions of pews, were sold to the following: Jesse Murdock, Thomas Southworth, Mary Ellis, Hannah Ellis, Ellis Griffith, Hiram Tillson, Zenas Tillson, Aaron Nott and Stephen Cushman.

THE SECOND SEPARATION

The incorporation of the South Precinct was a compromise to save the division of the town which the radicals declined to accept. In November, 1733 and again in March, 1733-34, the town voted down a petition of the new town advocates, whereupon they filed their petition with the General Court. The old town sent Joseph Thomas and Samuel Bradford to oppose the movement and nothing came of it. The following year a committee was named in town meeting to treat with the disaffected element, and the temper of the advocates of division may be seen in the committee report which said: "we cannot agree upon anything." In 1738 another petition was entered with the General Court, but the petitioners were given leave to withdraw and for a half century the question was hushed.

During this period the country was engaged with momentous issues, which held the old town together. It is evident that the advocates of division were residents of South Meadows, the Lakenham people standing with the opposition, and as the population to the South increased, the agitation increased in proportion. During the war days it was found advisable to compromise with the sentiment and one-third of the town meetings were held in "Mr. Howland's meeting house" while the South Precinct had been granted some of the privileges that go with the full fledged town. But as usual, compromises are only postponements of the main issue and the agitation continued.

In 1780, the question found its way into town meeting only to be voted down. Then followed our critical period in which questions of finance transcended all others—in fact the town may be said to be trembling on the verge of bankruptcy—but in January, 1788, the people had so far recovered that the question again was forced to the front, only to be lost by the decisive vote of 40 to 7. As the petitioners had entered their petition again with the General Court, Deacon Thomas Savery, Thomas Gannett, Capt. John Bradford, John Chamberlain and Capt. Benjamin Crocker were delegated by the town to enter a remonstrance. In the following June another petition was voted down by the apparent decisive vote of 33 to 3, but the question would not stay settled. The insignificance of the size of the negative vote in these two cases only signifies that the advocates of division had put the question before the town, while they were saving their strength for the final issue. February 19, 1790 was a spirited day in Plympton, and the days preceding were rife with agitation as both factions marshalled their strength for the final battle. It is evident the advocates of division had carefully measured their strength, and that they had also placed the issue so clearly before the General Court, that they felt positive that their efforts were to be crowned by

THOMAS HAMMOND, JR.

THE SECOND SEPARATION 137

success this time, and when the question was put by the moderator on the day named above, the town of Carver* was ushered into existence by the vote of 97 to 76. Nothing remained but to secure the charter, settle the preliminaries, agree upon boundary lines, divide the poor, etc., and by June 10 their charter having passed its several stages, received the signature of Gov. John Hancock.

The first "legal meeting of the Inhabitants of the town of Carver" was held in "Mr. Howland's meeting house" July fifth following the granting of its charter in which business was transacted according to the following report:

1

"At a meeting of the inhabitence of the Town of Carver Regularly assembled agreeable to the foregoing act of the general cort and held at the North meeting house in Said town on monday July the 5th 1790 the meeting was opend with Prayer By the Rev. John Howland after which Franecis Shurtleff Esq was chosen moderator in Said meeting.

2

Made choice of Capt Nehemiah Cobb Town Clark for the year insueing he was acordingly Sworn by Franecis Shurtleff Esq.

3

mad choice of Dea Thomas Savery, Capt William Atwood and Samuel Lucas jun Select men for the year insuing.

---

*The town received its name in honor of John Carver the first Governor of Plymouth who died childless.

4
made choice of Benjamin White, Samuel Lucas Jun and Barnabus Cobb assessors for the year insuing they ware accordingly sworn.

5
made choice of Franecis Shurtleff Esq Treasurer for the year insuing he was accordingly sworn.

6
Voted to chuse two Collectors for the year insuing.

7
Voted to Devid the Town into two Destricks for Collections, to be Devided as it was Last year.

8
Made choice of Jonathan Tilson for the North Destrick agreed with for 8d on the Pound and was Sworn.

9
Made choice of Caleb Attwood for the South Destrick the year insuing agreed with for 8d on the Pound and was Sworn.

10
Made choice of Jonathan Tillson Constable for the North Destrick the year insuing.

11
Made choice of Caleb Attwood Constable for the South Destrick the year insuing.

12
Made choice of Nathaniel Atwood grand juryman for the year insuing.

13
Made choice of Timothy Cobb Tithing man for the year insuing.

14

Made choice of Benjamin Cobb Sevear of high ways for the first Destrick for the year insuing, maid choice of Lieut Joseph Shaw for the second Destrick made choice of Capt. Benjamin ward for the third Destrick made choice of John Muxam for the forth Destrict.
the 4 above Survayors ware Sworn.

15

Made choice of James Vaughan and Lieut John Shaw fence Vuers for the year insuing.

16

Made choice of Carver Barrows and Isaac Cobb for Hogreves for the year insuing.

17

Voted that Mr. Issacher fuller keep Susannah Cole till fall meeting at the Rate She was bid of at the Last May neeting.

18

Voted that James Vaughan keep Patience Pratt till fall meeting for one shilling and fore pence per week.

19

Voted that the Select men agree with Joseph Robbins how he shall keep Elizabeth Boardmen and how much he shall give for the improvement of her Estate.

20

Voted that Franecis Shurtleff Esq and Capt Nehemiah Cobb be a Committy to join with the Selectmen as a Committy to Settle the Accomps with the town of Plymton.

21

Voted to agurn this meeting till the fall meeting."

The final report of the committee appointed to settle with the town of Plympton was rendered in 1795 by which it appears that the new town was indebted to the old town to the amount of 18 pounds and 18 shillings. Against this amount there was a set off amounting to 6 pounds 3 shillings and 8 pence, being school allowance for Samuel Lucas for the years 1788 and 1789, which deducted made the net debt of the town of Carver to the mother town of 12 pounds 14 shillings and 4 pence. By way of assets that came to Carver as a dowry there were 2968 paper dollars in the treasury of Plympton, Carver's share of which was adjudged to be 1385 dollars. This sum was constituted of Revolutionary reminders known as Continental money, apparently and absolutely worthless except as curios, and Nathan Cobb was constituted the agent of the town to dispose of these "dollars" as "best he could." There is no evidence to indicate that he found a market, for in the saying that has come down to us they "were not worth a continental."

The first town meeting was held in the North Meeting house but the custom of calling a portion of these meetings in the South Meeting house was begun in 1792. The old building near Lakenham cemetery soon went to decay and all of the legal meetings were held in the South building for a few years or until the new buildings at the Green and at the centre of the town were erected in 1824 when the custom of meeting at different sections was renewed. The accommodations of these buildings proved unsatisfactory and all of the town meetings were held in the South Meeting house which came to be known as "the Town hall," being specially prepared for that purpose in 1854. This building was the sole town meeting place until 1881, when it began to divide the honors with King Philip's hall.

An agitation for a town hall sprang up in 1840, but the proposition was rejected by the voters; and again in 1850 and 1854. In 1880 the agitation was renewed, and in view of the degenerate condition of the old building the advocates of the new hall triumphed and the town hall since used was opened to the public in 1887.

Tythingmen were annually elected for upwards of fifty years but their election was little less than the following of a custom as the sentiment of the age was against the spirit that evolved such an officer. Never did one of these officers succeed himself, the last to be elected being James Savery, Eliab Ward and Ellis Griffith in 1847.

The town voters annually settled the question of whether hogs and cattle might be permitted to run at large. Hogs had to be "ringed and yoked according to law," but horses and cattle went unfettered. To regulate the custom hogreaves and horsereves had to be chosen but their duties began to wane about 1825 when the town refused to give the practice the sanction of its approval and the duties of these officers soon fell to the modern field driver. Inspectors of nails were also chosen in the early record of the town.

When domestic animals were permitted to run at large, a town pound was essential, and these have continued through the regime of the field-drivers, the later votes authorizing each field driver to make his own pound or use his own domains for that purpose. The Town Pound was located opposite and a little to the north of the Baptist church. It was seven rails high, three panes square, and furnished with a gate, lock and key. It was repaired for the last time in 1855.

In 1814 according to custom the town became the owner of a hearse and erected a hearse house near the town pound. The town also purchased a set of burial clothes which were used in common. In 1826 sextons were elected by the town and their compensation fixed at one dollar per funeral. In 1841 a new hearse was provided and the house repaired. The building was repaired for the last time in 1855. Soon after this (1868) the custom of providing a public hearse was discontinued at a lively town meeting in which the hearse was championed by George P. Bowers and opposed by William Savery.

After the prevailing custom of caring for the poor when the town was incorporated each individual case was disposed of in open town meeting by setting the ward up at auction and striking him or her off to the lowest bidder. In cases where the pauper was so undesirable that a satisfactory bid could not be obtained it was left in the hands of the Selectmen. In the process of evolution this system soon became unpopular. The poor were on the increase, bidders were scarce, and the voters were driven to look for another system.

To purchase the simplest article of wearing apparel called for a vote in town meeting. The matter would be discussed pro and con, rules of parliamentary procedure would be strictly adhered to, while the question before the house was whether Joseph Cobb should be given a contract to make a pair of shoes for Patience Pratt for six shillings. At the first town meeting of Carver it was voted that the poor be continued in the hands of those who bid them in at the last Plympton town meeting. By the effect of this vote "Isaker Fuller was to keep the Cole woman until Fall at the rate she was bid off in May," "James Vaughan was to keep a woman named Robbins until Fall meeting for one shilling and four pence per week," while the Selectmen were authorized to agree upon terms for which Joseph Robbins should keep Elisabeth Boardman and how much he should give for the improvement of her estate. Among other Town ordinances illustrating this system of caring for the poor were these: The town would assist Amaziah King to build a chimney; Thankful Bumpus' child was left in the hands of the Selectmen "to see that it was not abused;" Edward Stetson was authorized to keep Isaac King until he was twenty-one with "the Town's allowing him twenty dollars for his trouble;" a family was ordered to stay with "his wife's brother in Middleboro;" a ward was voted two dollars and a barrel of herrings to assist him in supporting his family; the Selectmen must see if they can get Cuffy Collins kept for what the Town receives from the State; Samuel Lucas could draw $3.92 for finding an indigent woman a pair of shoes, a gound, a petticoat and two shirts; the Selectmen were authorized to bind out Lydia King until she was eighteen. Such were the troublesome questions that came before the town meetings of the early days.

By 1805 the poor problem had become such a burdensome one in the opinion of the voters that the Selectmen were instructed to collect all of the Town wards, bring them into Town immediately and buy or build a house for them at the lowest possible cost. Nothing came of this vote, however and ten years later another effort was made towards a more centralized and economical system. At the regular March meeting it was voted to postpone the sale of the poor until May. A system developed so rapidly that at the May meeting a committee composed of Samuel Shaw, Thomas Hammond and Hezekiah Cole was named to find a place where the poor could be gathered and to estimate the cost. As a result of the deliberations of this committee its chairman, Shaw, agreed to take the poor at his house. The offer was accepted and Samuel Shaw became keeper of the town's poor, a position he held for ten years. Shaw owned a large farm between the Quitticus road and Cedar brook, residing in a house near the brook and keeping the poor in another of his houses which stood on the corner of Rochester road and Quitticus road. During this decade the poor were well cared for and un-

THE BAPTIST CHURCH—BUILT 1824
Centre of Old Home Meetings

THE SECOND SEPARATION

der the supervision were kept at work as far as their strength and competency would admit. Making cloth for the town from flax purchased by the agent formed a good part of their labors.

In 1826 the salable paupers were again sold at auction while the undesirable ones were left in the hands of the Selectmen. This old system had not come to stay, for the following year the Selectmen were instructed to see what they could buy a small farm for and in 1829 the town voted to build a poor house and Thomas Cobb and Jonathan Atwood was the committee to select the site and contract for the building. The committee followed their frugal instincts so closely, no doubt urged by the town vote to buy a "small building" that the building proved too small and after a year's experiment it was discarded and the poor again fell to the care of the Selectmen. This first poor house† owned by the Town stood on the corner of Rochester road and the road that leads to Beaver Dam road and after several fruitless efforts to remodel it, it was placed upon the market where it remained for nearly twenty years before a purchaser was found. In 1841 the Selectmen recommended trading it for the Winslow Wright farm,* but their proposition did not receive the approval of the town.

---

†The poor were first gathered in a house owned by Samuel Shaw, which stood on the site of the residence of E. E. Shaw. The first poor house stood on the site of the residence of Mrs. P. J. Barrows, and which was burned.

*The Winslow Wright farm, was that now owned by James P. Kennedy.

In 1840 the novel plan of selling the poor singly and then setting them up in a body with the understanding that if the bid in a lump was less than the aggregate of single bids, the bidder of the lump should be accepted. Under this experiment Thomas Hammond was the successful bidder for the lump sum of $471. Financially his speculation was not a success and he was subsequently granted an additional fifty dollars.

In 1843 the Selectmen were instructed to view the farms in town that were for sale, but owing to sectional feeling over the location no agreement was made. Two years later Jonathan Atwood, Eliab Ward, Ebenezer Cobb, Asaph Atwood and Henry Sherman were constituted a committee with authority to purchase a poor farm and as a result of their labors the last poor farm came into the possession of the town. This farm was bought of Capt. Joseph Holmes but it was known as the Deacon Savery place, being the former residence of the town's first Selectman, Thomas Savery.

A share of the dissatisfaction of the poor management of the early times arose from a lack of centralized agencies. A Board of Overseers was chosen in 1838 and again in 1845 but the method at that time did not touch the popular favor and permanent Boards were not elected until 1852. Since that year the Almshouse under the management of the Overseers has been the unquestioned system governing the poor department.

THE SECOND SEPARATION 147

In the march of events the dawn of the 20th century found almshouses as conducted in small towns out of favor. Still more centralized possibilities are hinted at as public sentiment advances and country poor houses may be considered a thing of the past. Consequently there is no agitation looking towards replacing the house burned in 1909 and it is probable that a better system will be developed from the unscientific methods now in vogue in this humanitarian branch of municipal government.

A provision for education, meagre as it may seem to us, was among the early duties of New England town fathers. At first the limit of efforts consisted in a vote in Town meeting instructing the Selectmen to hire a school master. The labor of the master was mainly during the Winter months and there was no minimum or maximum limit to the age of his pupils. School houses and books were not provided, and the seeker for "learning" was expected to interest himself or herself to the extent of procuring books and of finding a place where the school might be held in session provided there were pupils enough to render it necessary. From this beginning developed the District School system which was well under way at the time the town was incorporated, the Districts having been organized under the direction of the Precinct.

The initial move of the Town of Plympton for a school was at a town meeting in 1708 when the freeholders voted to have a school and instructed their Selectmen to hire a school master.

Two schools were established at that time, one at Colchester and one at Lakenham, but in 1716 the master was authorized to spend one fourth of his time at Lakenham and one fourth at South Meadows. By this it appears that one half of the school money was devoted to the South which at the time had established two schools.

In 1734-5 the South Precinct (recently incorporated) was exempt from a school tax provided it maintain a school of its own, and by 1755 while the town voted to have a school in each Parish the South Precinct was left to control its own, Samuel Shaw being the authorized agent to hire a master, and Capt. Barnabas Shurtleff, Dea. Crocker and Samuel Shaw constituted a committee to "model" the Districts in the South. This may be considered the basis of our school system.

There were three Districts at that time, Lakenham, Popes Point and South Meadows, Dea. Crocker representing the first District, Capt. Shurtleff the second and Samuel Shaw the third. At the time Carver was incorporated three districts more had been carved out of the Precinct and at a town meeting in November, 1790, Benjamin Crocker, Consider Chase, Samuel Lucas 3d, Capt. William Atwood, Benjamin White and Caleb Atwood were named as a committee to re-model the school Districts in town and apportion the money. In 1802 a seventh District was established known as the Federal District and made up of the families residing around the Federal Furnace, and in 1851 the Western part of District

No. 4 was set off as a separate District No. 8. With occasionally voting a family from one District to another, and a general vote in 1843 annexing the Federal District to No. 4 and the "Snappit" District to No. 1, these Districts continued up to the time the District system was abolished. After the two Districts named were merged Summer schools were maintained at Federal and Snappit, those old districts drawing their proportional part of the school funds for Summer schools while scholars over eight years of age attended other schools in Winter.

The town's authority in the school was an agent elected in town meeting from the District, but the schools were in the control of the patrons of the school who resided in the District, and in some of the last years of the system the town showed its hostility to the growing sentiment in the direction of town control by voting to permit each District to elect its own agent. Each District built and paid for its own school house, the management of the schools was in the hands of District officers, and resenting the approaching town control it was frequently voted "that the Prudential Committee be the School Committee required by law."

There were various plans of dividing the school money which was raised in a lump sum and assessed by the town Assessors. At first it was divided according to the polls and estates in each District. Later is was divided according to the number of scholars in each District, and as the battle between the advocates of the Town and the District systems waged hotter the town showed its colors by voting that each District should draw all the school money paid into the town treasury within its limits.

For several years after the town's incorporation there were but two school houses within the municipality Districts 2, 3, 5, 6, and 7 holding their schools in private buildings. The first building in the Lakenham District stood directly south of the Green; the second building was built in 1849 and used until the present school house was opened in 1903. The original Popes Point school house stood on the east side of the river a short distance west of the residence of George W. Atwood; the building now in use was erected on its present site in 1854. The first building in the Center District stood opposite the residence of Mrs. Maria Y. Shurtleff and used until the present Primary school house was erected in 1850. The old school house of South Carver stood near the Indian land east of the brook. Upon the secession of the western section forming District No. 8 the old building was discontinued and the present school house erected which was opened for school purposes in 1852. The first building in Wenham stood opposite the present school house which was built in 1855. "Snappit," once a populous village, erected its first school house on Snappit Green; the second building built about 1850 was moved to North Carver in 1880 and fitted for a Grammar school. Federal District never had a school house; the original building in District No. 8 stood east of the residence of Capt. William S. McFarlin which was moved to its present location near Bates Pond in 1900. In 1890 a small school house was built near East Head bogs but owing to the vacilating population of that section it was in use but a few years.

In addition to the public schools there were private schools in operation in the southern section of the town in the first half of the nineteenth century conducted only during the summer months and supported by private subscriptions. The school was first held in the South Meeting house, the front seats being used. Later a small building was erected where afterwards stood the blacksmith shop of Ellis Maxim, and in 1833 through the efforts of John Savery and Ezra Thompson a school building for summer use was erected on the Ridge near the Israel Thomas place. This was in use but a few years. It is a significant fact that the total annual enrollment has not materially varied since the town was incorporated.

The High school was established in 1897, holding its sessions in the Town Hall until the High school building was erected in 1899.

The first town appropriation for schools was thirty pounds, equal in the exchange of the times to two hundred dollars. This annual allowance was annually increased until it reached eleven hundred dollars when the system was abolished in 1869.

In considering the appropriations up to this point it is essential to remember that the system of "boarding around" was in vogue, the teachers being compelled to board a proportional time with each patron of the school. The teacher whose lot was cast under this regime could tell entertaining stories of her experience, and while it may seem something like a hardship the teacher could get an insight into the nature and requirements of the pupils which the modern trained educator looks upon as a thing beneath her dignity.

The leading citizens of the town were unalterably wedded to their system, and as the statute required a vote on its abolition once in three years beginning with 1859 the matter was one of continual agitation. In 1863, 1866 and 1869 at the regular March meetings the friends of the system easily prevailed; but at a special meeting in May, 1869, the majority voted to submit to the inevitable and a committee composed of Thomas Cobb, John Bent, John Shaw, Jesse Murdock, H. A. Lucas, Frederick Cobb and Andrew Griffith was elected to appraise the several school buildings in town. An effort to reconsider was made at a meeting June 20th, called upon petition of George P. Bowers and twelve others but the majority refused to recede.

Among the opponents of the change who fought to the end was William Savery. Believing the cause of education would be injured in passing the control of the children and the schools into alien hands he stubbornly resisted the change. Mr. Savery had taken an interest in the schools in many ways. He furnished a large bell for his

THE HAMMOND HOMESTEAD
At Wenham

THE SECOND SEPARATION

own school District; he had presented each District in town with a library of forty-two volumes each; and for several years he had added one hundred dollars annually to the town's school appropriation. Benjamin Ellis and E. Tillson Pratt were also interested in the schools to the extent of leaving substantial endowments for their encouragement.

THE TEMPERANCE MOVEMENT

Evidently the remorse over the evils of intemperance was not marked enough in the eighteenth century to make any impression on public sentiment. Certainly late in said group of years the remorse was not of such a type as to interfere with a society of meeting house promoters which voted to provide ardent spirits, not only for those who were to do the tugging and sweating at the raising of their structure, but to those who attended in their capacity as curiosity seekers, and "liquor sufficient for them all" is written boldly in the records.

Then again it is evident that here and there, some lonely soul condemned to serve its probation in advance of its time was the target of wise remonstrance or biting sarcasm as perchance it ventured to suggest that it was not the part of wisdom for one to get crosslegged in body and mind often enough to hazard his dependents on the public charge. And this sentiment grew little by little until it produced a revolution in public sentiment and the anti-tipplers became the dominant force.

This town seems to have been afflicted with the evil early and hard. Its taverns, located about midway between the rum importing towns of New Bedford and Plymouth with stages making their periodical stops; its furnace stores making a specialty of rum and molasses; and with its merchants* with an eye ever out for business looked after the supply. And the furnacemen subjected to extremes of heat and cold, with ample spare time and a constant credit gave a back ground for the demand.

And so the tavern became the centre of the evil on which the invaders trained their artillery. Around these taverns were centred the excitement, the society, the loafers, for no where else was the opportunity. And there was the news, for there were no newspapers and the only mails came lumbering along in the stages. A letter from New York was marked twenty five cents due and precious glad was the recipient to pay the price, for it was a rare treat to hear from such a remote point of creation. And then if a well-to-do spendthrift happened to be a passenger on the stage he would be sure to stop to warm his frost bitten fingers and incidentally stand treat for the house, and it would be little less than a misfortune to be reckoned among the absentees. For these reasons, and others unmentioned, the loafers and the news seekers and the smoke-after-supper furnacemen felt it a duty to be at the tavern

---

*Benjamin Ellis and Skipper John Bent were rivals in the iron trade, rum trade, etc. Ellis was eminently successful, but Bent failed to land, hence looked upon his rival with suspicions. Meeting at a town meeting when the agitation against rum selling was at its height, Ellis accosted Bent in this bantering way: "What do you say Skipper? The ministers say they are going to send us to ——— for selling rum. What do you say to that?" The Skipper improved his opportunity with his piping answer. "I don't believe they can do that. But they may send some of us there for mixing too much of Sampsons pond water with it."

THE TEMPERANCE MOVEMENT 157

every night and the sounds of revelry made their mark ultimately upon the public conscience.

Thus it comes to pass that when we look back to that tide called temperance movement which assumed shape and motion about eighteen hundred and twenty five, the old tavern lit up with its glowing fires and merry with its jostling joking loafers breaks upon our vision with the glare of a noonday sun.

That there was just cause for the movement does not admit of contradiction; that public sentiment laid dormant so long invites comment. Drunkenness everywhere, pauperism on the increase, farms passing to the store keepers, even at funerals the inebriety of those in official capacities shocked the sensibilities of the mourners. And so we do not marvel that when the unlucky number had been reeled off of the nineteenth century the voters in town meeting assembled, with no opposition on record, decided "to have a stroke in the warrant for the May meeting for taking up rum."

The State had taken hold of the subject with its legislation when in 1825 the Selectmen of Carver were instructed to use their influence for the suppression of the evils of intemperance in town according to law; and two years later Ezra Thompson, Samuel Shaw and Thomas Adams were constituted a committee to enforce the laws relating to Taverners and Retailers. In their report the committee says:

"Your committee have viewed with grief the increased progress of dissipation in the town of

Carver and feel anxious that some arrangement might be made which will come within the limit of the authority of the town to check the progress of that evil which in our opinion is the principle cause of the multiplied crime and poverty which the inhabitants of the town are becoming noted for, and your committee are of the opinion that these evils are promoted by a want of due observance of the laws by the licensed houses and stores in town."

As a step towards the solution of the problem the committee recommended:

First.

That a committee of three be chosen by ballot to act with the Selectmen in posting in the licensed places the names of those who are known to be notoriously intemperate.

Second.

That a committee of seven be elected to be known as a Committee of observation to make a note of every violation of the laws and report to the Selectmen.

Third.

The Selectmen to take cognizance of such complaints and when proved to annul the license and commence action against said parties.

These recommendations were accepted by the town and for the first committee, those making the suggestions were named. The committee of observation was composed of Dea. Levi Vaughan, Jonathan Atwood, Thomas Hammond, Joseph

THE TEMPERANCE MOVEMENT

Barrows, Lieut. John Shaw, Levi Sherman and Ebenezer Dunham.

While these committees may be assumed to have worked with determination along the lines mapped out, the evils of intemperance did not disappear, if in fact there was any visible cessation.

In 1829 John Savery took up the problem in a special town meeting. As a result of his efforts an inquisition was named composed of Benjamin Ellis, Ezra Thompson, Jesse Murdock, Lot Shurtleff, Jonathan Atwood, Capt. Samuel Shaw, Alvin Vaughan, Capt. Thomas Cobb, Capt. Levi Vaughan, Levi Sherman, Benjamin Ransom, John Savery and Lewis Pratt. The prescribed duties of the inquisition were to watch over the habits of their fellow townsmen and if in their judgment any were found spending too much of their time around the taverns a report signed by any three of the committee brought the matter to the attention of the Selectmen. The time of this method was brief but it was the means of placing several under guardianship and out of the reach of the greedy retailer.

In 1832 the Selectmen were under instructions to post the names of those "who were misspending their time and property by the excessive use of intoxicating liquors," and Rufus Sherman, Samuel Briggs, Lot Shurtleff, Thomas Maxim, John S. Lucas, Isaac Dunham and Ebenezer Dunham, constituted a standing committee for the prosecution of illegal liquor sellers.

This first outbreak of the temperance movement failed to eradicate the evils of intemperance and the first promoters became disheartened. There naturally came a lull in the efforts while the need of corrective steps did not abate. The efforts of those who were recorded against the evil were centered in efforts to enforce the laws against illegal sales, until 1856 when an attempt was made to regulate the traffic by the adoption of the Town agency plan.

According to his bond the agent was to sell "to be used in the arts, and for mechanical, chemical and medicinary purposes and for no other." Very little was called for in the arts, or for mechanical or chemical purposes, but the records show that it was used liberally for medicinal purposes. With few exceptions the 8,500 sales recorded while the plan was in vogue were for medicine. A well known resident who had served the town in various public capacities headed the list May 28, 1856, with one gallon of gin and one gallon of New England rum for medicinal purposes.

The agency was continued nearly twenty years but it failed to eradicate the evils of intemperance; and this fate reached also the State prohibitory law that followed and the local option rule of later days.

Working outside of the channels of legislation, and on moral suasion lines, have been instituted several temperance societies.

Wankinquoah Division, No. 135, Sons of Temperance, was organized Nov. 3, 1859, in Bay State hall with the following charter members:

THE METHODIST EPISCOPAL CHURCH

William S. McFarlin, John Murdock, Benjamin Harlow, Elisha M. Dunham, Hiram O. Tillson, Andrew Griffith, Ephraim Griffith, Isaac Harlow, Simeon Harlow, Joseph T. McFarlin, Solomon F. McFarlin, Joseph T. Shurtleff, Alonzo Shaw, Lucian T. Hammond, William Hammond and Jason Atwood. These ladies were also initiated as visitors: Mrs. Mary A. Murdock, Mrs. Nancy B. Perkins, and Misses Eliza Shaw, Amelia Sherman, Harriet Atwood, Lucretia McFarlin, Mercy J. McFarlin, Lydia Atwood, Deborah Bumpus, Hannah Tillson, Helen Griffith, Eliza Ellis, Mary E. Shaw, Harriet Tillson, Lois Smith, Hannah Smith, Elizabeth Maxim, Elizabeth Shaw, Lydia Shaw, Melissa Atwood and Carrie B. Griffith. This order continued in active operation until the surrender of its charter, Oct. 10, 1872.

Five years later Echo Lake Lodge, I. O. G. T., was organized in the same hall with the following charter members: William S. McFarlin, Alfred C. Covill, Lucie H. Gill, Lizzie Leach, Ella Lovell, T. T. Vaughan, Edward Vaughan, J. A. Vaughan, Eben Crowell, Bell Faulkner, Nannie Douglass, Emma Blake, Frank Case, Charles Sherman, Laura Shaw, Ella Sears, William Miller, C. F. Tillson, Elmer Shaw and Emma Souther. The charter of this society was surrendered in 1881.

Winthrop Lodge, I. O. G. T., No. 247 was organized in Winthrop hall, Oct. 28, 1889, with charter members as follows: William S. McFarlin, Nelson F. Manter, Thomas P. Manter, James E. Brett, Ira B. Bumpus, Zelotus K. Eldredge,

Albert F. Atwood, Jason B. McFarlin, John B. McFarlin, Silvanus L. Brett, Hannah A. Brett, M. Elvira Briggs, Lizzie M. Schouler, Z. W. Andrews, Emma F. Manter, Amanda J. Adams, Ella F. Manter, Sarah J. Swift, Ida M. Tillson, Mabel M. McFarlin, Nellie W. Shaw, Edward C. Shaw and Hannah W. Atwood. The efforts of this society resulted in the building of Good Templars hall.

The Carver W. C. T. U. was organized April 14, 1893 with twenty five members. Mrs. Mary Tobey was the first President; Mrs. Dessie Vaughan, Secretary and Mrs. L. C. Vaughan, Treasurer. April 26th of the same year the Carver L. T. L. was organized with Mrs. P. Jane Barrows as President.

The South Carver W. C. T. U. was organized Feb. 26, 1884, with Mrs. D. M. Bates, President, and Mrs. John S. Cartee, Secretary.

THE BAPTIST CHURCH

Somewhere around the year 1760 a cloud no bigger than a man's hand appeared on the horizon of the orthodox world of the South Precinct of Plympton. Witness a vote of said body-politic in March, 1763 when without ceremony and not without apparent spite the freeholders voted not to abate the taxes of those calling themselves "Baptes" on the list of Collector Elkanah Lucas. Rowland Hammond was among the first to break with the established church, and assisted by a little band of agitators, he made life worth living among his neighbors before and after the Revolution.

It would be a matter worthy of protracted comment if there were not a little mite of human nature in those days, so what of it if an occasional tight fisted tax payer did make a stone Easel of the new faith as a shield against the darts of the Publicans? But there is not an apology for evidence to indicate that the devotees of the young sect were not as sincere a band of reformers as those heroic souls that came over in the Mayflower.

Gradually gaining in numbers and enthusiasm, by 1788 the rulers of the Precinct were compelled to notice them, and Thomas Savery, Capt. William Atwood and Isaiah Tillson were sent out as pickets to investigate affairs around South

Meadows and find out who really were, and who were not, Baptists. The Committee trudged down to the affected region and learned to their satisfaction that there were a few heretics in the woods, and upon the information thus obtained the Precinct Assessors were instructed to post notices to the effect that those who called themselves Baptist must file certificates with said Board if they wished to be in line for abatements. Rowland Hammond and Frances Bent had been outspoken Baptists so long that they looked upon this move as a means of humiliation and they refused to register. And for their particular benefit the Precinct ordered that they must produce a certificate from a Baptist Elder if they would escape the wrath of the tax gatherer.

In April, 1789, William Shurtleff, Nathaniel Atwood, Noah Pratt, Billa Bryant, John Tripp and Mrs. Abigail Lucas met together to discuss the situation. After thoroughly considering their numerical strength (weakness), their financial straits and the rashness of withdrawing from the old church, they postponed temporarily the launching of the proposed society. But in June, 1791 the devotees of the new faith had reached a stage in which they felt justified in taking active steps towards the organization of their church. John Tripp was instructed to transcribe the Articles of Faith of the third Baptist church of Middleboro, and these with a few alterations became the Articles of Faith of the first Baptist church of Carver. After taking counsel of Elders Bachus of Middleboro, and Nelson of Taunton, the

THE BAPTIST CHURCH 165

little group adjourned to July when the following signed the covenant: William Shurtleff, Nathaniel Atwood, Seth Barrows, Benjamin Ransom, Noah Pratt, Billa Bryant, Rowland Hammond, John Tripp, Levi Shurtleff, Ruth Faunce, Mercy Shurtleff and Priscilla Shurtleff.

The society set out in earnest to arrange for the ordination of a pastor and after a few harmonious meetings it was voted to ordain as the society's first preacher one of its charter members, John Tripp.

The Council which convened Sept. 27th, 1791 was composed of Elder Isaac Bachus and Dea. Alden from the first church of Middleboro; Elder George Robinson and delegates Lothrop and Howard from Bridgewater; Elder Ebenezer Nelson and Stephen Nelson from Taunton; and Deacons James and George Shaw from the third church of Middleboro.

A contest for the position of deacon was settled by the decision of the society to elect two and both Rowland Hammond and Billa Bryant realized their highest aspirations. Elder Tripp was a faithful laborer who found a place for himself in the hearts of his co-workers, and he enjoyed the complete confidence of every member of the society. During this period the society had the use of the South Meeting house and many came into the church from the Fresh Meadow Village. The society flourished under the labors of its first minister and at the beginning connected itself with the Warren Association. Elder Tripp was released in November 1798 to be ordained over the

Baptist church of Hebron in the district of Maine to which charge he carried a warm recommendation from his first church.

For seven years following this ministry the society was without an ordained leader. While too poor financially to support a minister it was too aggressive to compromise fully with the old society, and frequent church conferences were held while the whip was in constant use. Occasional public services were held in which Elders Samuel Abbott, Ebenezer Nelson and Ezra Kendall lent their assistance. In the year 1804, Elder Kendall appears to have been the pastor of the church. Federal village was a favored place of meeting where at the residence of Moses Wright baptisms were celebrated and the church received communionists which in after years became the staunch defenders of the faith.

In the summer of 1805 a new day dawned upon the society—a day marked by great enthusiasm—and which added materially to its numbers although its financial standing was little improved. In November of that year David Bursell having become a member of the society was called to its ministry. The sentiments breathed in the formal call, as also in Bursell's reply, did not seek to belittle the financial weakness, and it was under the most gloomy skies that the new minister began his labors. He was ordained in June 1806 by a Council composed of Elder Simeon Coombs, Peter Hoar, Barnabas Clark and Moses Perras of the second church of Middleboro; Elder Samuel Nelson, Elisha Clark and Joseph Shaw of the third

THE BAPTIST CHURCH

church of Middleboro; and Elder Samuel Abbot, Abitha Briggs, Ebenezer Briggs and Deacon Briggs of the fourth church of Middleboro.

Under the ministry of Elder Bursell the society gained materially in membership but it was continually submerged in matters of finance. The meetings and public services were held at various places, sometimes at the South Meeting house, sometimes at the Spruce church,* and often at private dwellings. The residence of Lieut. Caleb Atwood was a favorite place of meeting, being centrally located for South Meadows, South Middleboro and Federal. At this period the society had an active membership over the Middleboro line and in 1812 it was voted to advise the Middleboro branch to withdraw and organize a fifth Baptist church for that town.

The society was incorporated June 22, 1811 with the following charter members:

Benjamin Shurtleff	William Atwood
Flavel Shurtleff	Asaph Atwood
Lot Shurtleff	Jonathan Atwood
Ebenezer Shurtleff	Joseph Atwood
Gideon Shurtleff	Lazarus Atwood
Abial Shurtleff	Samuel Atwood
Gideon Shurtleff, Jr.	Samuel Atwood, Jr.
Frances Shurtleff	Stephen Atwood
Nathaniel Shurtleff	Levi Atwood
Nathaniel Shurtleff, 2nd.	Caleb Atwood
Peter Shurtleff	Abner Atwood
Thomas Shurtleff	John Atwood

---

*Now the South Middleboro M. E. church.

John Atwood, Jr.
Joshua Atwood
Nathaniel Atwood
William Atwood, 2nd.
Samuel Shaw
John Shaw
Silvanus Shaw
Silvanus Shaw, Jr.
Levi Shaw
Abigail Shaw
Benjamin Ward
Benjamin Ward, Jr.
Samuel Lucas
Carver Barrows
Seth Barrows
Ephraim Griffith
Huit McFarlin
Bethnel Tillson
David Vaughan
Joseph Ellis, Jr.
Ellis Shaw
Joseph Robbins
Eli Thomas
Benjamin White
William Murdock
Ebenezer Dunham
Jabez Maxim
Jabez Maxim, Jr.
Thomas Maxim
John Bumpus
Isaac Cushman
Hosea Lucas
Cornelius Dunham
Calvin Lucas
John Appling
Lewis Pratt
Swanzea Hart
John Shaw of Middleboro
Ephraim Ward of Middleboro
Gideon Perkins of Middleboro
Nathaniel Shurtleff of Middleboro

Elder Bursell was followed by Elder Cummings and these Elders left the Baptist church about the same time that Rev. John Shaw severed his connection with the old society, and at this point the rivalry between the two societies abated. Neither was in a position to ordain a minister, and while each should constantly repair its sectarian walls, they travelled together for nearly a half century. Then turning their backs upon the past, and unhampered by the necessity of modifying articles of faith, in a modern age each was free to carve out its own fortune.

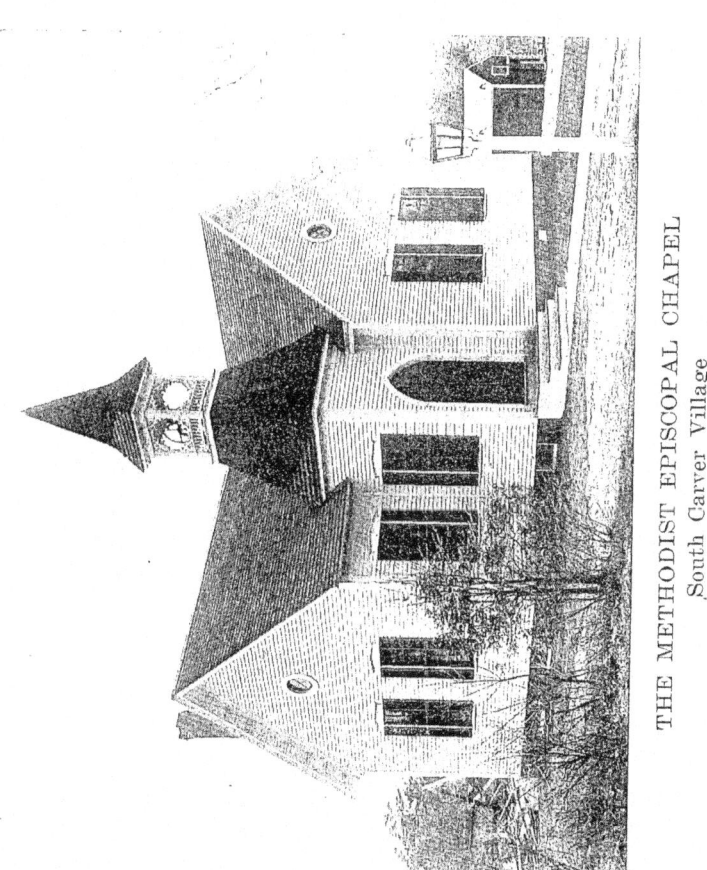

THE METHODIST EPISCOPAL CHAPEL
South Carver Village

THE BAPTIST CHURCH 169

To add to the discouragements of this year 1815, both societies were without a meeting house. The temple of the mother society, after eighty-five years of wear and tear, had become too rickety for safety, and after fruitless efforts to repair the structure or build anew, the societies began to utilize the school houses. Religion had decayed with the meeting house to such an extent that the leaders became alarmed at "the state of religion in the town," and through their united efforts resulted the memorable revival of 1820-23. Missionaries were sent into the south end of the town, and while the people of that section declined to connect themselves with either of the old societies, they were aroused to repair their old meeting house, which was started on its final career. Many converts were made during these revival years for both of the societies, and as a practical result the new church building at the Green was built in 1823 and the Central temple the year following. The fact that two edifices were erected indicates that in the minds of the leaders the line of cleavage between the societies was irreparable.

Up to the middle of the century the societies continued to travel together, and even for twenty-five years longer the Congregationalists held services in the Baptist temple by virtue of shares of ownership, when the church was not in use by the Baptists. During these years, however, each society held its own church conferences and also frequent public services under ministers of its own persuasion. In 1834 the Articles of Faith of the First Baptist church of Boston were adopted as the faith of the Carver society. The decade 1840 to 1850 was marked by still further divisions in the church. The most potent factors were the Advent movement at the North and Methodist and Universalist movements at the South.

This first half of the nineteenth century was a period marked by much activity in the sectarian world and all evidence points to the fact that the Baptist church of Carver played its part with vigor. The church was without a pastor the greater part of the time, but during this period the temple was erected and its membership largely increased.

Its field was a large one, covering the Southern half of Carver, South Middleboro and a section of Rochester. It received an influx of communicants from South Middleboro and for a year or more it was called the Baptist Church of Carver and Middleboro. Its services, previously to the building of its meeting house, were held in the South Meeting house, the Spruce Meeting house, and at private residences at Federal, South Carver and Fresh Meadows.

Not only did the society work determinedly to make converts, but it watched carefully after the welfare of its devotees. A member failing to attend a regular meeting was visited by a committee and required to show cause "why they had not been up to their duty in attending the church to which they belonged." While there were numerous counts of unscriptural conduct, not a few of the committee's duties consisted in enquiring after "the state of mind" of the suspect. In

THE BAPTIST CHURCH 171

those early days of the disintegration of the church the Baptist church of Carver made an heroic effort to hold its own. Second only to heresy as a disturbing factor was the alarming increase of intemperance that showed itself from 1825 to 1850, and this gave the church committees many subjects for investigation.

Ministers

John Tripp	1791—1798
Ezra Kendall	1804
David Bursell	1805—1810
Abraham Cummings	1811—1814
James Parsons.	1821
David Curtis	1832—1833
Samuel Glover	1838—1839
John B. Parris	1842
Caleb Benson	1850—1851
J. M. Mace	1852—1853
C. S. Thompson	1864—1865
William Leach	1865—1870
Henry C. Coombs	1872—1873
Noah Fullerton	1875—1879
Joshua F. Packard	1883—1887
Willard F. Packard	1887—1890
James J. Tobey	1890—1893
C. A. Parker	1894
Joseph Ellison	1895—1899
H. Y. Vinal	1900—1901
Albert Leach	1902—1903
A. Davis Graffam	1904
George H. Lockhart	1905—

Temporary preachers not included in preceding list:

Elder T. Smith	1819
Rev. Asa Niles	1834
Rev. Perez L. Cushing	1858
Rev. Samuel Cheever	1871
Rev. Walter Chase	
Rev. H. W. Buckles	1881
(Newton Theological School.)	
Rev. Wellington Camp	1882
(Newton Theological School.)	
Rev. E. Hatfield	1883
(Newton Theological School.)	

Clerks

In the early days of the church the minister made the records on loose sheets of paper. Neither he nor the clerks that followed signed their records. In 1806 this church named a committee to gather the loose records and copy the records in a book. John Drew, who served as clerk one year, was not a member of the society, but acted with it under a vote of the church. The following served as clerks of this church:

John Tripp	1789—1798
John Drew	1802
Jacob Shaw	1803—1805
Samuel Lucas	1806—1807
Ebenezer Shurtleff	1808—1850
Jacob Shaw (Middleboro branch)	1809
Horatio A. Lucas	1853—1887
James A. Vaughan	1888

THE BAPTIST CHURCH

Deacons

Rowland Hammond,	1791—1801
Billa Bryant,	1791—1808
Jacob Shaw,	1802—1818
Joseph Robbins,	1809—1833
Ebenezer Dunham,	1810—1820
Ebenezer Shurtleff,	1820—1850
Ebenezer Atwood,	1823—1851
Ephraim Dunham,	1851—1883
Horatio A. Lucas,	1854—1887
Samuel W. Gould,	1884—1892
James A. Vaughan,	1890—
E. Allan Lucas,	1893—

THE METHODIST CHURCH

Rev. Lorenzo D. Johnson conducted revival meetings in France* school house in the spring of 1831, during which many conversions were made for the Methodist faith. The larger part of these conversions were residents of the Fresh Meadow village, and on May 18th of the above mentioned year Charles Ryder, as leader, organized a class, with the following members: Anna Ryder, Sumner Atwood, Thomas Maxim, Mary Atwood, Ichabod Shurtleff, Patience Maxim, Susan A. Maxim, Sylvia Shurtleff, Thomas Maxim, Jr., Edward P. Bumpus, Alice Bumpus, and Sullivan Gammons. This class at once affiliated with the Reformed Methodist denomination and entered upon its designed work with enthusiasm, holding its public services in school houses and private dwellings under the leadership of Elders Pliny Brett and Nathan T. Clark.

In 1836 a second series of revival meetings were held, as a result of which the society materially increased in membership and then decided to adopt the Methodist Protestant church discipline. For the succeeding thirty years it was known as the Methodist Protestant church of South Carver. In the words of Charles Ryder, its

---
*School house in South Middleboro, France St.

promoter, it "protested against the M. E. church government but adhered to all its fundamental truths of Methodism as taught by Wesley its great founder."

With the spirit of a new society, the lack of material things did not hinder the growth of the church. During the following seven years public services were held part of the time, as before, in private residences, school houses, and in the South Meeting house. By 1843 the army had swelled to such proportions that the leaders felt justified in taking active steps toward the building of a meeting house, and in April of that year, under a warrant issued by John Savery, Esq., Charles Ryder, Thomas Maxim, Jr., Thomas Maxim and Seth S. Maxim, as proprietors, voted to build a meeting house, and to insure its construction they signed for the necessary number of shares. The building was nominally erected under the pew-plan.

Charles Ryder, Thomas Maxim and Ichabod Shurtleff were chosen trustees and also building committee, and so strenuously did they carry on the work that the edifice was dedicated on October 20th of the same year. On that day, also, pews were struck off to the following, who became the first proprietors: Atwood Shaw, Aaron Nott, Charles Ryder, Thomas Maxim, Thomas Maxim, Jr., Seth S. Maxim, Ichabod Shurtleff, John Maxim, David Bates, John Thomas, Betsey Bumpus, Sumner Atwood, Nathaniel Shurtleff, Nathan Avery, and Matthew Cushing.

The construction of the building was financed by the trustees, Charles Ryder being a continual

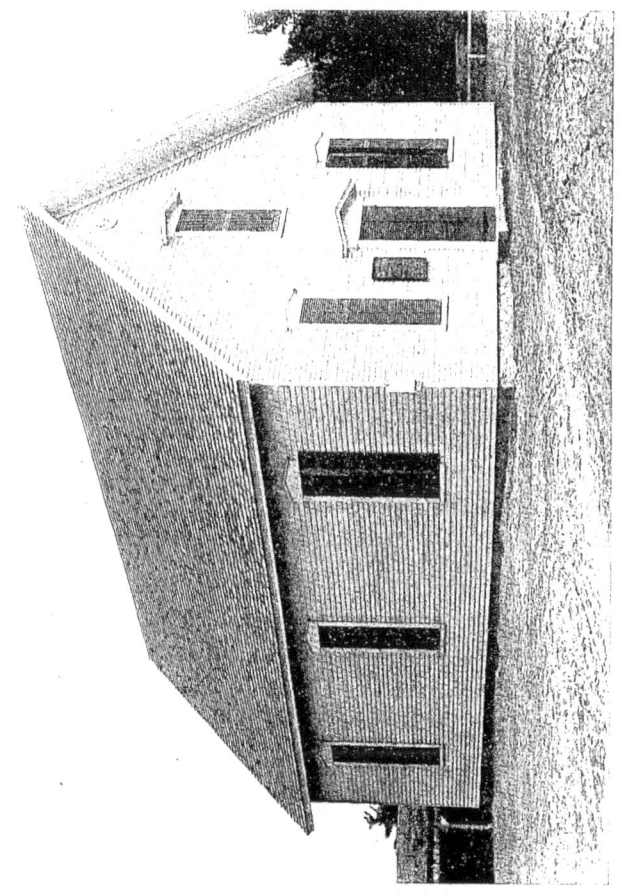

THE ADVENT CHRISTIAN CHURCH

THE METHODIST CHURCH

creditor, and to his generosity and disinterestedness the project owes much of its success.

From this point stretching through nearly two decades a remarkable unity marked the labors of the society. The first quarterly conference was held in the church July 17, 1847, with Rev. John Melish presiding. Charles Ryder was chosen secretary and Thomas Maxim, Ichabod Shurtleff and Seth S. Maxim standing committee. In February, 1850, Ichabod Shurtleff was chosen as the society's first delegate to an annual conference.

Beginning in December, 1857, the most remarkable revival in the history of the society was ushered in. Services were conducted in the vestry for upwards of one hundred consecutive nights, and forty names were added to the church register.

In 1859 camp meetings were held in the grove belonging to Sumner Atwood, easterly from his residence; and in 1860 began the collections for the Home Missionary cause.

Following this for six years the society waned. Some of its stanch and active members had enlisted in the army, while the Union society was making inroads in its membership. In this weakened condition the church arranged for bi-weekly services in conjunction with the church at South Middleboro, Rev. E. W. Barrows supplying both societies. The following year this plan was discontinued, and Rev. Mr. Barrows became the settled minister of the Carver church. But his ministry was not destined to end without dissensions and in 1865 he became the first settled minister over the Union society, carrying with him some of the leaders in the Methodist society. The year following, discouraged by these dissensions, the church voted to ask for a supply from the M. E. conference, and under the ministry of Rev. T. Marsh the Methodist Protestant church became affiliated with the Methodist Episcopal government.

During his second ministry Rev. Mr. Hunt agitated the erection of a chapel in South Carver village with such success that the edifice was dedicated in December, 1896.

THE UNION CHURCH

THE METHODIST CHURCH 179

Ministers

Elders Pliny Brett, Nathan T. Clark	1831—1850
William Tozer	1851
T. M. Hall	1852
William Tozer	1853—1856
Pliny Brett	1857—1858
S. Y. Wallace	1859—1861
E. W. Barrows	1862—1864
C. Carter and R. M. Dorr	1867
Elisha M. Dunham	1868
Eben Tirrell	1870
R. M. Dorr	1871
Paul Tounsend	1872—1873
Edward Williams	1874—1876
A. B. Besse	1876—1877
William I. Ward	1878
H. W. Hamblin	1879
J. B. Hamblin	1880
Charles Smith	1881
E. A. Hunt	1882—1885
John S. Fish	1886—1889
J. E. Duxbury	1890
W. E. Manley	1891
T. P. Fisher	1892
E. A. Hunt	1892—1897
E. G. Babcock	1898—1902
Charles G. Johnson	1903—1906
E. A. Hunt	1907—1911
Robert E. Bisbee	1912—

THE ADVENT CHRISTIAN CHURCH

This society had its inception in the decade 1840-1850, when fourteen members of the orthodox church, converted to the doctrines of William Miller, withdrew from the old church. These primitive members of the Advent church were Louisa L. P. Chase, Persis Lucas, Winslow Pratt, Benjamin Ransom, Levi Ransom, Lucy Ransom, Phebe Ransom, Rebecca Ransom, Joseph Robbins, Jr., Patience Robbins, Eunice Vaughan, Isaac Vaughan, Phebe Vaughan, Waitstill Vaughan.

The peculiar mark of this society in stationing ministers to work with them instead of over them has been attended by the natural consequence, and most of the pastors of the church have had other occupations than that of preaching. Isaac Vaughan was their first leader, deserving the title of Elder if it was never conferred. He furnished a room in his residence near the centre of the town which was used as the meeting house of the devotees until the breaking out of the Civil war. There the regular services of the sect were held, and there also revival meetings called together old and young from all sections of the town.

When advanced age compelled Mr. Vaughan to relinquish the leadership, Benjamin Ransom assumed the responsibility for the work, furnishing a room in his residence near the Wenham school house, which was the headquarters of the Advents until the chapel was built in 1870.

Up to this point the sect were held by no organization, being a spontaneous coming together of those who subscribed to a common faith, but when the chapel was erected a formal church society was organized and the Advent church assumed the regular form, although it affiliated with no state organization until several years later.

Under the conditions above noted the devotees of this faith have held regular services since they came together in 1845, and since their chapel was erected, although there have been years when there was no pastor laboring with them, their meeting house has never been closed.

William E. Hathaway joined the sect in its early days and became a prominent worker, assuming the leadership with Benjamin Ransom when he was given the rank of Elder. Aside from his work as a preacher, he formed a wide acquaintance in the county as a peddler of dry goods. Elder I. I. Leslie was also a well known preacher of that period, serving the society a short time, and at intervals, after the chapel was built. Dr. J. R. Boynton was associated with Elder Leslie in the first year of the organized work of the society, and became its settled pastor late in the year 1870. Under the ministry of Elder Boynton, small pox appeared in Wenham, and it fell to him as a physician to treat those afflicted with the malady.

For a few years the society worked in conjunction with the Plymouth church, and between 1875

LEWIS PRATT, JR.

THE ADVENT CHURCH

and 1880 Reverends John M. Curry and Frank Shattuck served both societies.

Those who have been leaders of the faith since its establishment in Carver, either as elders or ministers, have been:

Elder Isaac Vaughan	1845—1860
Elder Benjamin Ransom	1860—1870
Elder William E. Hathaway	1860—1875
Elder I. I. Leslie	1870—1875
Elder J. R. Boynton	1870—1875
Rev. W. Smith	1876
Rev. John M. Curry	1876—1880
Rev. Frank Shattuck	
Rev. Charles H. Sweet	1880—1883
Rev. Alfred R. Meade	1906—1910
Rev. Burt J. Glazier	1910—

The clerks since the organization of the society:

Rev. J. R. Boynton	1872—1875
Austin N. Vaughan	1876—1879
Daniel W. Nash	1880—1909
Julia F. Hammond	1910—1911
William E. W. Vaughan	1912—

Those who have been chosen deacons:

Levi Ransom	1870
James Breach	
Dr. N. M. Ransom	1877
D. W. Nash	1897
William E. W. Vaughan	1904

THE UNION SOCIETY

There appears to have been no intent on the part of the builders of the South Meeting house to break away from the established church. Their purpose was to erect a temple and induce the regular minister to hold a part of the Sunday services there as a convenience to the residents at this end of the Precinct who were located a distance from the old meeting house. But spurned by the rulers of the church, and fought every inch of the way by the conservatives, the proprietors of the new temple were forced into a receptive mood, and when the old order began to crumble the heretics who had stepped out of the ruts found a forum in the South Meeting house. The Baptists who were the first to make the break were without a meeting house, and they found a welcome in this building; later the Universalists utilized its accommodations, and in this way the short-sighted policy of the old church unconsciously paved the way for its dissolution.

Thus it came about that when the descendants of the proprietors faced the problem of replacing the decaying structure with a modern church building under the guidance of William Savery in 1853 sectarianism was omitted from the subscription paper. The subscribers met in November, organized as proprietors, and voted to build their new building on the pew plan. William Savery was clerk, and Nelson Barrows treasurer of the organization. The temple was completed and turned over to the proprietors in 1855. An organ and bell were presented by William Savery and Jesse Murdock, and July 28th of that year, with an elaborate program, the edifice was dedicated "to the public worship of God."

The society was non-sectarian, and the dedicatory exercises were participated in by Baptists, Congregationalists, Universalists, Unitarians and Methodists, and following the custom the society has always given a hearing to various denominations.

At a subesquent meeting of the proprietors their affairs were vested in a Board of Trustees, which became the permanent form of government, and at the same meeting was adopted the name of the society, The Union Society of South Carver.

Services have usually been held only during the Summer months, with ministers supplied by a pulpit supply committee made up from different sects, and with two exceptions this has always been the custom of the society. During the first year's series of services denominations were represented as follows: One Episcopalian, two Baptists, two Unitarians, three Congregationalists, four Universalists and five Methodists.

At the annual meeting in 1861 the following resolution was adopted unanimously:

That a subscription list, as usual, be put in circulation to raise funds by voluntary contributions for support of preaching in the Union church the

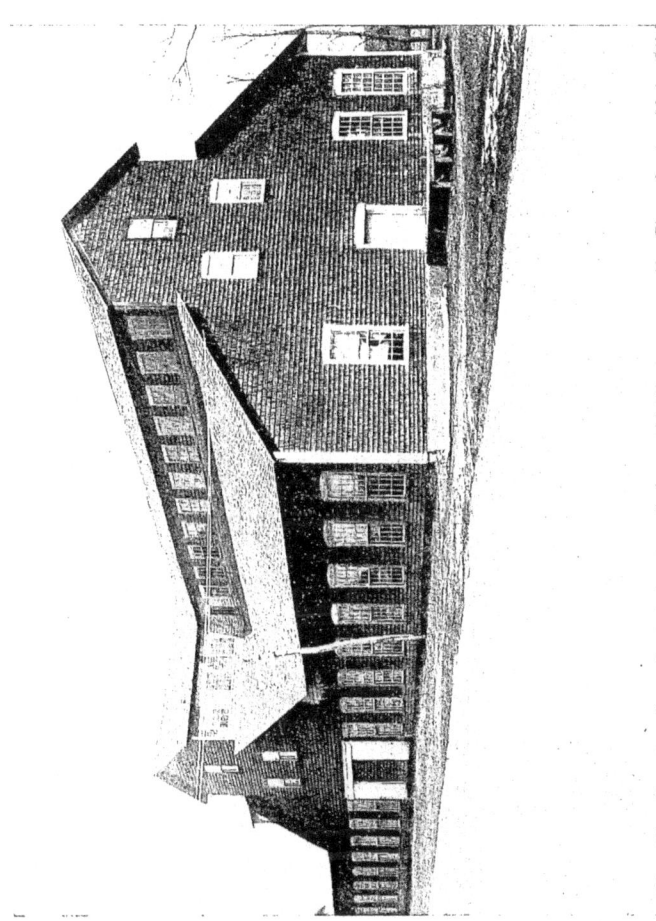

THE CHARLOTTE FURNACE BUILDING

Now Used as a Cranberry Screenhouse by the Cranebrook Co.

ensuing year; but if the present war-like position of the country continues the funds thus contributed shall be appropriated to the comfort and necessities of our Carver citizen-soldiers now abroad, or those that may hereafter go, for the defence of our country; or to the support and honorable maintenance of their families while absent, as the Trustees of this Society shall deem best calculated to secure the greatest good.

Accordingly, the church was closed during that year and the funds used agreeable to the resolve. The same custom was followed through the succeeding three years.

The church was opened again for public worship in 1865. Rev. E. W. Barrows, who had been stationed over the Methodist society, had developed a following among the members of the Union society, and at the annual meeting in that year steps were taken to settle him as the minister of the Union church. The free use of the edifice was proffered the friends of Mr. Barrows and William Savery appointed agent to confer in the matter. As a result Rev. Mr. Barrows occupied the pulpit as the first settled minister of the society. But his ministry was of short duration, and the following year the society resumed its former custom.

The church was opened but six Sabbaths this year, three of these services being conducted by Rev. George L. Smith. A Swedenborgian in theology, Rev. Mr. Smith developed such a strength in the society that he became its second and last settled preacher, ending his ministry in 1873.

The building was now out of repair, and this with the outlay necessary for a new organ taxed the finances of the society, and the church was closed for the year 1874. The year following it went back to its first custom of supplying the pulpit through an undenominational supply committee—a custom that has been continued without a lapse.

The last decade of the century revealed the weakness of a church founded on the pew-plan, and the annual meetings of the proprietors dwindled to stereotyped and lifeless meetings. As a matter of fact, the changes of time had almost capsized the little craft. Proprietors had died, moved away or assigned, and even the bona fide pew holders that were left were weary of time and they saw the necessity of placing their society on a more modern and permanent basis. As a result of this agitation the society was incorporated in 1908 with sixty-three charter members under the old name: The Union Society of South Carver.

Following is the list of the original proprietors, many of them heirs of the proprietors of the South Meeting house. It was their first intention to erect this building on the site of the old one:

Thomas Wrightington (1), Daniel Shaw (2), Joseph Atwood (3), Thomas Southworth, Jr., (4), Jesse Murdock (5, 8, 27, 33, 35), Matthias Ellis (6, 15, 32), George P. Bowers (7, 14), Joseph Barrows (9), Ellis Griffith (10, 20), Stephen Atwood (11), Marcus Atwood (12), Stephen Cushman (13), Capt. Samuel Shaw (16), Sampson McFarlin (17), Ira C. Bent (18), Capt. Henry C.

THE UNION SOCIETY 189

Murdock (19), Miranda, Lucius, George W. Atwood (21), John Murdock (22), Zenas Tillson (23), Oren Atwood (24), John Shaw, 2d, (25), Silas Shaw (26), Bowers and Jenkins (28, 29), Salmon F. Jenkins (30), Polly Savery (31), Hannah Weston (34), Andrew M. Bumpus and John Bradley (36), Perez Shaw (37), Jacob Holmes and Eli Southworth (38), Thompson P. Thomas (39), William B. Gibbs (40), William Savery (41, 43, 44), Samuel Vaughan (42). Transfers from original ownership were made by warranty deed, supposed to be recorded with Plymouth County Registry of Deeds.

Presidents of the Society

Jesse Murdock	1853—1874
Capt. Daniel Shaw	1875
George P. Bowers	1876, 78—80, 82—84
Capt. H. C. Murdock	1877
R. C. Freeman	1881
Peleg McFarlin	1885—1904
Alfred M. Shaw	1905—1907
Thomas M. Southworth	1908

Treasurers

Joseph Barrows	1853—1865
Rufus C. Freeman	1867—1868
Nelson Barrows	1869, 72, 84
Peleg McFarlin	1873—1883
Ellis Maxim	1885—1895
Josiah W. Atwood	1896—1908

Secretaries

William Savery	1853—1895
John Bent	1896—1908

Those who served as trustees in the life of the proprietors:

Marcus Atwood
Lucius Atwood
Josiah W. Atwood
S. Dexter Atwood
Joseph Barrows
D. M. Bates
Ira C. Bent
John Bent
George P. Bowers
John S. Cartee
Rufus C. Freeman
William B. Gibbs
Andrew Griffith
Henry S. Griffith
S. F. Jenkins
A. R. Kinney

Thomas Maxim
Peleg McFarlin
Jesse Murdock
Henry C. Murdock
John Murdock
William Savery
William E. Savery
Daniel Shaw
John F. Shaw
Samuel Shaw
Alfred M. Shaw
Ichabod Shurtleff
Perez Smith
Thomas M. Southworth
Augustus F. Tillson
Samuel Vaughan

HON. PELEG McFARLIN

FURNACES AND FOUNDRIES

The dawn of the 18th century broke upon a New England busy in the twilight of a new era, and the folly of relying upon importations for many of the necessities which could be made at home came to the attention of the people. Under such conditions Yankee ingenuity was developed, and a spirit of enterprise quickened into life the dormant resources of the Old Colony.

Three factors were essential to the equipment of an iron manufactory of that age, and these three abounded in the South Precinct of Plympton. The swamps and lakes were bedded with iron ore; the hills were burdened with good coaling timber; and the swamps and hills combined formed numerous water privileges without which there was no power to operate a plant. If the question of transportation entered into the reckoning, the proximity of the locality to tide water on either coast must have been a favorable point. Sea shells that abounded on the coast furnished the lime necessary for separating the iron, and these shells with native charcoal served the purposes of the smelting furnaces until lime and anthracite became articles of commerce and smelting furnaces were supplanted by cupola furnaces about a century later. As these smelting furnaces are a thing of the past, a brief reference to the conditions under which they were operated, with a description of their mechanical construction, deserves a place in history.

Selecting a site where a dam could be constructed the arch or furnace was located so as to make a connection with the water wheel. The furnace was built of stone, lined with fire brick, and leading up to the top house which was built over the arch was made an inclined runway up which the ore, shells and coal were carried in a wheelbarrow. The building extended from the tophouse and in cases of large plants wings were added all leading to the furnace.

Along the walls of the wings bunks were constructed in which the workmen slept, for the blast usually lasted a month and the iron was trickling constantly from the furnace. When the temp* was full it must be taken away and so the work was in continuous progress, moulders moulding and casting at all hours of night and day, for when the fires went out the process must begin over again.

The general superintendent of the works assumed the title of skipper; the man stationed over the tophouse and whose duty was to feed the furnace with coal, ore and shells was called the topman; while his assistant who worked around the base performing all sorts of work that did not fall within the prescribed duties of any other employee took the appropriate name of gutterman.

---

*Temp was the technical name of the stone trough which received the iron as it trickled from the furnace.

FURNACES AND FOUNDRIES

The fires were kindled in the furnace about one week in advance of the opening of the blast.

A store was a necessary adjunct of a furnace for business was done largely on credit and barter. Molasses, W. I. rum, codfish and pork were the standard stock in trade and accounts were carried from year to year. Often the skipper took the contract to furnish the men and their supplies in which case the regular allowance of rum was a clause in the indenture. A review of these "low-ance" accounts reveals a temperance lecture of the times. Many of the employees appear to have more than their share of black marks while some have but few if any records. It is probable that the thrifty turned their marks to their financial advantage.

The power for operating the plant was derived from the combination of a bellows, a water wheel and a huge beam weighted with rocks and extending out into the road. The wheel carried the end of the beam down and opened the wind chest, and after being freed from the wheel the weight on the beam ejected the wind by closing the bellows.

Coaling developed among neighboring farmers as a business incidental to the furnaces. The numerous "coalpit bottoms" seen about the woods is standing evidence of this industry, for a century has not restored the life-giving quality of the soil. Brush making was also an industry, but the market for the product of the saw mills made by the demand for lumber in making the flask*

---

*Flask is the technical name of the boxes in which the moulds are made. That part of the mould that is lifted is called the cope, and the part that remains on the floor is called the nowel.

and furnace buildings was the largest incidental industry.

The casual traveller through the quiet village called Popes Point would be impressed by the dark color of the soil and without a suggestion might be justified in assuming that once upon a time a blast furnace spit out its coal dust and cinders which as refuse went to harden the road bed, leaving literally "footprints on the sands of time." And if the traveller had a historical curiosity, he might ask how the place came to receive its name.

The name appears in Old Colony records in 1704, but as such names grow by usage sometimes years before they get sufficiently grounded to give them a place in the public records, it is probable that the name was used long before the dawn of the 18th century.

As a part of the lower South Meadows this vicinity attracted the settlers as they branched out from old Plymouth, and forty years after the landing of the Pilgrims, Thomas Pope and George Watson held land grants. The property of Pope, forming a point of land at the junction of Watson's Cove brook and the Weweantic came to be known as Popes Point, a name that in after years was applied to that region. Watson took the land further up the brook in what is now known as Rocky Meadow cove. Among Watson's descendants was a grandson, Jonathan Shaw, who probably came into possession of the property through inheritance and who ceded the water privilege with sufficient of the adjacent land for the first iron manufactory that embarked in that business in Plympton.

The village of Popes Point reached the prime of its glory during and shortly after the Revolution. The Shurtleff family had prospered nearly a century on the estate eastward of Quitticus road, and Barnabas was one of the promoters of the first furnace; Capt. Joshua Perkins with his family lived on the old farm on the easterly side of the Lakenham road while a son Luke had a blacksmith shop on the site later occupied by Bents mill and a residence where stands the shop of Rufus L. Richards. A saw mill was located on the other branch of the brook where it crosses the Rocky Gutter road and later the blacksmith shop of Abial Thomas stood on the Middleboro side. Coal houses, ware houses and dwellings that have long since gone to decay went to make up the thriving village.

The furnace building stood on the east side of the road between the Stephen Atwood farm and the John Bent homestead. The raceway and brook were filled in by the orders of the town in 1845. The store stood on a site northerly from the Stephen Atwood house, on the corner of Pope's Point road and the Rocky Gutter road; the boarding house on the opposite side of the Carver road a little to the north. The furnace building was a structure that excited the pride of the village people. The water wheel that furnished the power was a massive affair standing thirty feet in the air. Long after the works were discontinued the wheel stood as a plaything for the village boys and girls of the neighborhood.

In 1735 Jonathan Shaw, whom we have seen inherit the property from his grandfather, ceded the privilege and land on Watsons Cove brook conditionally as may be seen, to Isaac Lothrop, Esq., Isaac Lothrop, Jr., Lazarus Lebarron, John Cooper of Plymouth; and George Barrows, Samuel Lucas, Elisha Lucas, Barnabas Shurtleff, Abel Crocker, Isaac Waterman, Isaac Churchill, John Shaw and Joseph Lucas of Plympton—"for divers good causes but principally and more especially for the encouragement and ye erecting of a furnace or new iron works at a place called Popes Point in ye town of Plympton—at a place on said land where it shall be most convenient to locate a furnace, coal house or coal houses, pot house or pot houses, dwelling house or dwelling houses, or any other building that may be necessary for carrying on said business — also right to a dam already made on Watsons Cove brook and flow land from Sept. 1st to March 31st. — two acres of land for a coal yard and mine yard — the deed to remain in force so long as the men, or the major part of them, keep up the furnace or iron works."

Such was the indenture that gave birth to the industry that built up the village of Popes Point. As the smelting was done with wood and charcoal, an incidental business of making charcoal was established which has left its marks in numerous sterile spots in the surrounding country, farmers for miles around engaging in the work as a side issue. Ore was brought for miles from Carver and adjacent towns and this was no small feature of the industry of the times.

FURNACES AND FOUNDRIES 197

Hollow ware comprised the bulk of the products of this plant. Pots, kettles, tea kettles,* cauldrons, flat irons, bake pans, and fire dogs or andirons were the staple articles of manufacture. The furnace was in operation upwards of a century, a record equaled only by the Charlotte. A few of the last years of the operation of the plant was as a cupola furnace; the last blast was in 1836.

Among the proprietors after the first firm had dwindled away were Skipper John Bent, Skipper Nathaniel Shaw, Seth Morton, Major Branch Harlow, Thomas Weston, and last of all Samuel Briggs and Joshua Eddy under the firm name of Briggs & Eddy.

It is easy to look back to those farmer-residents of 1735 and note what enthusiasm was kindled in their souls at the prospect of the establishment of an iron manufactory in their community. As the monotony of agriculture was the rule of their lives, importing their ware in the main, little was known of the art of making it, and the curiosity of the inhabitants must have been aroused as they watched the progress of the new industrial venture, and perhaps our curiosity would be aroused too if we could witness the way the first iron moulders went about their task.

The boys and girls wandering over the region, little dreamed of the intrinsic value of the ore under their feet, for their untrained eyes saw nothing but repulsive dirt in the red water that

---

*A favorite tradition says the first tea-kettle made in America was moulded in this furnace. This tradition is not supported.

trickled from the springs, but older heads saw the opportunity, hence by the time Popes Point village began to thrive as a manufacturing community most of the residents of the South Precinct of Plympton had become workers of iron, or vitally interested in some of its incidental branches.

The operation of Popes Point furnace created a demand for bog ore that gave life to industrial Plympton and the swamps and ponds were regarded as valuable properties. A rich bed of this ore was found in Sampsons pond and tributary coves which was being turned to a source of profit to the abutters when the officials of the town raised the point that the bog was public property. The matter found its way into Town meeting in 1749, where the private claimants were defeated and agents appointed to guard the interests of the public. After a few years of clashing between these factions the courts decided in favor of the private claimants and the pond passed to the control of George Barrows and Bartlett Murdock who in 1758 signed an indenture whereby a line was established extending from a point on the northerly shore to a point near the connection of Sampsons brook, Barrows to have the ore on the westerly side of the line, and Murdock the ore on the easterly side, while each was bound to guard the property of the other against poachers.

In 1760 Bartlett Murdock began active work towards the construction of his first furnace and in 1761 seven-eighths of the land and business was conveyed to the following which comprised the promoters and first partnership that operated Charlotte* furnace: James Hovey and William Thomas of Plymouth; James Murdock, Nathaniel Atwood, Benjamin Shurtleff, Peleg Barrows, John Bridgham, Frances Sturtevant, Benjamin Barrows, Nathaniel Atwood, Jr. and Joseph Barrows of Plympton; and Robert Sturtevant and Benjamin Curtice of Halifax.

A few years later Lieut. Thomas Drew began to buy straggling shares of the company and in 1784 he had come into possession of 23/32 of the business, which in that year was transferred to Joshua Eddy of Middleboro. After six years of control, Eddy sold the plant to a partnership of local investors and furnacemen. These early owners conducted the business through the most trying years of their country's history.

The plant had not been fairly established when it was hit by the ante-revolutionary times with their agitations and unsettled business standards. This period was followed by seven years of destructive war to be followed in turn by the critical

---

*Charlotte furnace is supposed to have taken its name from Queen Charlotte, wife of George II, who was on the throne when the works were established. This name also, later abbreviated to "The Furnace," was applied to the village surrounding the works, and not until after the Civil War did it acquire its modern name of South Carver.

In 1872 Matthias Ellis, Peleg McFarlin and Nathaniel S. Cushing embarked in the iron business in Kentucky at a place and postoffice named Charlotte Furnace in honor of this furnace. When the enterprise was conceived iron was selling at sixty dollars a ton, but when the new firm placed its first shipment on the market the price had dropped to sixteen dollars. Hence the brief career of the Southern adjunct.

period during which the country was in a state bordering on anarchy. Throughout this period, stretching from 1760 to 1790, the finances of the country were in such a chaotic state as to render stable business impossible, the currency varied in purchasing power from the low level in the ante-war years to the most alarming inflation in the life and decline of the Continental currency, and the best to be expected in the line of business rested in barter. To this system the early operators of the furnace adjusted their business with as good degree of success as could have been expected under such circumstances.

The new firm that assumed control of the business in 1790 was composed of Benjamin White, Bartlett Murdock, Jr., Rowland Leonard & Co., Nathaniel Atwood and Skipper John Bent. These were all practical furnacemen whose lessons had been learned in the school of experience in the days that turned the hard side to the front and under their management the plant was destined to reach the highest point of success in its career up to that date. Coupled with the practical knowledge of affairs on the part of the management was the improvement in the condition of national finances and the well established confidence and stability under the Constitution.

A decade of prosperity naturally ensued. As native ore could not be procured in abundance to meet the demands of the increasing business, Jersey ore was imported through Wareham wharfs, while an increased demand came for shells, coal, lumber and ore of neighboring farmers. As a

HON. JESSE MURDOCK

result of the business for 1793-94, the first really successful year of the firm, the owners had on hand as dividends 157 tons, 2 cwt. 3 qr. and 10 lbs. of ware valued at nine pounds per ton.

Each of the proprietors assumed his place in the industry. Murdock, White and Bent were blacksmiths and they found useful employment for their accomplishments around the plant making flasks, ironing flasks, repairing, etc. Leonard & Co. and Atwood furnished supplies and made themselves useful in any way which came within their limits. Nathaniel Standish was the most prominent employee, and in addition to his skill as a moulder and maker of iron he practiced his natural instinct for business in boarding the moulders, furnishing the "lowance rum," etc., through which the balance due him at the end of the year compared with the amounts due the owners. Bartlett Murdock and John Bent of the firm also improved their spare time at their trade as moulders.

The following are known to have shared in the prosperity of the furnace during the decade either as employees or furnishers of supplies:

Moulders

David Bonney	Thomas Barrows
Seth Bonney	Elijah Crocker
Joseph Bonney	John Samson
Nathaniel Standish	E. Bonney
Jabez Loring	Nathaniel Bonney
Ichabod Tillson	Benjamin Cartee
Robert Sturtevant	Union Keith

John Freelove
Lieut. Caleb Atwood
Benjamin Waterman
T. Rogers Waterman
Jabez Hall
Caleb Benson
Elisha Murdock
Samuel White
Joseph Ellis

Benjamin Ellis
Bartlett Murdock, Jr.
Bartlett Murdock
John Bent
Ichabod Waterman
Salmon Washburn
Nathaniel Shurtleff
John Murdock
Stephen Bennett

Topmen

Experience Bent
Ebenezer Atwood
Obed Griffith
Swanzea Hart

Salathiel Perry
Henry Richmond
Noah Wood
Simeon Morse

Guttermen

Thomas Shurtleff (minor)
Thomas Barrows

Nathaniel Shurtleff

Among the employees of this period who were destined to play an important part in the development of the iron industry in this region were Benjamin Ellis and Bartlett Murdock, while John Savery, as a ten year old boy, loafing around the works may be presumed to have there received the inspiration for his future career. Ellis and Savery began their careers as guttermen and later developed into moulders. From November, 1794, to February, 1795, Ellis earned as a moulder 27 pounds, 10 shillings and 4 pence equal to thirty dollars per month which at that time was considered princely wages. When not engaged at his trade he improved his time housing coal or at any job that came within his reach, and he was considered the best all-round furnaceman connected with the works. In the light of subsequent events it is easy to read the nature of his dreams for in 1800 he began to buy shares in the business and by 1808 he owned a controling interest. In this broader field he retained the services of Bartlett Murdock and John Savery until each had graduated from his school to establish iron works of their own.

The marital connections of Ellis served to keep the business in his family. He married a daughter of Bartlett Murdock, Jr., and in 1810, while he held 13/24 of the business the balance was owned as follows: Jesse Murdock 7/24, Deborah Murdock 2/24, Joseph Ellis and Benjamin Shurtleff 1/24 each. The firm now assumed the name of Benjamin Ellis & Co. under which it was conducted with success for a half century.

In the early years of the industry, traders among neighboring farmers found profitable employment peddling ware. Moulders accepted a portion of their wages in the products of the plant which they peddled and traded between blasts. In some instances ware passed as tender notably in the construction of the South Meeting house by whose proprietors it was accepted from its promoters on subscription both on account of construction and later on account of repairs.

The furnace building stood on the southerly side of the dam on the site on which the last building was built in 1874. The plant was destroyed twice at least by fire, once about 1808 and again in 1872. A boarding house was conducted in connection with the foundry; also a building for housing the employees called the Lodging House. This latter building stood northerly from the furnace building on the north side of the dam.

The store in connection with the plant which stood near Furnace pond on the northerly side of the road was the centre of activities for there the moulders and farmers met for business and social purposes. The business interests were not confined to the management and its employees for it included many of the thrifty of this and surrounding towns who carted coal and ore to Charlotte and opened ledger accounts with the company. Liquors were sold over the counter by the glass, gill or pint and charged on account. Farmers found their provisions at the store and received credit for ore, coal, lumber, hides, pork, etc. The more thrifty ones even deposited cash on account and received interest on unsettled balances. Thus the store of B. Ellis & Co. partook of the nature of a banking house, and in this institution local capitalists found an opportunity for investment while the young firm found capital with which to conduct its increasing trade before bank discounts became general accommodations of commercial life.

The second war with Great Britain gave Ellis his opportunity. Whether he shared the prevailing sentiment which was arrayed so bitterly against that conflict or not, he did not permit his political prejudice to interfere with his business instincts and he hastened to sign contracts with the general government which severely taxed his ability to fulfil. But by sub-contracting and rental of other plants he emerged from the deal with a financial strength that placed him in the front ranks of New England manufacturers. The most important of the out-side plants pressed into service was the idle works up the Cranebrook which B. Ellis & Co. conducted through the rush under the superintendency of Col. Bartlett Murdock.

After the war was ended, and with a surplus of capital, the firm was in a position to extend its trade. It began to own its vessels through which ore was landed at Wareham, and an extensive teaming business flourished between the plant and the wharf. Vessel loads of ware were also sent up and down the coast from Bangor to New Orleans. The Maine trade thus established continued through the various managements of the plant to the end of the career of Ellis Foundry Company.

Jesse Murdock inherited the sceptre from Ellis and during the last half of this management he was the guiding genius of the business. In 1860 the firm of Benj. Ellis & Co. was dissolved and the new firm of Matthias Ellis & Co. assumed control of the business. This new company was composed of Matthias Ellis, Joseph Ellis and Charles Threshie,* and under this management the busi-

---

*Charles Threshie was a native of Scotland who settled in New Orleans, where he engaged in the hardware trade with Joseph Ellis, who migrated to that city from Carver. When the Civil War broke out the partners sacrificed their business and hurried North through lack of sympathy with the Southern cause. Mr. Threshie continued as a leading spirit in the foundry management until his death in 1873.

ness was continued until it was incorporated under the name of the Ellis Foundry Company in 1872. The corporation stock was owned by Gerard Tobey, Peleg McFarlin and Edward Avery. Peleg McFarlin was the treasurer and general manager of the corporation until its dissolution in 1904.

The earliest products of the plant were hollow ware of a common assortment which included crane pats, long leg kettles, spiders and andirons. Tea kettles were made from the beginning and the plant was always regarded as a hollow ware centre. Up to 1860 tea kettles were made in four part flasks with a dry sand core when twelve was considered a day's work per man. At this date the two part flask, green sand core, came into use and the product of the day's labor was doubled. The manufacture of aluminum tea kettles and other aluminum ware began in 1885.

During the war of 1812-14 cannon balls and other missiles of war were turned out, and following the war the furnace kept pace with material changes. Franklin fire place frames, Dubois and Hathaway stoves were among the principal products of this period. In the decade 1830 to 1840 the furnace was changed to a cupola furnace and charcoal was supplanted by anthracite.

With this change came also a change in the products of the plant. Continental and Cape Cod cook stoves became popular sellers, followed closely by airtights, cabooses, coral and box stoves, and in the last days of the plant gas burners and Arbutus Grand ranges.

FURNACES AND FOUNDRIES

The manufacture of farmers boilers was started about 1860, and these proved to be the most popular products of the foundry. They were shipped in large quantities to the Western and Pacific States and to European countries. During the last half century of the operation of the plant there was a wide diversity in its products. This included all forms of hollow ware, both iron and aluminum, frames, grates, sinks, funnels, cauldrons, stable fixtures and miscellaneous jobbing.

The last crew that operated this plant, and also the last crew to operate a foundry in Carver was composed of the following: Donald McFarlin, foreman; Carl Z. Southworth, melter; William and Joseph Hayden, assistant melters; Nelson F. Manter, carpenter, and the following moulders: Frederick Anderson, Z. W. Andrews, Albert F. Atwood, Samuel B. Briggs, Lemuel N. Crocker, E. Lloyd Griffith, Orlando P. Griffith, Orville K. Griffith, Charles Kelley, John B. McFarlin, Edward Paro, John Piercon, Ephraim E. Stringer, Charles F. Washburn, George H. Westgate, Howard G. Westgate, Rufus S. Westgate and John A. Winberg.

Federal furnace was established in 1793 on the site of a saw mill. Long after this plant had been abandoned one of the survivors of the last crew that operated it was roaming under the decaying structure with a well known character of that locality hailed as Uncle Ben Wrightington. Uncle Ben was not versed in letters to the extent of being able to distinguish one figure from another, but when his companion asked him when the furnace was built he understood the nature of the question. "Come here," he replied in his characteristic style, and leading the way to the crumbling arch and brushing the dust from a huge rock that entered into its construction he pointed to the date chiseled out of the granite. For the first two decades of its history this plant was known only as the furnace but after it was operated for the manufacture of shot for the war of 1812-14 it acquired the name which comes down to us.

It is not probable that there was any settlement of importance in that region at that time. Uncle Ben resided on his old homestead to the south on the corner of Federal road and Mayflower road, attracted no doubt by the mill that had been operated on the stream, but with this exception the country was a wilderness until the furnace building with its store, boarding house and one or two dwellings, gave rise to the thrifty little village in the woods. For several years beginning with 1808 a school was maintained in that vicinity.

The original partnership which established and operated the furnace was made up of veterans of the Revolutionary cause with Gen. Silvanus Lazell as the moving spirit. The General was a pioneer in the development of the iron trade and being impressed with the natural advantages of the locality in 1793 he purchased of Capt. Joshua Eddy two-thirds of the water power, saw mill and other buildings with several acres of land and transferred a one-half interest in his purchase to Gen.

EBEN D. SHAW

Nathaniel Goodwin, John Reed, Dr. James Thatcher, Dr. Nathan Hayward and Friend White, all of Plymouth.

Reed transferred his interests to Goodwin in 1796; Lazell sold his claim in 1817 and Goodwin died in 1818. It is not probable that this first firm operated the plant more than ten years. It was idle when the second war with Great Britain broke out when it was rented for a limited time.

Benjamin Ellis who had signed contracts with the government leased this idle plant and put it in motion under the superintendency of Col. Bartlett Murdock. The war was unpopular and this management interested in the conflict in a business way found it advisable to employ a watchman for protection against incendiaries. And this precaution was not altogether fruitless, for a would be incendiary was detected by the watchman in the act of applying the torch but was prevented from accomplishing his purpose by a gun from the monitor. Imagination ran riot for a time but it was finally decided that the culprit was one well known sympathizer of the anti-war cause.

The plant was not destined to remain idle after the lease of Ben. Ellis & Co. expired. John Bent was a practical furnaceman who had served an apprenticeship at Popes Point, Charlotte and possibly another furnace from which he had been advanced to the position and style of skipper. This was but a degree below that of proprietor, and being squeezed out of Charlotte by the rising power of Ben. Ellis, the skipper saw in the idle works up the Cranebrook one more opportunity of gratifying his ambition to take the last degree in the iron trade. Hence in 1817, in company with Timothy Savery of Wareham, he came into possession of the works and started them in operation under the firm name of Bent & Savery. The firm fell short of the desired end and in 1828 the plant was sold to a partnership composed of John W. Griffith, Seabury Murdock, Alvin Perkins, Caleb Wright, Stephen Wright, John Bumpus, Hervey Dunham, Henry Wrightington and Marstin Cobb. The purchase was not a profitable one and the new firm did not succeed in operating their works.

It is probably that the management of Bent and Savery ended the blast furnace regime and when the firm of ? ? ? ? ? ? and Holmes took the business for a brief time in 1830 a cupola was placed in front of the old arch which was discarded but not removed. The exact time this firm operated the plant is not evident but it had remained idle a year or more when the last firm started the wheel in 1837.

Ellis who had made his fortune in the iron trade had become interested in a young protege whom he had found in Plymouth and saw in the Federal furnace an opportunity, and he said to his young friend George P. Bowers, "why don't you and Joe Pratt hire the Federal furnace and go in business for yourselves?" Although a sanguine youth the thought of getting so high at one step as to be the proprietor of a furnace had not bothered the boy's mind, and as for Pratt it transpired that he had no ambition to stoop so low. Pratt was a

SCREENHOUSE OF FEDERAL CRANBERRY CO.

school teacher with a taste and ambition for literature, who had conducted the little school on Indian Brook about four years and at that time he was under contract for a large school in a neighboring town.

Squire Ellis had full faith in the opportunity, and young Bowers was a plausible talker, and the possibilities of business advancements were painted in such glowing colors before the vision of the school master, and so persistent, that a literary career was demolished, a teaching contract annulled, one more son-in-law secured for Squire Ellis, and a new firm launched called Bowers & Pratt.

Through the interest of their benefactor the works were put in good condition and when the young associates met on the field with their force of employees everything appeared bran new. The owners seem to have been more interested in keeping up appearances than in earning dividends, for the firm was under contract to pay an annual rental of one hundred dollars and every cent of it was to be expended in repairs.

Bowers & Pratt soon yearned for a larger field. It seemed to them that their chances for advancement were penned in Plymouth woods. In confirmation of their judgment it must be seen that conditions had radically changed since the Federal furnace was founded. All of their raw materials must be imported and all of their products exported. Bog ore, what there was left, laid useless in the neighboring swamps, coaling timber stood on the hills but it had no place in the new methods of operating iron works, and a larger centre with modern facilities for handling freight and workmen, seemed to be indispensable. In such a frame of mind the firm started its wheel in 1841, but the breaking of their dam in October of that year abruptly ended their enterprise on the Cranebrook. They decided not to repair the break, but moved their business to Roxbury where they established the Highland Foundry Co.

The furnace was originally, and for the greater part of its active operation, a hollow ware manufactory. Pots, kettles, spiders, bake pans, andirons, etc., formed the bulk of its output. Government supplies were made in 1812-14, and Bowers & Pratt commenced the manufacture of stoves.

In the last jolly days* of the old plant Bowers & Pratt lived there, unmarried, and proprietors

---

*The nature of the iron trade gave rise to a spirit of fun and repartee that has enriched our traditions, and there is unmistakable evidence that the employees of the furnaces were the best patrons of the taverns. Every moulder had a nickname and when a new man or boy entered the shop a christening was in order and many of the old furnacemen are known only by their sobriquet to the present generation. At a time when the employees of Charlotte who lived within hailing distance of the works raised pigs as a side line a custom developed of visiting each other after the day's work was done to compare pigs, and on these social calls the treat was an iron rule. Naturally this custom was abused by some who had no interest in the size of porkers, but who did have an interest in the treat. On one occasion a moulder known as Capt. Gurney, who had no pig, thus accosted a fellow workman whose sobriquet was Bug, after the day's work:

"Well Bug, guess I'll come down and see your pig tonight. Going to be at home, ain't you?"

"Don't make any difference whether I'm at home or not," retorted Bug, "you can come just the same. The pig will be there."

FURNACES AND FOUNDRIES 213

of the boarding house. Betsey Atwood and Hope Tillson were cooks; Ellis Shaw, carpenter; Zoath Wright and Joseph Bent, ware dressers; Skipper Edmund Bump, melter. Salmon Atwood headed the list of moulders making heavy andirons, and from the nature of his work doomed to take the last or cinder iron every day; John Bump, Lewis Pratt, Ephraim Pratt (killed in a California mine), Sylvanus Griffith (drowned in Boston harbor), Lothrop Barrows, Isaac L. Dunham, George Cobb, James Wright, Harrison Shaw and Chandler Robbins.

In 1819, a temporary plant was established at Slug pond near Wankinco. This was conducted by Ben. Ellis & Co. under the superintendency of Lewis Pratt, only during the Winter months until 1824. The probable object of this plant was to utilize the ore from the Wankinco swamps, and as cinder iron was carted to the works from Charlotte the works may have been a pig manufactory. It is known that only the coarsest of moulding was done there, and during this period Ellis & Co. supplied raw iron to plants in Wareham and Taunton.

The Pratt & Ward furnace was built by Col. Benjamin Ward and Lewis Pratt in 1824. Established on the dam and water privilege now used as a reservoir by South Meadow Cranberry Co. The firm dissolved in 1827.

The first furnace in Wenham was built by Lewis Pratt near Wenham brook in 1827. The products of the plant at that time were fireplace iron ware, wagon wheel boxes, andirons, stoves, and castings for Plymouth merchants. Charcoal furnace changed to anthracite in 1834. Foundry was kept in operation until it was burned in 1840.

In 1841 Lewis Pratt and son (Lewis) bought the Pratt & Ward buildings, water privilege, etc., moved the cupola and flasks from Wenham, and began the operation of this foundry which they continued until 1852 making stoves and hollow ware. In that year the firm dissolved, and Lewis Pratt, Jr., moved the cupola and flasks back to Wenham and rebuilt the foundry on Wenham brook, in 1855, which he conducted in company with his sons until it was again burned in 1866. The works were immediately rebuilt by Matthias Pratt and burned again in 1869. It was rebuilt by Matthias and Joseph Pratt and operated until 1887, when it was abandoned and its proprietors established their works at Campello. Stove repair work and funnel irons were the main part of the products of this foundry during its later years.

In 1844 a foundry was established by Benjamin Cobb and others near the present residence of Alton C. Chandler. It was in operation about four years when Cobb retired from the partnership to establish the firm of Cobb & Drew in Plymouth. The buildings were removed about 1860.

In 1841 David Pratt established a foundry on Wenham road near the swamp southerly from the present residence of Eben S. Lucas. It was operated by horse power but a few years. The buildings were moved to Wenham brook in 1868 by Pratt brothers and burned the following year.

FEDERAL VILLAGE
Abodes of Employees during Harvest Season

FURNACES AND FOUNDRIES

The enterprise started here was the inception of the Walker & Pratt foundry of Watertown.

About 1825 for a short term Joseph and Nelson Barrows operated a small plant between the Union church and the Barrows homestead. A unique feature of this plant was its method of obtaining the power which consisted of the swinging of a huge log. The log was operated by a muscular negro and this form of furnishing power was one of the earliest impressions of Lewis Pratt who witnessed the manœuvre while passing the plant when a very young boy.

For a few years during the decade beginning with the year 1800 a furnace was in operation on Fresh Meadow dam near the site of the N. S. Cushing mill. Little is known of the plant or of the nature of its output except that John Bent, Joseph and Nelson Barrows were interested in the business and worked there.

In 1850 Silas Bumpus conducted a furnace with horse power near his residence in South Carver. Caboose stoves, grates, funnels, etc., were made for the Charlotte furnace company. This plant was in operation but a few years.

THE CRANBERRY INDUSTRY

The swamps which had furnished the residents of this region with pasturage and hay during their first century, with bog ore for the operation of their furnaces during the second century, proved to be ideal ground for the cultivation of cranberries and thus formed the basis of the industrial life for the century following the decline of the iron trade.

While the records show that cranberries were used as an article of food in earliest Colonial days the fruit did not become a staple article of commerce until late in the 19th century and even that period was well beyond its prime when a methodical attempt at cultivation was made. Through the earlier years the berries were regarded as common property, but after their place in commerce was established marsh owners looked more carefully after their property and gleaning gradually disappeared. Flooding for winter protection and the annual mowing of grass constituted the only encouragement of the old school of growers* and in the industrial development following the close of the Civil war the farmers first began the cultivation as it is now practiced.

---

*Benjamin D. Finney, who built a dyke for flooding a marsh in 1856, is claimed to have been the first to encourage the growth of cranberries by artificial means.

After marsh owners came into undisputed possession of their property, cranberry harvesting began to develop as an industry. A popular method of harvesting was "by the halves," that is the laborer held one half of the day's harvest for his labor while the owner took one-half as rental of his marsh. Screening and packing were also of a primitive order. A windy day was necessary for the operation when a sheet was spread upon the ground and the screener, with a measure of berries held above his head gradually shook them out, the wind removing the chaff as they fell upon the sheet. The fruit was then packed in discarded barrels of varying dimensions.†

Shipments were consigned to agents in Boston, New York and Philadelphia, and these commissioners acted as distributors until the custom of selling for cash came into vogue. The increasing demand for the fruit that grew up in the West made buying an attractive speculation and the operator found a promising field between producers and consumers. Co-operative selling did not become an influential factor until the dawn of the 20th century.

From the hygienic standpoint the experiences of the harvesters of the earlier days of the industry would now be regarded as a hardship that would call for an investigating committee. The marshes

---

†The contents of the barrel is now regulated by state laws, while a movement is on foot to establish a national standard. The disposition of national legislators to make the contents of the package too large has aroused the interest of the growers.

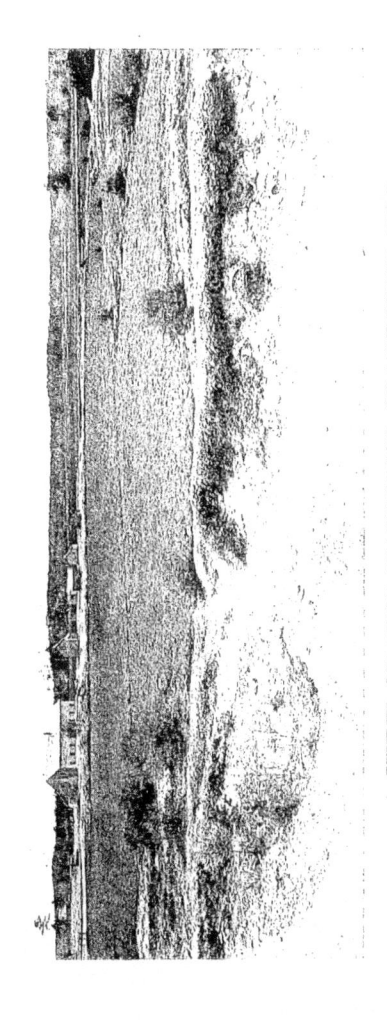

A VIEW OF THE WANKINCO CRANBERRY BOG
Largest Single Tract Bog in the State

were always damp and in wet seasons they were breeding places for rheumatism and kindred complaints. The older laborers wisely refrained from a contact with the water but the boys took no such precautions. Long files of shivering barefoot boys lined out on the marsh awaiting the signal for attack and when the word was given they would drop into the icy water with shouts of laughter and boyish pranks, and the knees were numb with cold before the sun was high enough to impart its heat.

The New Meadows, comprising five hundred acres of natural cranberry bog, was the most famous of these early marshes. It proved to be valuable property as the trade developed and employees gathered for the annual harvest from Carver and surrounding towns. Prominent among the growers of the old regime were Sampson McFarlin, Luther Atwood, Benjamin D. Finney, Joseph and Benjamin W. Robbins, John Dunham, George Shurtleff, Eben and Earl Sherman, P. W. Bump, H. A. Lucas, Ephraim Griffith, Nathan Ryder, Nathaniel S. and Matthew H. Cushing and Atwood Shaw.

Cultivation as it was later practiced began in the decade 1870-80. Among the first to train the plants were Thomas Huit McFarlin,* Chas. Dexter McFarlin, Alfred M. Shaw and George P.

---

*Thomas H. McFarlin, whose residence was near the New Meadows marsh, was a pioneer in the development of the industry. Noticing a large variety he transplanted a few of the vines and started cultivation of what proved to be one of the most popular varieties, the McFarlins. Mr. McFarlin died in 1880.

Bowers, the latter being the first to embark in the business on a large scale. Charles D. McFarlin* expended upwards of one thousand dollars on one acre constructing more on experimental than on financial grounds. Every root was dug from the mud, and ditches were boarded and a spirit level used to insure a proper grade.

In 1878 George P. Bowers who had interested capitalists in the possibilities of the trade, began active construction on the East Head bogs which have proved a model, ideal sand, mud, drainage and water, making it one of the most valuable bog properties in town. Chief among those interested in the operation of the Bowers company was Abel D. Makepeace who a year later began work on the large swamps around Wankinco which ultimately developed the largest single tract bog in the State. The success of the East Head and Wankinco companies gave an impetus to the industry that made Carver the banner cranberry producing section and up to the year 1900 this one town raised one fifth of the total crop of America.

The status of the town is seen in the following statistics:

Acreage under cultivation in 1890.................. 750
Acreage under cultivation in 1912...............2461

---

*Charles D. McFarlin migrated to California in the gold excitement period. On his last visit east in 1874, he became interested in cranberry culture and constructed the bog as stated in the above record. He returned to the Pacific coast in 1876 and embarked in the business of cranberry culture near Coos Bay in Oregon, which he continued until his death in 1910.

THE CRANBERRY INDUSTRY

Assessors valuation of cranberry bogs in
  1900 .... $335,510.00
Assessors valuation of cranberry bogs in
  1912 .... $1,106,600.00

Total crops of the town as per assessors reports:

1904	66,278 barrels
1905	25,407 "
1906	62,531 "
1907	70,383 "
1908	55,336 "
1909	85,598 "
1910	60,640 "
1911	59,545 "
1912	66,043 "

While the berries were gathered only from the natural marshes Fall frosts constituted the principle discouragement of the growers. Mud and water, the natural environment of the vines, precluded the development of the various insects and parasites that appeared in such proportions when the vines were removed from their natural conditions in the process of cultivation.

Marked changes in the methods of harvesting and packing have followed the development of the industry. The crops were gathered from the natural marshes by hand assisted rarely by the long handle rake. In the early days of cultivation the crops were handpicked and hand screened while the chaff was blown out by a fanning mill. In the decade 1880-90 the snap machine came into use, and in the following decade it was the main means of harvesting. At this time the manufacturers of fanning mills began to study the theory of bounding boards from which separators that would remove the bad berries were evolved. At the beginning of the new century scoops began to displace the snap machines, while separators were improved and with grading attachments to remove the small and poor berries, and the cost of picking and screening lessened. The practice of grading the fruit on lines of variety, size and color came in with the co-operative packing and selling companies.*

---

*About 1895 an attempt was made to organize a co-operative company through the Cape Cod Cranberry Sales Co., but with little success. The New England Cranberry Sales Co. was organized in 1907.

ALBERT T. SHURTLEFF
First Civil War Volunteer from Carver. Lost an Arm at First Bull Run. Clerk in War Department at Washington fifteen years following the War.

MILITARY HISTORY

Under the charter of William and Mary military duty was compulsory. This arose through customs then in vogue among European nations, and through the necessity from the prevailing state of society, and every town had its training green. The dangers from attacks from the Indians had not disappeared, while the scramble for territory between the French and English, rendered preparations for defence a perpetual duty.

This custom accounts for the prevalence of military titles. Captains, Lieutenants, Ensigns and Sergeants appear very common as prefixes in the records of the times, and even followed the holders to the grave where they were chiseled on the slate headstones.

There were two companies in the town designated as the North Company and the South Company.

The Revolution served to renew this custom and after the constitution was adopted, military duty came in as a marked factor in civil government. For fifty years after the town of Carver was incorporated the old order was continued and annually the commanding officer issued his summons to his subalterns. Following was the form required by law to be served on all non-commissioned officers and privates:

To ——————— Sir:

I warn you to appear at the house of James Ellis, Inn Holder in Carver on Friday the eighth inst., at one o'clock P. M., equipt as the law directs for military duty.

Those who arose to the highest ranks were as follows, with the date of commission:

Colonels

Bartlett Murdock	1823
Benjamin Ward	1826

Majors

Nehemiah Cobb	1790
John Shaw	1796
Benjamin Ellis	1812
Stillman Shaw	1829

North Co.

Captains

Nathaniel Shaw	1762
Frances Shurtleff	1781
Nehemiah Cobb	178–
John Sherman	1790
Barnabas Cobb	1796
Abijah Lucas	1802
Joshua Cole	1806
Thomas Cobb	1815
Levi Vaughan	1818
Israel Dunham	1822
Charles Cobb	1827
Benjamin Ransom	1829
Anthony Sherman	1833

CAPT. WILLIAM S. McFARLIN

MILITARY HISTORY 225

Lieutenants

Nehemiah Cobb	1781
Isaac S. Lucas	1790
Lemuel Cole	1796
Joshua Cole	1802
Isaiah Tillson	1806
Levi Vaughan	1815
Benjamin Lucas	1818
Israel Dunham	1821
John Lucas	1822
Benjamin Ransom	1827
Asa Barrows	1829
Lewis Holmes	1833

Ensigns

Frances Shurtleff	1762
Joseph Shaw	1781
Barnabas Cobb	1790
Abijah Lucas	1796
Nathaniel Vaughan	1802
Thomas Cobb	1806
Benjamin Lucas	1815
Israel Dunham	1818
John Lucas	1821
Asa Barrows	1827
Anthony Sherman	1829
Thomas Cobb	1833

South Co.

Captains

Benjamin Ward	1787
John Shaw	1793
Ichabod Leonard	1797
Gideon Shurtleff	1800
Elisha Murdock	1804
Benjamin Ellis	1808

Samuel Shaw	1812
Bartlett Murdock	1815
Joseph Shaw	1818
Benjamin Ward	1819
Lothrop Barrows	1822
Stillman Shaw	1827
Stephen Griffith	1829

Lieutenants

Samuel Shaw	1809
Luke Perkins	1812
Joseph Shaw	1815
Benjamin Ward	1818
Ira Murdock	1819
Stillman Shaw	1824
Stephen Griffith	1827
Daniel Shaw	1829

Ensigns

Benjamin Ellis	1804
Samuel Shaw	1808
Luke Perkins	1809
Bartlett Murdock	1812
Benjamin Ward	1815
Ira Murdock	1818
William Murdock	1819
Daniel Shaw	1828
Oren Atwood	1829
Silas Bumpus	1832

The system died a natural death when the causes that called it into existence once passed, and the last of its May trainings and musters were little less than farces. While the law remained on the statute books, through public sentiment it had become obsolete, and the captains "warnings" were considered optional by the recipients. It was at one of these last trainings that William S. McFarlin* who was destined to play a prominent part in the modern militia, was initiated in his military career. The annual warning was left at the home of Sampson McFarlin who had lost interest in the company of which he was legally a member, and young William, then just entered his 'teens, shouldered the musket and started to obey the summons as a substitute. When the name of Sampson McFarlin was called during the roll call, the boy fairly staggering under the weight of his gun, stepped forward and shouted "here." The shout of laughter that went up from the assembled militiamen, made an impression on the boy's memory that never left it. Thus the old military system passed.

A movement for a company under the modern system was made by Thomas B. Griffith in 1852 in consequence of which, Co. K, 3d Regiment, was organized, and which voted to take the name of "Bay State Light Infantry." The armory of the company was in the South Meeting House, which at that time was remodeled and equipped for the purpose. The first officers elected by the company were as follows:

        Capt. Matthias Ellis
        Lieut. Seneca R. Thomas
          " William S. McFarlin
          " Benjamin Ward
          " Joseph W. Sherman

---

*Solomon F. McFarlin, son of John, also reported as a substitute for his father.

HISTORY OF CARVER

Non-commissioned officers:

Sergeant Solomon F. McFarlin
" John F. Shaw
" Ansel Ward
" Philander W. Bump
Corporal Alvin C. Harlow
" Ira B. Shaw
" Augustus F. Tillson
" Thomas W. Wrightington

Privates

Robert W. Andrews
Samuel S. Atwood
Joseph Atwood
Simeon H. Barrows
Pelham W. Barrows
Charles H. Bennett
David M. Bates
J. Henry Bump
George Cobb
Marcus E. Cobb
Marstin F. Cobb
Erastus W. Cobb
John S. Cartee
Nathaniel S. Cushing
Charles H. Cole
Thomas C. Cole
Charles H. Chase
Joseph S. Chandler
Ebenezer Dunham
Elisha M. Dunham
Henry A. Dunham
Charles W. Griffith
Andrew Griffith
Rufus Hathaway

Ephraim T. Harlow
John B. Hatch
Wilson McFarlin
Elisha Murdock
John Murdock
Abisha S. Perry
Enoch Pratt
John M. Maxim
Josiah Robbins
John Shaw, 3d
Bartlett Shaw
Gilbert Shaw
Cephas Shaw, Jr.
Oliver Shaw, 2nd
Abiel Shurtleff
Joseph F. Shurtleff
Perez T. Shurtleff
William F. Shurtleff
Andrew G. Shurtleff
Levi Shurtleff, Jr.
Marcus M. Tillson
Hiram O. Tillson
Hiram Tillson
Alvin S. Perkins

Thompson P. Thomas
Andrew S. Tibbetts
Adoniram W. Vail

James Waterman
Isaac C. Vaughan
John Witham

Two years later, Capt. Ellis, having been promoted to the rank of Lieut.-Col., Lieut. Seneca R. Thomas was elected Captain and Second Lieut. William S. McFarlin advanced to the rank of 1st Lieut. In 1858, Capt. Thomas resigned and Lieut. McFarlin was chosen Captain. The new captain was a military enthusiast and excellent drill master, and he brought his command to such a degree of proficiency, that it was reputed the best drilled company in the regiment. In 1860, George F. Cobb had been elected 1st Lieut.; Thomas B. Griffith 2nd Lieut.; and John Dunham, 3d Lieut.

The third regiment being one of those selected from which to make up the State's quota of the first call of Pres. Lincoln, Capt. McFarlin and a few of his command went down as "Minute men of '61." Thomas B. Griffith started with the detachment, but was ordered back as recruiting officer to fill the depleted regiment.

The Civil war ended the career of the company as an organization, and it was depleted to fill the various calls for volunteers. In 1868, a company was organized which elected Thomas B. Griffith as captain, but it held but a brief sway, for Captain Griffith was promoted to major and the members of his company who desired to remain in the militia were merged in other companies. Since that time young men of the town who have desired a place in the militia, have been connected with the Standish Guards of Plymouth.

CARVER IN THE REBELLION

United in spirit, but differing as to methods, the town entered enthusiastically into the struggle for the preservation of the Union. From the stormy days of '61 to the fateful April 19th of '65, there was no cessation of labors. In Bay State hall and in town hall beneath, public meetings were continually fanning the spirit of patriotism and made it possible to say, when the battles were over, that the town in the woods had done her share.

Many special town meetings were called to consider war problems. In May, 1861, it was voted to add enough to the pay of volunteers in addition to the allowance of the State and national governments, to make it twenty-six dollars per month. In July, 1862, the town committed itself to the policy of paying bounties. Strong opposition to this system was encountered from those who doubted its wisdom. At the same time, it was voted to constitute the first to enlist as the recruiting officer and to give the first five an additional five dollars.

In December following, it was voted to recall all offers of bounties for nine months men and a pledge of one hundred dollars for each enlistment necessary to fill the town's quota substituted. This amount was raised in 1864 to one hundred and twenty-five dollars and made to cover all calls or anticipated calls. In December, 1864, an offer of fifteen dollars for a raw recruit and twenty-five dollars for a veteran, was offered to anyone who would produce those volunteers before the fifth of the ensuing January.

Of the volunteers from this town, nine died on battle fields and twelve in hospitals, making a toll of twenty-one lives sacrificed in the conflict. Five of these viz.: Bartlett Shaw, John S. Robbins, Wilson McFarlin, Joseph F. Stringer and Allen S. Atwood, lost their lives through the second battle of Bull Run.

CARVER VOLUNTEERS

Under the ante-rebellion, State militia Co. K, 3d Regiment, was known as the Carver company, William S. McFarlin, captain. When Pres. Lincoln's first call reached him, Capt. McFarlin gathered as many of his soldiers as possible in the time given and started for the front. Those who answered this summons and who are now designated as "The Minute Men of '61" were:

    Capt. William S. McFarlin
    1st Lieut. John Dunham
    2d Sergeant Hiram O. Tillson
    3d Sergeant Robert P. Morse
    3d Sergeant (rank) Henry White

Hiram B. Tillson	James H. Stringer
Isaac B. Vail	George E. Bates
Josiah W. Coggeshall	Joseph F. Bent
John M. Cobb	John D. Sanborn
George H. Shaw	Jonathan W. Shaw
Linas A. Shaw	Joseph F. Stringer

MAJ. THOMAS B. GRIFFITH

CARVER IN THE REBELLION

The company was mustered into service, April 23 and May 6, 1861, and sent to Fortress Monroe and Hampton, Va. Mustered out of service at Long Island, Boston Harbor, July 22, 1861.

Co. D. 1st Reg. R. I. M.
Albert T. Shurtleff

Enlisted April 17, 1861. Mustered out of service November 30. Wounded at first battle of Bull Run and taken prisoner. Right arm amputated July 24. Confined in Libby prison and released October 7, 1861.

Co. B. 1st Battalion Maine Volunteers
Ezra F. Pearson

Enlisted at Augusta, Me., March 25, 1865. Mustered out of service April 5, 1866.

Co. D. 44th Reg. M. V. M.
William E. Savery

Mustered into service Sept. 12, 1862; mustered out of service at Readville, June 18, 1863.

Co. B. 3d Reg. M. V. M.

Mustered into service Sept. 26, 1862. Mustered out of service at Lakeville, June 26, 1863.

Capt. Thomas B. Griffith
2d Sergeant Charles W. Griffith
Corporal George H. Shaw
Corporal Andrew D. Merritt
Corporal John M. Cobb

Jonathan W. Shaw. Mustered out June 2, 1863.
John Murdock, musician.
Alonzo D. Shaw. Died at Stanly hospital, Newberne, N. C., April 18, 1863.
James H. Bates, musician. Mustered out at Boston, 1863.
William H. O'Connell. Discharged May 9, 1863, on account of disability, and died Sept. 30.

Stephen T. Atwood
Ebenezer E. Atwood
Josiah W. Atwood
Jesse M. Shaw
Charles H. Chase
Ansel B. Ward
Sidney O. Cobb
John B. Chandler
William B. Chandler
William Irwin
Joseph F. Cobb
Nathaniel B. A. Bates
Joseph G. Washburn
Nathaniel Shaw, Jr.
George W. Tillson
Ellis D. Dunham
Henry A. Dunham
Lorenzo N. Shaw (wagoner)
Edward W. Shaw
John A. Stringer

This company was in engagements at Winston, Goldsboro and Whitehall, North Carolina.

Co. C. 18th Reg. M. V. M.

Mustered into service between Nov. 2 and Dec. 16, 1861, for three years.

Capt. William S. McFarlin. Resigned on account of disability Oct. 19, 1862.
1st Sergeant Bartlett Shaw. Killed at Bull Run Aug. 30, 1862, before receiving commission as 1st Lieut.
2nd Sergeant Linas A. Shaw. Wounded at Bull Run Aug. 30, 1862. Discharged for disability Aug. 1863.
3d Sergeant Henry White. Mustered out Sept. 2, 1864.
3d Sergeant Pelham W. Barrows. Discharged for disability at Harrison's Landing, July, 1862.
4th Sergeant Albert W. Perkins. Discharged for disability, January, 1863.
Corporal James H. Stringer. Died at Camp Winfield Scott before Yorktown, April 29, 1862.
Corporal Eli Atwood, Jr. Died Dec. 14, 1862, from wounds received at battle of Fredericksburg.
Corporal Wilson McFarlin. Supposed to have been killed at Bull Run Aug. 30, 1862.
Corporal Levi Shurtleff, Jr. Died at Governors Island, N. Y., Oct. 7, 1862.

THE SOLDIERS MONUMENT

Isaac B. Vail. Discharged for disability Jan. 3, 1863.

Josiah W. Coggeshall.

Joseph F. Stringer. Killed at Bull Run, Aug. 29, 1862.

Marshall A. Washburn. Discharged for disability, Sept. 1862, at Fortress Monroe, Va.

Elbridge A. Shaw. Died at Gaines Mill, Va., June 14, 1862.

Peleg B. Washburn. Discharged from service on account of disability.

Thomas S. Dunham. Discharged for disability Oct. 10, 1863.

John B. McFarlin. Discharged for disability April 3, 1863.

John M. Maxim. Promoted to Corporal. Wounded at Bull Run Aug. 30, 1862. Taken prisoner and paroled. Discharged for disability April 8, 1863.

Daniel B. Dunham. Lost left arm at Petersburg, July 15, 1864. Discharged Oct. 20, 1864.

Micah G. Shurtleff. Promoted to Sergeant July 1, 1863; to Orderly Sergeant Sept. 1. Wounded at Bull Run Aug. 30, 1862; and at Fredericksburg Dec. 13. Mustered out at Boston Nov. 25, 1864.

James F. Shurtleff. In battles with his brother, Micah G., and mustered out with him at Boston Nov. 25, 1864.

Charles F. Pratt. Musician, Regimental band. Re-enlisted for three years Feb. 1864.

Henry F. Shurtleff.

Isaac Shaw, 2nd. Discharged from the service, April 8, 1863, at Annapolis, Md.

Benjamin W. Dunham. Died at Convalescent Camp, Alexandria, Va., Oct. 26, 1862.

Isaiah F. Atwood. Transferred to Invalid Corps March 16, 1864. Discharged from service Sept. 17, 1864.

Allen S. Atwood. Wounded at Bull Run Aug. 30, 1862, and died Sept. 7, at Carver hospital at Washington, D. C.

Harvey Finney. Wounded in battle May 10, 1864, and died June 26 at Campbell hospital, Washington, D. C.

Samuel B. Barrows. Promoted to Corporal.

Thomas Atwood. Discharged for disability June 28, 1862.

Co. C. 32nd Reg. M. V. M.

Sergeant Hiram O. Tillson. Mustered in Nov. 27, 1861; promoted to Orderly, Nov. 12, 1862; to 2nd Lieut., April 21, 1863. Wounded at Shady Grove church, May 30, 1864, and discharged for disability Oct. 26, 1864.

3d Corporal Lucian T. Hammond. Died at Harrison's Landing, Va., July 30, 1862.

Co. E. 20th Reg. M. V. M.

Lucius E. Griffith. Mustered in Aug. 8, 1861. Died at Mt. Pleasant hospital, Washington, D. C., Nov. 6, 1862.

Joseph F. Bent. Mustered in Sept. 10, 1862. Wounded at Balls Bluff Oct. 21, 1861; and at Charles City Cross Roads, Va., June 30, 1862; taken prisoner to Richmond and paroled after thirty days and exchanged. Discharged for disability Aug. 29, 1863.

Co. G. 38th Reg. M. V. M.

Mustered in Aug. 20, 1862.

Sergeant Josiah E. Atwood. Died at Brashear City, La., July 11, 1863.

William W. Pearson. Musician. Discharged Feb. 1, 1864, from disability resulting from accident on the steamer Morning Light.

George E. Bates. Died at Baton Rouge, La., May 21, 1863.

CARVER IN THE REBELLION 237

George H. Pratt. Wounded Oct. 19, 1864, and died the following day at Winchester, Va.

Levi C. Vaughan. Discharged for disability April 16, 1864.

Perez T. Shurtleff. Discharged for disability, April 16, 1864.

James McSheary. Died at Fortress Monroe, Jan. 13, 1863.

John B. Hatch. Discharged for disability, May 27, 1863.

Jesse F. Lucas.

Job C. Chandler.

John Breach. Died at New Orleans, May 11, 1863.

Benjamin H. Savery. Discharged for disability, May 14, 1863.

Levi Ransom, Jr.

Co. E. 23d Reg. M. V. M.

Edward S. Carnes. Mustered in Dec. 4, 1861. Re-enlisted Dec. 2, 1863. Wounded in skirmish near Cold Harbor, June 9, 1864.

John D. Sanborn.

Benjamin F. Fuller. Mustered in Sept. 28, 1861; mustered out Oct. 13, 1864.

Co. G. 45th Reg. M. V. M.

Jonathan W. Shaw. Mustered in Sept. 27, 1862; mustered out June 2, 1863.

Co. E. 32nd Reg. M. V. M.

William H. Barrows. Mustered in Feb. 20, 1862. Killed at Gettysburg, July 2, 1863.

Co. E. 18th Reg. M. V. M.
Mustered in Aug. 23, 1861.

John S. Robbins. Killed at Bull Run, Aug. 30, 1862.

Joseph S. Robbins. Wounded at Bull Run, Aug. 30, 1862, and discharged for disability, April 9, 1863.

Austin Ward. Discharged for disability Nov. 12, 1862.

Co. B. 7th Reg. M. V. M.

Frederick Atwood. Mustered in Feb. 17, 1862, and discharged for disability Feb. 6, 1863.

Co. E. 29th Reg. M. V. M.

Charles Atwood. Mustered in May 22, 1861.
William R. Middleton. Mustered in May 22, 1861. Discharged for disability Aug. 8, 1862.

Co. F. 38th Reg. M. V. M.

Henry T. Ward.

Co. C. 11th Reg. M. V. M.

John Kilroy. Mustered in Aug. 12, 1863; mustered out July 4, 1865.

Co. E. U. S. 1st Light Artillery

Hosea B. Morse. Mustered in Aug. 27, 1861. In 14 general engagements and 27 Cavalry fights. Wounded at Gettysburg. Mustered out at Fort Strong, Washington, D. C., Aug. 27, 1864.

Co. C. 1st Mass. Cavalry

Nathan Maxim. Mustered in Aug. 19, 1862. Taken prisoner at Aldie, Va., June 17, 1863; paroled July 23d; exchanged Sept. 1st. Mustered out with the regiment Oct. 3, 1864.

12th Battery

Robert B. Pearson. Mustered in Dec. 11, 1862; promoted to Sergeant.

Co. M. 4th Cavalry

Ansel B. Maxim. Mustered in March 1, 1864.

Co. B. 4th Mass. Cavalry

Edson C. Blake. Mustered in Dec. 23, 1863.

Co. I. 2nd Heavy Artillery

Manoah Hurd. Mustered in Jan. 1, 1864.

THOMAS SOUTHWORTH

Co. G. 4th Mass. Cavalry
Lucian B. Corban. Mustered in Feb. 21, 1864.

Co. G. 2nd Mass. Cavalry
Andrew A. Fuller.

4th Cavalry
Henry A. Hunting. Mustered in Sept. 17, 1864.
George Shurtleff.

2nd Mass. Heavy Artillery
Samuel Langley. Mustered in Sept. 20, 1864.
John Rardon. Mustered in Sept. 20, 1864.

3d U. S. Artillery
Edward Miller. Mustered in Sept. 17, 1864.

3d U. S. Infantry
Nelson Trudo. Mustered in Sept. 21, 1864.

11th Mass. Infantry
John Caples. Mustered in Sept. 17, 1864.

Veterans Reserve Corps
Thomas McMahon. Mustered in Sept. 17, 1864.
Samuel Ham, Jr. Mustered in Sept. 17, 1864.
George F. Tarbox. Mustered in Sept. 21, 1864.

2nd Mass. Infantry
Mustered in April 28 and 29, 1864.

Thomas McCabe	Thomas Haverty
William Wade	John Kelley

2nd Mass. Cavalry
Mustered in April 28, 1864.

Thomas Lalor	John Ray
Philip Anderson	Thomas Sullivan

In the Navy

On the Matthew Vassar, Sophronia and Eureka.

Stillman W. Ward. Ordinary seaman; mustered in Dec. 6, 1861; promoted to Masters mate, Dec. 1862; later promoted to Signal officer. In engagements at Fort Jackson, La., and at Vicksburg.

On the Matthew Vassar

Atwood R. Drew. Ordinary seaman. Entered service Dec. 6, 1861. Discharged for disability Nov. 10, 1862.

On the Racer, Columbia, Iron Age, and Montgomery.

Everett T. Manter. Sailor entered service as Masters mate Dec. 15, 1861; promoted to Ensign Dec. 14, 1862; in engagements on the Mississippi reducing Forts Jackson and Phillips and at Vicksburg. Taken prisoner Jan. 17, 1863, near Wilmington, N. C. In Libby prison five weeks.

On the Mystic

Levi Cobb.

On the King Fisher

Charles H. Holmes.

On the Saco

Adam Nicol, Jr.
Samuel Parker. Carpenter's mate.

On the Midnight.

Edwin O. Drew. Acting Ensign.
Samuel B. Runnels.
Philander J. Holmes.
Frances Y. Casey.
Joseph Y. Casey.

WAR OF 1812-14. POST OFFICES. SMALL POX. CEMETERIES. POPULATION

Although an inland town, Carver felt the influences of the second war with Great Britain, not only in the impetus given her industries, but in the conflicting political sentiments of the people. As a result of the division in sentiment, a special town meeting was called in 1812 as per the following petition signed by Thomas Hammond and others:

"Carver, Aug. 6, 1812.

To the Selectmen of Carver:

Gentlemen:

We, the Subscribers, Inhabitants of Carver, Pray you to Call a Town Meeting as soon as May be for the purpose of choosing some person of good and Regularity Character as a Committee of Safety in this time of Commotion and Political Division, and to adopt any other measures sd. town shall then think proper for the safety and well being of sd. town."

A world of insinuation can be read in this petition and we can see between the lines a glimpse of the issues of the day, but the majority did not share the consternation of these Federalists, and the committee was refused. On the contrary the town, against the prevailing sentiment of New England, supported the nationalist administration and voted an appropriation to bring the pay of the soldiers detached for actual service up to fourteen dollars per month, provided the State or national government refused to do it. This was later made to cover the services of those who were sent to Duxbury.

The furnaces of the town were in operation night and day, fulfilling contracts for shot and shell and this was resented by the ultra ante-war sentiment. Threats to burn the buildings of these plants were in circulation, and one plant situated in the woods, kept a night watch on duty as a safeguard against incendiarism.

Excitement reached its highest pitch, when the British took temporary possession of Wareham. Rumors of an invasion spread and Capt. Gideon Shurtleff who, as a boy had seen service in the Revolution, took his sword and riding through town on horseback, strove to arouse the patriotism of the people. Col. Bartlett Murdock was an eye witness of the British manœuvres in the neighboring town and on his way home at night, he stopped along the road to advise the farmers of their danger, but as the Colonel was well known as a practical joker he did not succeed in arousing the fears of the people. Several from the Carver militia shouldered their muskets and marched to assist in driving the enemy from the neighboring town, and one was worked to such a state of excitement, that he advocated firing on the ships as they made out of the harbor. When advised that the British had hostages for their protection he retorted: "The hostages no need to have been taken." The march of the militia from Plymouth up the Federal road to Wareham excited the imaginations of the people and doubtless created visions of carnage not justified by the circumstances.

POST OFFICES

The Carver post office was established in the first decade of the 19th century. Mail was delivered from the offices of Plymouth and Middleboro. John Shaw was the first postmaster and his successors have been James Ellis, Eliab Ward, Daniel Shaw, E. Watson Shaw, James A. Vaughan and Frank E. Barrows.

The North Carver office was established about 1835, with Rev. Plummer Chase as postmaster. He has been succeeded by William Barrows, Alvin C. Harlow, Benjamin Ransom, Jr., Rufus L. Brett, James C. Whitehead and Stewart H. Pink.

The South Carver office was established about 1850, with mails delivered from Wareham by teamsters. The postmasters have been Amos Adams, Matthias Ellis, Augustus F. Tillson, Peleg McFarlin and Thomas M. Southworth.

In the decade 1870-80, mail for residents of Wenham was left at the house of Albert Shurtleff, but the regular postoffice at East Carver was not established until ten years later with Ephraim Robbins as postmaster. His successors have been Alerton L. Shurtleff and George E. White.

SMALL POX

The appearance of small pox in 1777, created consternation in the towns of Plympton and Middleboro. The infected region was in what is now North Carver and East Middleboro and raged on both sides of the town line.*

The problem of confining the plague was taken up in a special town meeting, but municipal action appears to have been mainly in the negative. It was voted "that Jonathan Parker's family and Caleb Loring should not have the small pox in Jonathan Parker's house," and further, "that they should not be removed to Widow Ann Cushman's nor to the Widow Repentence Chandler's to have the small pox." But the malady, unmindful of town ordinances, continued to rage.

A movement was made to build a pest house on the Cranebrook, then at a safe distance from the settlements, but nothing came of it, and in lieu of it a committee was appointed to take the afflicted ones out of town. Failing in this delicate duty, the Selectmen were instructed to provide a place where the sick could be cared for.

---

*There were eight deaths in Middleboro, including Rev. Sylvester Conant of the First (Putnams) church, Zachariah Eddy, William Soule, Sarah Reading, Hannah Love, Widow Rhoda Smith, Joseph Smith and Bethiah Smith. These were buried in a field between Mahutchett and Rocky Meadow, which has since grown up. The late Otis Bent cared for the lot with fidelity, planting eight pines around it. After his death the pines were cut by lumbermen and nothing remains to mark the spot except an unmarked slab and one foot stone.

Dr. Jonah Whitcomb appears as the storm centre of popular clamor. As a practicing physician he may have desired to study the disease for the benefit of his profession, but whatever his motive may have been, he viewed the situation calmly and whether justified or not the town voted to prosecute him for inoculating Jonathan Parker's family. The suit was dropped, however, and the only rein on the doctor's activities was a town vote forbidding him the privilege of speaking in the town until the disease should abate. The disease in a mild form appeared in East Carver in 1873.

CEMETERIES

Carver cemeteries were of the conventional order. The older markers were of slate and the inscriptions were solemn warnings to those who lived to read them. The following quotations illustrate the system in vogue in the 18th and in the first half of the 19th century of making the dead speak to the living through the slab that stood above their resting place:

"Reader stand still and spend a tear,
Think on the dust that slumbers here,
And as you read the state of me
Think on the glass that runs for thee."

"The dear delights we here enjoy
And fondly call our own
Are but short favors borrowed now
To be returned anon."

"My time is spent,
  My days are passed,
  Eternity must count the rest.
  My glass is out
  My race is run
  The holy will of God is done."

"Reader, the time's at hand
  When you and all
  Into the dust
  With me must fall."

"Hither my friends just turn aside
  And read and see how young I died,
  And as you read consider well
  How soon you'll die there's none can tell."

"Here rests his head upon a lap of earth
  A youth to Fortune and to Fame unknown,
  Fair Science frowned not on his humble birth
  And Melancholy marked him for her own."

"All you who stop my tomb to see
  As I am now so you must be,
  Repent, repent, while you have time
  For I was taken in my prime."

Burials were made without reference to any plan, which is a handicap in the efforts to bring the plots under the modern order. Perhaps it is best that the resting places of the dead should stand as a monument to the simple ways of those whose pilgrimage ended there, for in the modern lot where the square plots are marked with white marble and polished granite, the most attractive spot is the old corner dotted helter skelter with reclining slate stones.

The Union cemetery is fortunate in the possession of the Jesse Murdock and Fanny Murdock endowments for general repairs, which with the many endowments for private lots insures the perpetual care and improvement of the ground and with the many costly monuments this cemetery has earned the name of: "The Mount Auburn of Plymouth County."

Lakenham cemetery, the oldest, most unique and from the historical standpoint the most interesting was endowed in 1912 by Mrs. Rosa A. Cole. Up to that year with few endowments for private lots the cemetery was neglected, and many of the inscriptions on the older stones had become indecipherable. The Wenham and Carver cemeteries have each a few endowments for private lots but none for general improvements.

Cushing's Field Cemetery

A small cemetery was located on a knoll near the N. S. Cushing residence. Many of the Bensons were buried on this plot, but the "burial ground" was discontinued before the present generation came upon the scene and with one exception the markers had been removed by boys.

Lakenham Cemetery

The land for Lakenham cemetery was given from the Shaw estate. Burials were made before the incorporation of the South Precinct and the location of the burial ground settled the location of the first meeting house. The oldest inscription is that of a daughter of Benoni Shaw (Rebecca?) which reads as follows:

> Here lyes a child
> of Benony Shaws
> Dyed April ye 4th
> in ye year 1718
> in ye 8th year of her age.

In 1736 Benoni Shaw, George Barrows and Jonathan Shaw were named by the Precinct as a committee "to clear and subdue their burial place." In 1741-42 a committee was chosen by the Precinct to see that each lot owner clear his own lot, and more than a century passed before the ground was cleared as we know it. Up to 1908 when the town voted to elect cemetery commissioners the plot was left to the care of individual efforts.

Wenham Cemetery

The land for Wenham cemetery was given by the Ransoms and Hammonds. Burials were made before the Revolution. There is no organization in connection with the ground, the Hammonds and Finneys caring for it until the town assumed control.

Carver Cemetery

The land for the Carver cemetery was given by the Shurtleffs from their large estate adjoining. In 1885 "The Central Cemetery Association of

LAKENHAM CEMETERY
The Oldest Section

Carver" was organized with the following officers: Thomas Vaughan, President; James A. Vaughan, Secretary; H. A. Lucas, Treasurer; and T. T. Vaughan, Perez T. Shurtleff, and Albert T. Shurtleff, Executive Committee; Mrs. P. J. Barrows, Mrs. P. J. Holmes and Mrs. A. T. Shurtleff, soliciting committee.

Union Cemetery

The land for Union Cemetery was given from the Barrows estate. The oldest inscriptions are for the year 1777 in memory of Nathan who died Oct. 22nd and Bethuel who died Nov. 2nd of that year, both sons of Jonathan and Lydia Barrows. The west addition was made through a gift from Maj. Thomas B. Griffith, and the ground was cared for during the last half of the last century by William Savery in an individual capacity. In 1906 the cemetery was incorporated as "The Union Cemetery of South Carver" with the following incorporators: Alfred M. Shaw, S. Dexter Atwood, Henry S. Griffith, Josiah W. Atwood, N. G. Swift, John Bent, Gustavus Atwood, Marcus Atwood, John F. Shaw and Mrs. Eldoretta McFarlin.

In 1908 the town voted to elect Cemetery Commissioners and since that year the unincorporated cemeteries have been cared for by the commissioners. The following have served in that capacity: Josiah W. Atwood, George E. Blair, George P. Lincoln, Eugene E. Shaw and Fred A. Ward.

The population of Carver according to the National census of 1790 was less than one thousand. It has varied but slightly as per the following, up to and including the year 1860 according to national census, and since 1860 the state census:

1790	847	1850	1186
1800	863	1860	1186
1810	858	1875	1127
1820	839	1885	1091
1830	970	1895	1016
1840	995	1905	1410

In the figures for 1895 were 1008 whites and 8 blacks. In 1905 the proportions were changed to 1231 whites and 179 blacks.

MISCELLANEOUS INDUSTRIES

Agriculture has been carried on in a general way from the days of the first settlers and with no great specialties until the development of cranberry culture. But beginning with the establishment of furnaces in 1733 manufacturing in varied lines has been the main source of the town's industrial activities.

The lumber trade ranks high in this line. Beginning with the up and down mills of old, mill men have kept pace with the times. The mills of longest record are Cole's at North Carver, Holmes' at Quitticus, Cushing's at Fresh Meadows, Vaughan's at Carver and Cushman's (now Shaw and Atwood) at South Carver. Shaw's steam mill at Carver is a modern plant. While box boards have formed the principal output of these mills, long boards, cedar boat boards, shingles, staves and heading have been manufactured at different times at most of the plants. Bent's mill at Popes Point and Barnes' mill at Swan Hold were busy plants in their day, while Eddy's mill on the site of the Federal furnace and White's mill on the Cranebrook later supplanted by the Shoestring factory were active centres in the days following the Revolution. The latter was in operation up to the middle of the last century.

While Holmes, Cushing and Cole did considerable cooperage business in the manufacture of nail kegs the trade was not fully developed until the output of cranberries created a demand for barrels since which time barrel making has been an important adjunct of the lumber business.

Making cloth from hemp and flax for home consumption was a necessity in the early days and extended well into the 19th century, when many of the older houses held looms among their keepsakes. But this industry disappeared under the development of modern mills.

The shoe trade had become quite a factor when the period of centralization set in. In the decade 1830-40 the annual output was about five thousand pairs of boots and shoes and this was increased until by 1860 small shops were scattered over the town many of the farmers taking it up as a side line working in connection with Bridgewater plants. In the boom days following the Civil war Chandler Brothers established a shoe manufactory under King Philip's hall where those who held to the craft found employment. The business disappeared from town finally in the decade 1880-90.

Sheep Raising

Sheep raising was an important factor in the early agriculture of the town, but this industry had nearly disappeared before the end of the 19th century when James A. Vaughan who held a dozen was the only sheep raiser in Carver.

The practice of letting the sheep run at large on the common lands was long continued after such

MISCELLANEOUS INDUSTRIES

lands had been divided. As this tract was not cultivated except in spots it was used in common well down to the 20th century, and private sheep marks were recorded with the town clerk by which the separate owners could reclaim their own at the end of the grazing season. When the custom was discontinued there were seventy-eight brands on record a few of which I give as specimens.

Consider Donham. A square crop off each ear and two slits in the end of each ear and a hole through the left ear.

Nathaniel Atwood. A square crop off the right ear and a slit in the end of the left ear.

James Savery. A swallows tail in the end of the right ear and a hapeney the under side of the left.

Sheep were turned loose in the woöds after the May shearing and when the season had advanced to a point where they could not live in the open they must be corraled and returned to the fold. This was sport for the boys who loved excitement and a severe test on their endurance. In the nature of sheep when their domain is invaded the first tendency is to scatter and each one will dart in a different direction. It required long runs over the hills and valleys, and no little patience and perseverance on the part of the boys to head them off but after the rattled Nannies had once been corraled in a herd they would hang together and no amount of driving could induce them to separate again. Thus after the exciting chase had ended driving them to the fold in a compact mass, and picking out the separate marks, was an easy proposition for the boys.

Another custom which grew up with sheep raising never received the sanction of law. Hunters in the woods for rabbits, foxes, or deer, frequently shot and dressed a fat lamb, and mutton was no luxury while sheep ran at large. The silly animals were an easy mark for dogs and great damage was inflicted on the herds by lawless canines. One farmer who was accused of shooting dogs that worried his sheep lost a large percentage of his herd one season and the field where the massacre took place is still known as Mutton Island.

In the popular fancy none of the varied industrial springs of the town holds a firmer place than the "shoestring" factory, that thrived for a generation. In 1852 William F. Jenkins a young man from Utica, N. Y., associated with George P. Bowers and ———— Inman, an inventor, in a firm styled Wm. F. Jenkins & Co. for the manufacture of cotton goods. The works were established on the Cranebrook on the water privilege of White's mills and through the enterprise of Mr. Bowers. Mr. Jenkins died in 1854 and a brother S. Freedom Jenkins became manager of the business. Sometime later it assumed the name of the Jenkins Manufacturing Co. or the Jenkins Braid Mill, but from the nature of its products its name of the Shoestring Factory could not be eradicated from the popular mind.

In the first years of the operation of the firm 1800 spindles were in motion, 50,000 pounds of cotton were consumed annually and 150,000 gross of shoestrings placed upon the market. While shoestrings always took the lead in its manufactures, its products varied with the demands of the times. Cord and braid were made extensively, and during the years that hoop skirts raged in the world of fashion the company did a thriving business covering the whalebone and steel that entered into the mechanism of the skirts.

The larger portion of the employees were girls who came from south eastern Massachusetts but largely Nova Scotia. The boarding house in connection with the plant was a mecca for the young and many of the girls married and are now prominent among the older generation of the town. The factory building was burned in 1880 in consequence of which the business was moved to Braintree, and the boarding house was remodeled for use as a cranberry apartment house.

In 1853 Thomas B. Griffith, Jesse Murdock, George W. Bent and Matthias Ellis formed a partnership for the manufacture of grates, under the firm name of Bent, Griffith & Co. The works were established on the brook that runs from Furnace pond, and a salesroom fitted in Boston. But eight employees were engaged during the first years of the project and about twenty-five tons of grates manufactured annually.

In the expansion days following the Civil war the plant increased its output, and Bent withdrawing from the firm its name was changed to Murdock & Co. At this time Maj. Griffith travelled extensively over Europe gathering styles and data from which the firm took front rank in its line and as a manufacturer of fancy household furnishings it had a national reputation. Brass moulding was added to the firm's facilities and brass castings by expert workmen from Sweden were finished in the most artistic manner. In 1877 the business was incorporated under the name of the Murdock Parlor Grate Co. The buildings of the firm were demolished by fire in 1885 when the business was moved to Middleboro.

HARRISON G. COLE

CHRONOLOGICAL EVENTS

1698. Rochester road laid out. Sampsons pond first mentioned. Jonathan Shaw ordained deacon.

1707. Plympton, seventh town of Plymouth County, incorporated. William Shurtleff first town clerk.

1717. Committee of two chosen to procure a schoolmaster.

1730. Moses Seipit appears in town.

1734-35. George Barrows, Nathaniel Atwood and Jabez Eddy elected first South Precinct herring committee "to take care that there be no stoppage in South Meadow river to obstruct or hinder the course of the fish either in their going up or going down sd. stream."

1737. School officers called trustees.

1738. Elisha Lucas elected Collector because incumbent "incapable of serving because of indisposition of body and mind." (David Shurtleff).

1740. Road laid out from Edward Washburn's and Silvannus Dunham's to the Meeting house.

1765. Town officers began to "take the oath respecting the bills of the neighboring governments."

1768. Laid out road from Barnabas Atwood's to Rochester road. School agents Seth Cushing, Isaiah Cushman, Joseph Wright, Dea. Lucas,

Capt. Shaw, John Shaw, Jr., and Joseph Barrows.

1773. Samuel Lucas and Caleb Cushman named as a committee to join with Wareham in a petition to the General Court for an act to prevent the destruction of fish.

1775. Dea. Thomas Savery elected Selectman of Plympton.

1779. Nathaniel Harlow elected agent to take care of the Tory land and hire it out to the best advantage.

1781. Laid out road from Nathaniel Atwood's to Rochester road. Committee elected "to reduce paper money to hard money." Reported in favor of a ratio of sixty to one. Great difficulty in providing horses and beef for the army.

1783. School agents: Dist. 7, Consider Chase; Dist. 8, Dea. Thomas Savery; Dist. 9, Capt. William Atwood; Dist. 10, Lieut. John Shaw; Dist. 11, John Muxam. Committee of Correspondence and Safety: Lieut. John Shaw, Isaac Churchill, Seth Cushing, Isaiah Cushman, Dea. Thomas Savery. Voted not to receive any of the "Refugees which had fled to the enemy for protection" and to hire out their land for the benefit of the town treasury.

1790. Carver incorporated.

1791. Laid out road from Lakenham road to Dea. Dunham's. Joseph Vaughan, Isaac Cushman and Abijah Lucas, first Herring Committee. Jonathan Tillson authorized to locate the bounds of the training field. Laid out road from Middleboro line to Ebenezer Blossom's.

1792. Laid out road from John Atwood's to Rochester road via. Gibbs pond. Atwood rebel-

CHRONOLOGICAL EVENTS

lion. John, Joseph, Samuel, Gannett, Nathaniel, Joshua and Lieut. Caleb Atwood refused to pay their Precinct taxes and 22 pounds were raised for their abatement.

1794. Committee chosen to survey the town and make a map.

1796. Road changed from East to West side of Ephraim Griffith's.

1799. Town paid a fine of $9.99 for neglecting to repair highways.

1804. Rev. John Howland died. Burial in Lakenham cemetery. Headstone inscription:

> Died, the Rev. John Howland, pastor of the church in this town being possessed of great patience and resignation he fell asleep in Jesus in full expectation of a glorious resurrection.
>
> Nov. 17, 1804. Aged 84 years and the 59th of his ministry.
>
> "Reader, the time's at hand
> When you and all
> Into the dust
> With me must fall."

1807. April 10th "four persons were dipped at the North end of Plympton by Mr. Ezra Kendall a Baptist minister from Kingston. Lived near Kingston line and were lead into error by Kingston Baptists. These were the first Baptists of Plympton." Record.

1809. Bounty of six cents on crow's heads; three cents on crow blackbirds; and one cent each on jaybirds and red winged blackbirds.

1811. Bounty increased to twenty-five cents on crows, eight cents on crow blackbirds and two cents each on jaybirds and red winged blackbirds.

1812. Laid out road from Joshua Atwood's to Asaph Atwood's to end at Clark's Coal house.

1813. Selectmen instructed to "call on Rochester and see if they can settle respecting the affairs of a black woman."

1815. Voted to recommend that all societies in town unite and hire one minister.

1826. I. and J. C. Pratt petitioned to be set off to the town of Wareham.

1842-44. School Committee reports published in Old Colony Memorial.

1843. Voted to disapprove of any one selling ardent spirits around the meeting house on town meeting days.

1851. Barn built on poor farm.

1852. Benjamin Ellis store built on the hill. Old store removed from its lot near the pond and fitted as a tenement. First house on Tremont street south of store.

1855. Libraries of fifty-five volumes each presented the schools in town by William Savery.

1855. Seventy acres devoted to cranberry raising valued at $1,622.50.

1856. Tillson Pratt and son appointed liquor agents of the town to sell for use "in the arts and for mechanical, chemical and medicinal purposes and no other." Those who served as agents under the system were Thomas Hammond, Charles W. Griffith, Robert W. Andrews and Ralph Copeland.

1861. Ladies of South Carver thanked by the town "for their offer to make clothing for the soldiers and otherwise contributing to their comfort." The ladies specially remembered Lieut. John Dunham with a revolver.

1861. Savery's Avenue. This unique driveway was built and presented the public by William Savery in 1861-2. It consists of parallel roads a distance of one half mile, shaded on each side and with a line of trees and shrubs between the two driveways. In January, 1861, Savery entered into an agreement with Eli Southworth, Jesse Murdock, Thomas Hammond, Tillson Atwood and Joseph Barrows, owners of the land through which the avenue was to extend, whereby said owners were to give the land and Savery to bear the expense of building the road. The owners bonded themselves to the amount of one hundred dollars and Savery to the amount of five hundred dollars, for the faithful execution of the agreement. The trees between the roads and on the outside of them were to be left standing "for shade and ornament for man and beast." Both roadbeds were Macadamized in 1907, a portion of the expense being advanced by the daughters of the builder, Mrs. Mary P. S. Jowitt and Miss H. D. Savery.

1872. Charlotte furnace buildings burned.

1873. Great Railroad fire.

1877. Tramp house built.

1881. E. D. Shaw Sons facing mill established.

1885. Federal Assembly, K. of L. organized. Charter surrendered 1889.

1889. Road commissioners elected.

1890. E. D. Shaw & Sons foundry built. Sold to Plymouth Foundry Co. in 1891.

1893-98. E. Herman Murdock Superintendent of Streets.

1895. Carver Public Library established.

1898. William Dischane, Arcade A. Patenaude, Felix Pouliot and Harry F. Swift volunteer for Spanish-American war.

1899. Road Commissioners elected.

1901. First macadam road built.

1902. Old Home Week observation instituted through the Library trustees.

1905. Soldiers Monument. The Carver Ladies' Soldiers Memorial Association was organized with one hundred members and the following officers: President, Mrs. P. Jane Barrows; Vice-President, Mrs. Charlotte Cole; Secretary, Mrs. Helen F. McKay; Treasurer, Mrs. Laura L. Finney. By collecting annual dues from its members, holding lawn parties and general contributions, with an appropriation from the town, funds were collected and the monument dedicated with appropriate ceremonies Decoration day of 1910.

1907. Capt. William S. McFarlin Sons of Veterans Camp 132, instituted with the following charter members: Arthur C. Atwood, Herbert F. Atwood, John E. Atwood, Frank E. Barrows, Arthur W. Burbank, Charles O. Dunham, William C. Hatch, Jesse A. Holmes, Edward C. Shaw, Elbridge A. Shaw, Isaac W. Shaw, William M. Shaw, Carlton Shurtleff, Oliver L. Shurtleff, Percy W. Shurtleff, George L. Spaulding, Horace D. Stringer, George P. Thomas, Frank F. Weston, Seneca T. Weston.

1908. Frederick Andreson, Frank E. Barrows and Abbott G. Finney elected Park Commissioners of Carver. This was the starting point of the park system.

1908. The Woman's Alliance of Carver was organized July 15, 1908, with the following charter members: Delia Atwood, Laura A. Austin, Wilhelmina L. Cornish, Sadie F. Gibbs, Mabel Griffith, Mary P. S. Jowitt, Anne Richmond McFarlin, Eldoretta McFarlin, Helena McFarlin, Sarah F. Mc Farlin, Veretta McFarlin, Anna R. Savery, Ethel Savery, Hattie D. Savery, S. Louise Savery, Gertrude F. Shaw, Nancy A. Shaw, Dora F. Tillson, Reba W. Tillson, Elva H. Washburn, Hattie D. Winberg. The following have joined the Alliance since its organization: Eleanor Barrows, Elizabeth J. Barrows, Catherine Costello, Julia Costello, Caroline Gibbs, Hannah Hawkes, Della G. Kenney, Mary Lincoln, Emma T. Moore, Jane L. Moore, Susan A. Murdock, Ethel V. Roy, Anna K. Shaw, Daisy Vaughan.

The East Head Game Preserve

In 1908 George B. Clark and James J. Ryan secured an option on the Turner estate with a view to the establishment of a sanctuary for the propagation of game birds. A company was organized consisting of Clark and Ryan, Charles W. Dimmick, Thomas W. Lawson, Paul Butler and others for the purpose of carrying out the project and the land came into the possession of the company with Henry S. Blake as trustee. A beginning was made in the line of plowing and sowing seeds to provide feed for birds, and in 1911 the premises were taken on a twenty year lease by the American Game Protective and Propagation Association of New York conditional upon the continued use of the estate as a game sanctuary. Charles W. Dimmick continues as managing director.

Active work began in 1912 when large flocks of ducks and pheasants were bred, also as experiments smaller flocks of ruffed grouse, quails, wild turkeys, silver and golden pheasants, etc. Enclosures were made with high wire fencing, some of them taking in the Bowers trout pond for the convenience of water birds. The buildings were remodeled, a large bungalo built for the use of the managers, numerous small buildings for winter protection of the birds, and a general improvement in the conditions necessary for the successful continuation of the work.

GEORGE P. BOWERS

LANDMARKS OF CARVER

Old Gate Road. Highway leading from the Advent church to the B. W. Robbins farm, once closed by a gate which had to be opened by travelers on that road.

Joel Field. At the corner of Rochester Road and Pine street. Once the farm of Joel Shurtleff.

Hemlock Island. Once a beautiful island on the west side of the cedar swamp densely wooded with hemlock and cedars. Noted also for its rank growth of ferns and for its thrifty painted trilliums. The natural beauty of the spot has been destroyed by lumbermen.

Province Rock. A large rock between East Head and Federal. Province Rock valley makes down to the South.

Bodfish Bridge. Spans the Cranebrook near the Z. A. Tillson homestead.

Shaky Bottom Bridge. Spans the brook leading from the Smith-Hammond cranberry bogs.

Tiger Field. A fertile spot in East Head woods under cultivation.

Skipper Edmund Place. The site of an old homestead on the westerly shore of Wankinco, so named from its former habitant Edmund Bumpus, who at one time was skipper in the Federal furnace. Mr. Bumpus was specially noted as a lover of flowers and for his ability in forecasting the weather.

Clarks Island. A place on Tremont street near the Wareham town line.

Fox Island, Wolf Island and Shaws Island. Spots of upland in the New Meadows swamp.

Goulds Bottom. A fertile field skirting the obsolete Federal-Wareham road.

Tillson Field. On the easterly edge of the New Meadows swamp. Once the home of the Tillsons.

Jacksons Point. A point of land making into New Meadows swamp from Popes Point road. So named from its original owner, Abraham Jackson.

Polypody Cove. A section of meadow on the Shurtleff farm supposed to have received its name from the rare ferns that grow there. Mentioned in Plymouth records in 1694.

The Plains. A level tract of land in West Carver.

Robinson Swamp. The bed of Cranebrook cranberry bog.

Egypt. A spot once thickly wooded between North Carver and Rocky Meadow in Middleboro.

Mt. Misery. A high hill between the railroad and the residence of Edgar E. Gardner. Said to be the highest elevation in Carver.

Meeting Road. Leads from Johns pond to Ocean house.

Swan Hold (sometimes Swan Holt). Mentioned in Plymouth records in 1662. Origin of name in dispute. Applied to the section East of Wenham.

Wenham. The section of the town now known as East Carver. The village went by this name until after the Civil War. First mentioned in Plymouth records in 1692. Supposed to have been named in honor of the old country home of one of the first settlers of that region.

Chris Springs. Former name of the pond now known as Bens pond south of Shoestring factory pond. So named from Crispus Shaw who resided on his farm near by. Sometimes called Chris Shaw springs. Triangle pond.

King Philip Spring. Near Carver green. Tradition says it received its name from Indians in King Philip war who stopped to wash their hands in the place on their return after their attack on Chiltonville. King Philip's hall received its name from the spring.

Herring Brook. Former name of stream that runs from Wenham pond to the Weweantic river.

Ocean House. Once a house standing on Main street south of Muddy pond bog.

Lothrops Forge. Site of the Centre Mill.

Pratt Place. Near Centre Mill.

Molly Holmes Place. Near First Swamp.

Barnes Mill. Saw mill that stood on the privilege now of the Swanhold Bog Co.

James Savery Place. The site of the homestead of Fosdick road south of Lakenham cemetery.

Lakenham. Name of North Carver village until the Civil War. So named in the grant of land to John Jenney in 1637. Origin of name unknown.

Bensons Forge. (Later called Leach's Forge.) Where N. S. Cushing's saw mill now stands.

Casey Place. The remnant of the Indian lands. So named from Augustus Casey, a South Carolina negro who married a daughter of Launa Seipet and reared his family on the old farm.

First Swamp. East of Carver Centre on the Plymouth road. Applied to the Ward farm and adjacent houses. Origin of name unknown.

Bowers Trout Pond. In 1862 George P. Bowers built a dam across East Head brook creating an artificial pond for the purpose of breeding and raising trout. Since known as the Bowers trout pond.

The Turner Place. In 1880 Job A. Turner of Scituate purchased a small tract of land on the east side of Barrett's pond and erected a cottage, library building, etc. Soon after that date he came into possession of three thousand acres around East Head and began clearing a farm. Several large fields were subdued and placed under cultivation. A larger house, with another cottage and a large barn were built near the Bowers Trout pond. Horses, ponies, cattle and poultry were raised. On the death of Mr. Turner in 1894 the farm was deserted and a few years later the Barrett's pond cottage and the trout pond house were demolished by forest fires and the property passed to the Game Preserve promoters.

Cobb Place. At Mahutchett, now used as a bog house by John W. Churchill. Once the Major Nehemiah Cobb homestead; later the Asa Barrows homestead.

Sixmile Brook. Frequently mentioned in earlier records. Not definitely located. Some have confused it with Huntinghouse brook but the latter was known by its present name from the earliest times.

Quitticas. Village in West Carver so named from the Indian word being surrounded by swamps.

Benson Cemetery. In Cushing field at Fresh Meadows where the first settlers were buried. The only headstone remaining marks the resting place of young William Morrison.

New Bridge. Spans the Cranebrook where it crosses Cranberry road.

Snappit. Corruption of Annasnapet the original name of the village in the north eastern section of the town.

Kidd's Island. In Wenham pond, so named from a traditional incident.

Pokanet Field. Near the river westerly from the residence of E. E. Shaw, so named from an Indian employee of the Shurtleffs.

Fresh Meadows. The village in the south western section of the town.

Shurtleff Park. Donated to the town as a public park from the Shurtleff estate by Benjamin Shurtleff, M. D. in 1908.

Carver Green. In 1736-37 Benoni and Jonathan Shaw deeded a tract of land to the Precinct to be used as a common. This became the training green of the Precinct and later of the town going by the name of Lakenham Green. After the civil war it assumed its modern name of Carver Green.

BIOGRAPHICAL SKETCHES

HON. BENJAMIN ELLIS

Benjamin Ellis was born in Plympton June 3, 1775. He died in Carver April 18, 1852, leaving an estate of two hundred thousand dollars. Considering his environments, his lack of early training and education and the times in which he lived, this marks him as a Captain of Industry.

There is nothing to indicate that his parents were above the ordinary people in the business world, when at the age of eighteen their son learned the trade of a moulder at Charlotte furnace. His rise was so rapid that in fifteen years he owned a controlling interest in the works and was recognized as a Baron in the trade. He had mastered all sides of the craft and after he became a Proprietor, he was in a position to give assistance to any of his employees whenever they were bothered with their parts.

His recognized ability made him a valuable man in the political world and he held numerous positions of trust and responsibility. Thrifty farmers who had spare capital, handed it over to Squire Ellis for investment with no further concern of the consequences.

He was the leader in Carver town meetings for nearly half a century, holding the position of

Moderator at no less than fifty-three of these legislative gatherings. He represented his town in the General Court at eight different sessions, was a representative to the Constitutional convention of 1820; and a State Senator at the sessions of 1825 and 1832, in which body he was known as the Cast Iron Senator.

After the close of the war of 1812-14, and with plenty of capital, Mr. Ellis became a ship owner and extended the trade of his furnace through these vessels which he sent up and down the coast. Lewis Pratt, one of the trusted Lieutenants of Ellis, was often an agent accompanying the vessel to trade the cargo of iron products for butter, corn, cheese, pork, molasses, rum, etc.

Personally Mr. Ellis was not a magnetic man, and it was only through his recognized ability that he captured the confidence of his neighbors. He was gruff in his intercourse with men and naturally unpopular. Comparing him with his compeer Col. Murdock, one who knew them both said, "They were both men of great capacity for accumulating wealth, but one could hold on to it while the other could not." The one that could was Benjamin Ellis.

He was twice married. First to Deborah Murdock by whom he had Hannah, (married Daniel Weston), Deborah, (married Dr. Samuel Shaw), Charles Clinton, Lucy B. (married Samuel Tisdale), Benjamin S. and Harriet N. (married Jesse Murdock). Second to Mary Savery, daughter of Peleg; by whom he had Louisa J. (married Joseph Pratt) and Matthias.

HORATIO A. LUCAS

WILLIAM SAVERY

The subject of this paragraph, oldest child of John and Polly Savery, was born in Carver, Oct. 26, 1815. He married Mary Page Van Schaack of Albany, N. Y., and with the exception of twenty years in New Jersey and New York their long lives were spent in Carver where in 1850 Leyden Cottage was built on the northerly shore of Sampsons pond.

Mr. Savery began his business career at an early age being associated with his father in the iron trade in Jersey City and New York. His life was a busy one, and in addition to his foundry business he was at one time engaged in the lumber business being one of the first to utilize a portable mill.

He also took an interest in public affairs and held numerous positions of trust. As an illustration of his spirit he practiced medicine in his earlier years enjoying quite an extensive practice but always without compensation. He took a deep interest in the schools and highways of his native town adding materially to the town's appropriations for several years. One of Mr. Savery's most unique and lasting monuments is Savery's Avenue which he built and presented the town in 1860.

MILES PRATT

Son of David and Sarah was born in Carver, Sept. 17, 1825. His early days were spent on his father's farm and when the foundry was built at Wenham he became a furnaceman as moulder and partner. About 1850 he embarked in business on Marthas Vineyard, and after remaining there a few months he went to Boston and engaged as salesman for a Blackstone St. stove dealer. A short time after this he started a store of his own but receiving a liberal offer he sold out. He thus found himself out of business but with a good stock of capital, and his foundry proclivities asserting themselves he built a foundry at Watertown. When the Civil war broke out he received a large contract for making missiles of war in connection with the Arsenal, and for three years his shop was in operation night and day, with two sets of moulders and for a part of the time two cupolas. The profits of this contract landed him among the wealthy manufacturers, and taking the Walkers in company with him he established the Walker & Pratt Foundry Co.

LEWIS PRATT

A son of Lewis and Hannah (Bonney) was born in Carver, April 4, 1819. Strictly speaking perhaps Mr. Pratt came as near to that condition "born in the iron business" as it is possible for one made up of human flesh. His father was a furnaceman and his mother's family was described locally as "the greatest iron founders in America." And young Lewis went soon after his birth to the Wankinco hills to reside with his parents where his father was operating the Slugg furnace. Thus his earliest recollections reverted to the industry and he had actually seen in opera-

A VIEW OF THE EAST HEAD GAME PRESERVE
Bowers Trout Pont in the Distance—Pheasant Yards on the Right

tion all of the furnaces and foundries of Carver. Though but five years of age when he left "The Slugg" he distinctly remembered seeing the plant in operation, and of being rowed around the furnace pond by Cephas Shaw, one of the moulders, on a raft. Shaw was ever a marvel in the memory of Mr. Pratt. He broke iron nails and rods with his fingers, lifted large pigs and performed other feats that were a marvel in the eyes of the boy. He also remembered seeing the Baptist church in process of construction and after the building had been framed he thought it must be the largest building in the world. Such impressions which Mr. Pratt recalled in his old age were very amusing to him and he gave the writer this bit of philosophy: "Whether one is a child or an adult things that he cannot do or understand are apt to impress him far in excess of their importance and unless he is on guard he may ascribe them to the supernatural."

ARAD BARROWS

Arad, son of Nelson and Nancy (Bisbee) Barrows was born July 22, 1819. He left Carver in 1838 locating at Albany, N. Y., but went to Philadelphia the following year where he engaged in the iron business with Peleg Barrows Savery and continued the business until his death.

He was interested in military affairs serving as Aide-de-camp on the staff of the Governor of Pennsylvania with the rank of Lieutenant Colonel. At the breaking out of the Civil war he took an active part in looking after the welfare of the soldiers, serving as President of the Union Volunteers Refreshment Saloon until the end of hostilities in 1865. He held numerous positions of trust but never held political office. He was a man of positive opinions on religious and political questions. A rock ribbed Republican and a Puritan-Quaker in religion although he never spoke the language or wore the garb of the sect.

He married Ellen Bailey who with a son William Nelson and a daughter Mrs. Katherine Ingham survived him. He died at Atlantic City, N. J., in 1888, where he located the previous year on account of failing health.

ROSA A. COLE

Rosa A., daughter of Benjamin and Lavina (Sherman) Cobb was born in that part of Carver called Wenham, March 27, 1841. Four years later her father who had been operating a small foundry in Wenham moved to Plymouth where in company with William R. Drew he established a larger stove making plant under the firm name of Cobb and Drew. In 1855, the buildings in Plymouth having been destroyed by fire, the business was moved to Kingston and the manufacture of tacks, rivets, etc., added to the business of the firm. Thus at the age of fourteen Rosa, as she had come to be known, became a resident of Kingston. In 1865 she married Leander S. Cole of Carver.

Mrs. Cole was a woman of marked business ability and upon the death of her father in 1868 she became active in the management of the business being associated with Byron C. Quinby. After his death in 1907 the business was incorporated, Mrs. Cole holding a large share of the stock, and up to the date of her death serving on the Board of Directors. She died at her home in Kingston, Feb. 4, 1911.

The success of her business enterprises was such that she had means and time for charitable work. She was one of the incorporators of Jordan Hospital in Plymouth and active in its management. Her charitable bequests aggregated nearly one hundred and twenty-five thousand dollars and among them one thousand dollars each to the Carver Public Library and for the benefit of Lakenham Cemetery in Carver.

BENJAMIN SHURTLEFF, M. D.

Benjamin Shurtleff, son of Charles and Hannah (Shaw) Shurtleff, was born in Carver Sept. 7, 1821, on the old Shurtleff farm that has been in the possession of his family since it was originally granted to his ancestor William in 1701. He attended Carver schools, Pierce Academy in Middleboro, and was graduated from Harvard Medical School in 1848. While a student at the medical school it was his fortune to witness the first surgical operation on one made insensible to pain through the inhalation of ether, and he was said to be the last survivor of those who witnessed that great event. Dr. Shurtleff served on the School Board of Carver in 1844 and 1845.

He went to the Pacific coast in 1849, sailing Jan. 27th, and arriving in San Francisco July 6th. For a brief time he served as a mine prospector, then took up the practice of his profession in Shasta. He returned to his old home in 1852, when he was married to Miss Anne M. Griffith and returned to California.

He was Shasta County's first Treasurer; in the State Senate for 1861-62-63; County Physician ten years, and a Presidential Elector in 1872. In 1874 he moved to Napa, from which town he was elected a member of the Constitutional Convention of 1878; was the first Mayor of Napa; President of the Board of Directors of Napa State Asylum sixteen years; life member of the Society of California Pioneers, and of the Harvard Alumni Association. He died at his home in Napa Dec. 22, 1911. As a mark of the esteem with which he held his native town he presented Shurtleff Park to the public.

JOHN SAVERY

John Savery, son of Peleg, was born in Plympton, Aug. 26, 1789. He was destined to a career in the iron trade, which he began at Charlotte Dec. 29, 1807. He mastered all sides of the craft from topman to Proprietor. Among his experiences as moulder, in which he had commendable pride, was the fact that he moulded shot for the war of 1812-14. After he became interested as a Proprietor, he was associated with Benjamin Ellis, and leaving the partnership, he

ANDREW GRIFFITH
His Record as a Municipal Officer has not been surpassed in the History of the Town

operated a plant in Albany for a few years. In 1838, in company with his son William, he established the Phenix Iron Works in Jersey City, and soon after the firm of John Savery's Sons Co., a well known hardware house of New York city of the last century.

Aside from his business duties he took a prominent part in politics, holding the position of Representative to the General Court at four different times. He married Polly, daughter of Capt. Eli Atwood, by whom he had William, Polly (married Alexander Law), Hannah Perkins (married Samuel A. Shurtleff), Waitstill Atwood (married George Peter Bowers), and John (died in infancy).

HON. THOMAS SAVERY

Thomas, son of Peleg and Hannah (Perkins) Savery, was born in Plympton, Oct. 25, 1787. His early life was spent in Carver, where he entered Charlotte furnace as a gutterman in 1806. He was speedily promoted to a moulder, but left the furnace and moved to Wareham soon after his marriage. In the town of his adoption he became a business and political leader. He served as a Selectman, Representative in the General Court, County Commissioner, and for the years 1853 and 1854 on the Governor's Council. He married Betsey, oldest daughter of "Left" Joseph Shaw, by whom he had three children, John, born Nov. 3, 1815, being the only one who survived him. He died May 15, 1873.

COL. BARTLETT MURDOCK

Bartlett, son of Bartlett, Jr., and Deborah (Perkins) Murdock, and grandson of Bartlett, the founder of Charlotte furnace, was born in Plympton Dec. 7, 1783. His mother, left a widow at an early age, showed excellent business ability, and continued her interest in the firm. Inheriting the family traits, young Bartlett became a moulder in the family works, where his promotion was rapid. Becoming a partner of his brother-in-law, Benjamin Ellis, it soon transpired that Charlotte village was not large enough for the development of both, and Col. Murdock stepped over the line into Wareham, and established the Mt. Washington Iron Works at Tremont. He was a jolly soul, popular with his employees and neighbors, and his business career in his adopted town was marked with success. He married Hannah Atwood, by whom he had Uriel, Hiram (died in infancy), and Abigail.

HON. OLIVER SHAW

The subject of this paragraph, son of Joseph and Hannah (Dunham) Shaw, was born in Carver Feb. 5, 1831. At the age of eighteen he entered the foundry as an apprentice, and after working at his trade in foundries of Carver, Middleboro, Boston and Watertown, he became, in 1863, Superintendent of the stove works of Miles Pratt & Co., in Watertown. He served in this capacity, through the different managements

WILLIAM SAVERY

of the Watertown works, until his death, being one of the directors upon the incorporation of the business in 1877. He was one of the incorporators of the Watertown Savings Bank in 1872, and one of the original trustees; elected President of the Union Market National Bank in 1883; holding both positions to the time of his death. From 1870 to 1885 he was on the Board of Selectmen of his adopted town, the greater part of the time serving as Chairman. In the election of 1894 he was elected Senator from the Second Middlesex District, but died December 26th of that year, before the Senate to which he was elected was organized. He was married in 1855 to Miss Miranda Atwood of Carver.

DEA. THOMAS COBB

Thomas, son of Thomas and Hannah Cobb, was born in Carver Aug. 17, 1808. He was a direct descendant of Elder Henry Cobb, who landed in Plymouth in 1629, and who later became one of the best known residents of Barnstable County, and among his ancestors were such Old Colony families as Bennett, Holmes, Nelson, Morton, Churchill, Bryant and Shaw. He married Mary Hammond, by whom he had Almira H. (married William H. Barrows), Jerusha, Juliet, Thomas and Solon (Reverend). He was one of the best known men of the town in his day, and having served as Deacon of the church at the Green a period of fifty-two years, he was popularly known as Deacon Cobb.

Through a kindly disposition he made a lasting impression on all with whom he came in contact, and many of the present generation look back to their childhood days with pleasant memories of Deacon Cobb, who was the first to peddle pastry and candy through the town.

He died at his home near the Green, August 25, 1886.

GEORGE PETER BOWERS

George P. Bowers, who was destined to play a prominent part in the development of Carver, was a native of Leominster, where he was born in 1813. Among the traditional stories, more or less hazy, which illustrate his character, concerns the time in his early career when he was sent away as manager of one of Ben. Ellis' trading vessels. He was under orders to trade his cargo of ware for anything salable, and in due time his employer was startled by a letter from his agent to the effect that the cargo of ware had been traded for a cargo of warming pans, and that the agent was on his way to Cuba to trade the pans for rum and molasses. Shrewd Ben Ellis couldn't see any demand for warming pans in a tropical climate, but when the agent returned with the report that the pans were eagerly taken by the molasses manufacturers as utensils for handling their goods, his apparent blunder was forgiven.

Mr. Bowers was a bold operator, with unlimited faith in his ventures. Hence he was the promoter and one of the active managers of the only cotton mill the town has ever had, and also the first to engage in the cultivation of cranberries on a large scale. While he died before the industry was fully developed, the success of the East Head bog has confirmed his judgment, not only in the trade generally, but in his method of bog construction.

Mr. Bowers was twice married. First to Miss Waitstill A. Savery, and second to Miss Eliza A. Shaw.

MAJOR THOMAS B. GRIFFITH

As a strong individuality Major Griffith made a lasting mark. Before entering upon his business career he travelled extensively, shipping on two whaling voyages to South America and the Indian Ocean. After he retired from the sea he spent short terms clerking in Cincinnati and New York, and then returned to Carver, where he was employed as a clerk by Benjamin Ellis & Co. until he embarked in business for himself.

In addition to his military and business activities in Carver, he was one of the promoters of Onset Bay, settling there to establish a Spritualistic resort, when the land was unbroken oak hills, and he was a leading figure in the development of the resort. He was also one of the promoters of the United Fruit Company that met with marvelous success in the development of the fruit trade.

Major Griffith was born in Middleboro, near the Carver line, May 17, 1823, a son of Ellis and

Lucy M. (Bent) Griffith. He married in 1852 Hannah M., daughter of Isaac L. and Hannah Dunham.

EBEN D. SHAW

A son of Joseph and Hannah, was born Feb. 8, 1823. The iron trade was characteristic of his family, and he became a moulder at an early age, By 1850 he was operating a foundry of his own in Middleboro. In 1868 he started the David Pratt foundry at Wenham with horse power. He made a specialty of hollow ware, and is said to have been the first to utilize iron flasks for moulding. The following year he moved the business to Plymouth, and became one of the incorporators of the Plymouth Foundry Company on Water street. The last of his projects was the establishment of a charcoal facing plant at Carver, in company with his sons, Eugene E. and Frederick W., under the firm name of E. D. Shaw & Sons.

E. TILLSON PRATT

This best known of school teachers of Carver was born June 6, 1825, a son of Tillson and Elizabeth Pratt. His life was devoted to the cause of education, and he was an active enthusiast in the development of our school system. Upon his death he left his estate as a perpetual fund, the income of which goes to the benefit of the schools.

MRS. P. JANE BARROWS

Priscilla Jane, daughter of Joseph and Hannah (Dunham) Shaw, was born Aug. 1, 1832. She married Pelham W. Barrows.

Through her parents she was a scion of the first settlers of this region and of numerous Old Colony families. She was always actively interested in public affairs. When the news of the surrender of Gen. Lee at Appomattox reached her she hastened to the Baptist church, where she rang the bell as a signal for the general rejoicing. She was a promoter of the Carver Ladies' Soldiers Memorial Association, and served as its President until its object was achieved. She was also one of the promoters of the Old Home gatherings, where her extended acquaintances and democratic manners made her a happy medium. She was popularly hailed as Aunt Jane.

JOHN MAXIM, JR.

A celebrated local wit and writer, John Maxim, Jr., was born in 1795, in the house at Huckleberry Corner, where his eighty-eight years were spent. He was four times married, first Miss Susannah Pratt, second Miss Ellen Pratt, third Miss Sarah P. Mulford, fourth Mrs. Susan A. Lawrence.

At an early age he began to write for the local press under the nom de plume of Bemis, and for seventy years his contributions were noted for their originality. Many of his news items were made up in the form of rhymes, as:

> "On Saturday noon I saw a balloon
> And fixed my eyes upon her;
> To my delight she did alight
> In Huckleberry Corner."

Mr. Maxim entered the blast furnace and became a moulder of the old school, and through his native gifts he matched the jolly crews, and his jokes and repartee are proverbial. He attained his widest fame in the Presidential campaign of 1840, when he published a campaign songster that went through two editions and did its part in fanning the enthusiasm of that remarkable political contest. He travelled on the log cabin floats in this section of the State, singing from his song book at the rallies. His songs were witty hits on the political slang of the day, adapted to the popular melodies, and aroused great enthusiasm among the Whigs. The following may be taken as a sample, sung to the air of Yankee Doodle:

> "Thus was our nation sore oppressed
> By Little Martin Vanny,
> Who by next Spring must leave his nest
> For Harrison his granny.
> Martin's aristocracy
> Makes the people wonder
> Loco-Foco-ocracy
> To Whiggery knocks under."

In the Polk campaign of 1844 Mr. Maxim continued the same tactics, but with less enthusiasm. The following from one of his songs of the second campaign perhaps illustrates the Whig sentiment concerning the Mexican war:

> "Locofocos haste away
> To Mexico without delay,
> The fight began with Locos crew
> And now his men must fight it through."

Following these episodes he turned to the anti-slavery agitation, and following the Civil war he devoted his writing and songs to the cause of temperance. He was a musician, playing the violin, and a music teacher and composer of no little talent, but as a witty writer he made his most lasting impression. The following may be selected as characteristic of his style:

On the request of a young lady for a declamation for a school concert he handed her the following:

> "Young ladies all on you I call
> To pause, reflect, and think;
> Withhold your hand from that young man
> Who loves to use strong drink.

> "He's on the way to misery's day
> Which soon will overtake him,—
> If he looks fair as lilies are
> Young woman, O, forsake him.

> "He's not the boy to raise your joy
> But for a little season,
> For rum and gin his love will win
> And override his reason.

"Then you'll be left, of peace bereft
And all your comforts fled,—
Such is the fate of small and great
Who do rum drinkers wed."

REV. SOLON COBB

The most eminent of the pulpit orators who commenced their career in Carver, and who did faithful service in impressing the New England character on our American life, Rev. Solon Cobb, was born in Carver, Sept. 12, 1839, son of Dea. Thomas and Mary (Hammond) Cobb. He was educated in the public schools, and after a short experience as a teacher, he prepared for the ministry in the Theological schools at Andover, Mass., and Auburn, N. Y.

From 1864 to the date of his death he was in the service of the church at the following pastorates:

First Presbyterian church, Oswego, N. Y., 1864 to 1869.

Congregationalist church, Medway, Mass., 1869 to 1875.

Congregationalist church, Jacksonville, Fla., 1875 to 1878.

Central Presbyterian church, Erie, Penn., 1878 to 1894.

Point Breeze Presbyterian church, Pittsburg, Penn., 1894 to 1900.

He was married in 1865 to Miss Hannah D. Anthony of New Bedford, by whom he had one son, now pastor of the Presbyterian church at

MRS. ROSA A. COLE

Cambridge Springs, Penn. He was created a Doctor of Divinity by the University of Western Pennsylvania. He died at his home in Pittsburg, May 26, 1900.

ELLIS H. CORNISH, M. D.

Born in Halifax, Mass., Aug. 24, 1840. Educated in the public schools of his native town, at Pierce Academy, Middleboro, and graduated from Harvard Medical School. Taught school for brief periods in Middleboro and Bridgewater and began the practice of his profession at North Carver in 1868. He was married on Jan. 1st of that year to Miss Nancy Pratt who had been a pupil in his Bridgewater school.

His life was spent in Carver, where he enjoyed a large practice extending over the adjoining towns. He was noted for his sincerity, his sympathy for people in distress, and for an unselfish devotion to his profession. For over forty years he was a welcomed visitor in the homes of the afflicted, where his skill and integrity carried hope, and his chief motive was in doing good. He died at his home in South Carver, July 24, 1910.

HON. PELEG McFARLIN

Aside from his business career Mr. McFarlin developed marked talent as a writer and speaker. When the iron industry began to decline he entered heartily into the movement for tariff reform, taking high rank among the advocates of the principles of the New England Free Trade League. While the greater part of his work was devoted to political and economic questions, he wrote much from a purely literary standpoint covering a wide range of subjects. For twenty-five years the writings of Ruralis and Logan, nom de plumes over which he wrote, were features of the local press. His contributions in both prose and poetry dealt in an original vein with local history, tradition and general philosophy, and these contributions now afford a bright star in local annals. He was an all around writer—not a genius—for as he wrote: "A man of genius is, as a rule, erratic, and his title to fame almost invariably depends on some supreme effort. It would seem as if his soul possessed but one drop of the pure oil of genius, touched by a live coal from the altar of fancy, flamed forth with portentious brilliancy, lighting to the view of the world, a hitherto undiscovered realm of beauty. While yet the exalted vision lingers, he writes his name beneath the picture and 'tis his forever more.' And so with little men who tread the lower plane; and so with the modest dabbler with ink who writes the village news. His pathway is, for the most part, flower girt and easy, but he sometimes meets the stony hill and seeks its summit with toiling steps."

He was a versatile writer, confining himself to no particular style or hobby and playing much with humor and satire. Perhaps the most noted of his poetical sketches was "The Money Digger," in which he related in three chapters the locally famous story of the finding of Capt. Kidd's treasure on the island in Wenham pond. Yet he could turn to a serious vein, as note a quotation from a poem on "Autumn Days":

"Once more the gleaners bind their sheaves
    That mark the season's wane,
"Once more we note the rustling leaves
    Upon the harvest plain.

"The tardy morn, the hastening shade,
    The crickets in the grass,
Giving a voice to every blade
    To swell their evening mass.

"The falling fruit, the bending vines,
    The ripe and golden grain,
These, hold the sure and grateful signs,
    Of Autumn's generous reign.

"Thy precepts, Autumn, closer bind
    My trusting heart to thee,
And Nature never seems so kind,
    Nor smiles so sweet to me,

"As when the flowers begin to fade
    Along the darkened wall,
And one by one, within the glade,
    The leaves begin to fall."

PRECINCT OFFICERS, PARISH OFFICERS, CHURCH MEMBERS, TOWN OFFICERS

PRECINCT CLERKS

Joseph Lucas	1732—1740
Joseph Bridgham	1741—1745
Benjamin Shurtleff	1746—1757
Samuel Lucas	1758
Benjamin Shurtleff	1759—1760
Frances Shurtleff	1761
Dea. Lucas	1762
Samuel Lucas	1763—1765
Frances Shurtleff	1766
Samuel Lucas	1767—1768
Frances Shurtleff	1769—1779
Nehemiah Cobb	1780—1790
Abiel Shurtleff	1791—1799
Ephraim Pratt	1800—1818
Levi Vaughan	1819—1824
Lemuel Pratt	1825—1828
Ephraim Harlow	1829—1830

PRECINCT TREASURERS

Samuel Jackson	1732
John Cole	1733—1736
Samuel Jackson	1737—1741
George Barrows, Jr.	1742—1744
Joseph Bridgham	1745
Rowland Hammond	1746

John Shaw	1747—1750
Rowland Hammond	1751—1766
Samuel Lucas	1767—1780
Issacher Fuller	1781—1782
Dea. Samuel Lucas	1783
Samuel Lucas, 3d	1784—1786
Isaiah Tillson	1787
Nehemiah Cobb	1788—1790
Capt. Crooker	1791
Capt. Benj. Croker	1792
Nehemiah Cobb	1793—1810
Thomas Cobb	1811—1814
Ebenezer Doten	1815—1816
Rufus Sherman, Jr.	1817—1818
Thomas Cobb	1819—1822
Rufus Sherman, Jr.	1823—1825
Alven Vaughan	1826—1830

PRECINCT COLLECTORS

Jabez Nye	1732
Barnabas Atwood	1733
Abel Crocker	1734
John Shaw	1735
Elisha Lucas	1736
Jabez Eddy, Jr.	1737
Benjamin Shurtleff	1738
Ichabod Shurtleff	1739
William Lucas	1740
Joseph Pratt	1741
Nathaniel Shaw	1742
———— ————	1743
———— ————	1744
Samual Lucas	1745
Moses Shaw	1746
Jonathan Tillson	1747

PRECINCT OFFICERS

Samuel Tillson	1748
Bonum Nye	1749
David Ransom	1750
—— ——	1751
Moses Barrows	1752
Dea. Dunham	1753
Eleazer Crocker	1754
Joshua Perkins	1755
Cornelius Dunham	1756
—— ——.	1757
Eleazer Robbins	1758
Nathaniel Cobb, Jr.	1759
Nathan Cobb	1760
William Shurtleff	1761
Elkanah Lucas	1762
John Bridgham	1763
Nathaniel Cobb, Jr.	1764
Nathaniel Cobb, Jr.	1765
Azariah Whitton	1766
Consider Chase	1767
Barnabas Lucas	1768
Consider Chase	1769
Consider Chase	1770
Gideon Sampson	1771
Joshua Perkins	1772
David Wood	1774
Isaac Nye	1777
Eleazer Crocker	1778
Abial Shurtleff	1779
Elias Nye	1780
Gideon Barrows	1781
Peleg Barrows	1781
John Shurtleff	1782
John Shaw, Jr.	1782
Benjamin Cobb	1783

Isaac Shaw	1784
Isaac Shaw Lucas	1785
Jabez Churchill	1785
Barnabas Cobb	1786
Jonathan Tillson	1789
Isaac Shaw	1790
Consider Chase	1791
Benj. Shurtleff	1792
Nathaniel Vaughan	1794
Benj. Shurtleff	1795
Moses Dunham	1796
Ebenezer Doten	1797
Benjamin Cobb	1807
Thomas Cobb	1808
Asaph Washburn	1808
Levi Vaughan	1809
Thomas Barrows	1809
Stephen Shurtleff	1810
Nehemiah Cobb	1810
John Waterman	1811
Lieut. Isaiah Tillson	1811
Israel Dunham	1812
Stephen Shurtleff	1813
Hezekiah Cole	1814
Stephen Shurtleff	1814
Levi Vaughan	1815
Hezekiah Cole	1816
Charles Barrows	1817
Levi Vaughan	1818
Ephraim Pratt	1819
Ebenezer Fuller	1821
Job Morton	1825
Ephraim Harlow	1826
Thomas Hammond	1826
——— ———	1827

DEA. THOMAS COBB

PRECINCT OFFICERS 297

Ebenezer Fuller	1828
Ephraim Harlow	1829
Levi Vaughan	1830
Alvin Vaughan	1830

PRECINCT JANITORS

Eleazer Jackson	1735—1736
Samuel Barrows	1737
Isaac Waterman	1738—1739
George Barrows, Jr.	1740—1742
Lieut. Jonathan Shaw	1743—1744
Samuel Shaw	1745—1747
Samuel Barrows	1748
Samuel Shaw	1749
Abel Crocker	1750
George Barrows, Jr.	1751—1760
James Wallis	1761—1776
Issacher Fuller	1777
John Sherman	1778
Dea. Savery	1779
Issacher Fuller	1780
Jonathan Tillson	1781
Andrew Barrows	1782—1783
Dea. Thomas Savery	1784
Issacher Fuller	1784
Ebenezer Ransom	1784
Samuel Cobb	1784
Benjamin Cobb	1784
Jonathan Tillson	1784
Timothy Cobb	1785
Ebenezer Ransom	1786—1787
Benjamin Cobb	1788
Ebenezer Ransom	1789
Samuel Cobb	1790
Jonathan Tillson	1791

Samuel Cobb	1792
Benjamin Cobb	1793
Andrew Barrows	1794
Benjamin Cobb	1795—1796
Isaiah Tillson	1797
Jonah Bisbee	1798
Asaph Bisbee	1799
Job Cole	1800
Asaph Bisbee	1801
Calvin Howland	1802
Asaph Bisbee	1803
Job Cole	1804—1806
Ebenezer Fuller	1807
Benjamin Cobb	1808
Jane Bisbee	1809—1813
James Savery	1814—1815
Jane Bisbee	1816—1819
None	1820—1822
Job Cole	1823
Ephraim Harlow	1824

PRECINCT STANDING COMMITTEE

Those who served and the Year for which they served

Barnabas Atwood	1759
Nathaniel Atwood	1743
Ensign Nathaniel Atwood	1744, 45
Lieut. Nathaniel Atwood	1749—51, 54, 55
Charles Barrows	1830
George Barrows	1736, 57—61
Lothrop Barrows	1817, 23, 26, 28, 29
Moses Barrows	1748
Peleg Barrows	1812—15
Joseph Bridgham, Esq.	1749
Dr. Joseph Bridgham	1738—40

PRECINCT OFFICERS

Benjamin Cobb	1824
Nathan Cobb	1813—15, 24
Nehemiah Cobb	1802—11, 17, 18
Timothy Cobb	1787—90
Thomas Cobb	1819—22, 28, 29
Abel Crocker	1737—39, 41, 42, 46, 47
Dea. Abel Crocker	1752
Eleazer Crocker	1762—64, 70—83
Dea. Dunham	1756
Capt. Israel Dunham	1823, 26
Dea. Silvanus Dunham	1765—69
Richard Dwelly	1732—33
Benjamin Ellis	1816, 19
Ebenezer Fuller	1827, 30
Isaac Fuller	1787
Thomas Hammond	1812
Lieut. Eleazer Jackson	1734, 35
Samuel Jackson	1736
Abijah Lucas	1797—1802, 12, 16, 19
Elisha Lucas	1740, 46—48, 52, 53
Joseph Lucas	1733
Samuel Lucas	1732
Samuel Lucas	1791—96
Samuel Lucas	1825, 26
Samuel Lucas, 3d	1783—86
Lieut. Samuel Lucas	1734—36
Joshua Perkins	1785, 86
Benjamin Ransom	1825
Ebenezer Ransom	1737
Joseph Robbins	1830
Benoni Shaw	1743
John Shaw	1741, 42, 53
Capt. Joseph Shaw	1825—27
Nathaniel Shaw	1775—83
Nathaniel Shaw	1759, 60
Capt. Nathaniel Shaw	1763, 64, 70—74, 84

Samuel Shaw	1737—42, 44—48, 50, 57
Capt. Shaw	1761, 62
John Sherman	1803—11, 16
Levi Sherman	1824, 28, 29
Capt. Nathaniel Sherman	1794—1802
Abial Shurtleff	1787
Capt. Barnabas Shurtleff	1732—35, 43, 44, 49, 50—55
Benjamin Shurtleff	1758
Benjamin Shurtleff	1791—96, 98—1801
Lothrop Shurtleff	1820—22
Shurtleff, Esq.	1756
Edward Stevens	1803—11
Isaiah Tillson	1782, 84—86, 1891—93
Jonathan Tillson	1757, 58, 60
Lieut. Jonathan Tillson	1761—69, 80, 81
Daniel Vaughan	1770—74
James Vaughan	1797
Joseph Vaughan	1788—90
Levi Vaughan	1817, 18, 20—23, 26

PRECINCT ASSESSORS

With the Years for which they served. None were elected for the years 1805, 1820, 1826, 1827

Nathaniel Atwood	1746
Lothrop Barrows	1825
Joseph Bridgham	1741, 42, 46
Barnabas Cobb	1791, 92, 95, 97—1801
Nehemiah Cobb	1781—89, 90, 92, 93, 99, 1802—4, 7, 10
Eleazer Crocker	1762
Ebenezer Doten	1802—4, 6—19
Thomas Doty	1790
Richard Dwelley	1733

PRECINCT OFFICERS

Benjamin Ellis	1806, 10
George Hammond	1763—67, 72—77
Rowland Hammond	1743—45, 47—51, 53, 55—58
Thomas Hammond	1813—16, 28
Ephraim Harlow	1822—24
Elisha Lucas	1739—45, 47
John Lucas	1755, 59—62
Joseph Lucas	1732—34, 36—42
Lieut. Samuel Lucas	1735
Samuel Lucas	1748—51
Dea. Samuel Lucas	1752—54, 56—58, 71—83
Samuel Lucas 3d	1784—86, 88, 89
Samuel Lucas, Jr.	1790—97, 1800—4, 7, 8, 17—19, 21
John Murdock	1732—40
Luke Perkins	1809, 11, 12
David Pratt	1825
Lemuel Pratt	1821
Benjamin Ransom	1829
James Robbins	1759—61
Abial Shurtleff	1788, 89
Capt. Barnabas Shurtleff	1732, 34, 35
Benjamin Shurtleff	1743—47, 49—52, 54, 55, 59—62
Benjamin Shurtleff	1787, 90, 91, 93—99
David Shurtleff	1736—38
Francis Shurtleff, Esq.	1768—73, 78—87
Henry Sherman	1830
Levi Sherman	1822—25, 28—30
Capt. Nathaniel Sherman	1794—96, 98, 1800, 01, 06, 08
Thomas ———	1802
Jonathan Tillson	1748, 52—54, 56, 58
Lieut. Jonathan Tillson	1763—71, 74—80
Levi Vaughan	1811—19, 21—24, 28—30

PARISH OFFICERS

The parish, inheriting the form without the authority of the precinct, speedily adjusted its affairs to changing conditions. While collectors were chosen for two years their uselessness was so apparent that the obsolete office was abolished and the modern custom of appointing soliciting committees instituted. These committees—one for each school district in town, were instructed to collect the subscriptions and pay them over to the Treasurer. For a few years the position of janitor was set up at auction and let to the lowest bidder, but this custom was of short duration when the matter was left in the hands of the standing committee.

While the North and Centre societies maintained their union there was a semblance of life in the parish. The standing committee had charge of both meeting houses; members of both societies were on the committee; and the parish, by vote, apportioned the services between the houses of worship. From the time the union was sundered (about 1853) the meetings of the parish were little but duplicates of the North church meetings, although the custom was continued until 1896.

PARISH CLERKS

William Barrows	1831—1840
Thomas Cobb	1841—1854
C. H. Chase	1855—1857
Ralph Copeland	1858
C. H. Chase	1859

PARISH OFFICERS 303

Ralph Copeland	1860—1869
C. H. Chase	1870—1872
William W. Atwood	1873—1874
Benjamin W. Robbins	1875—1896

PARISH TREASURERS

Alvin Vaughan	1831—1833
Ephraim Harlow	1834
Dea. Levi Vaughan	1835—1844
Timothy Cobb	1845—1851
James B. Tillson	1852—1854
Ezra Lucas	1855—1856
Ralph Copeland	1857—1869
Rufus J. Brett	1870—1877
Theron M. Cole	1878—1896

PARISH STANDING COMMITTEE

Reuel Atwood	1854
William W. Atwood	1860, 62—67
Charles Barrows	1843—45
Capt. Lothrop Barrows	1836, 38—40
Rufus J. Brett	1856—59, 68—73
Benjamin Chase	1849, 51
Timothy Cobb	1842, 51
Thomas Cobb	1836, 37, 50, 51, 55—61, 68—82
Theron M. Cole	1895, 96
Thomas Cushman	1855, 56
Ebenezer Fuller	1831
Thomas Hammond	1842—46, 54, 55
Alvin C. Harlow	1853
Ephraim Harlow	1838—40
Ezra Lucas	1842
Capt. Benjamin Ransom	1833
Benjamin Robbins	1874, 75, 83—96
Chandler Robbins	1846—50

Joseph Robbins, Jr.	1831, 32
Ichabod Sampson	1852, 53
William S. Savery	1831—33, 50
Charles S. Shaw	
Henry Sherman	1834—40, 45, 52, 62, 67—95
Levi Sherman	1846, 48
Nelson Sherman	1896
Rufus Sherman	1834, 35
James B. Tillson	1847—49, 52, 54
Alvin Vaughan	1832—34, 37
Daniel Vaughan	1853
Ezra Vaughan	1857—60, 77—94
Isaac Vaughan	1835
Levi Vaughan	1843, 44

JOHN MAXIM, JR.
More widely known as Bemis, the bard of Huckleberry Corner

DEACONS, CONGREGATIONALIST CHURCH

Thomas Savery	—
Nehemiah Cobb	1807
Isaac Shaw Lucas	—
Levi Vaughan	1822
Nathan Cobb	1824
Thomas Cobb	1829
Thomas Hammond	—
Thomas Cushman	1857
William W. Atwood	1864
Job C. Chandler	1877
Charlotte E. Eames	1888
Theron M. Cole	1903
Benjamin W. Robbins	1903
Edgar E. Gardner	1912

MEMBERS OF CONGREGATIONALIST CHURCH

Through the loss of the records of Rev. Othniel Campbell there is no record of the church membership preceding the ministry of Rev. John Howland. But the list of subscribers towards the building of the first meeting house may be taken as a basis and it doubtless includes the active church workers for that period. The agreement and list of subscribers follow:

"Whereas we ye Subscribers Being by ye Providence of God Settled where we Live Very Remote from ye Publict Worship & being Desirous to accomodate our Selves & Familys with ye more convenient attending upon the Same Which

Can Not be Done without Bulding a Meting House Which we promas to Do at a Place called Laginham near to ye Buring Hill in ye Southerly Part of Plympton viz. on that Side of the Buring Hill next to Laginham brook on a Spot Left to Mr. Georg Bonum. To apoint and to begin to buld the sd House when the major part of ye Subscribers Shall Agree upon. Pursuant to sd Promis we each of us for our Selves Covenant and Promis to Give ye Severil sums herein Sett Down against our names In this list against names In this towards Bulding sd House that Is to Give Two Thirds in Specie For Bulding Sd House & ye other Third in money & to pay in ye same such time that shall be Desired by ye Major part of ye Subscribers & to pay ye Severil Sums unto Richard Dwely & Isaac Waterman or as they shall order & we do also Give to our sd Trustees above sd full Power——the Severil Sums Subscribed & Recover ye Same according as ye major part of ye Subscribers Shall Apoint & Agree upon for ye—— & for ye True Performance of ye Promis above sd we have Sett——with the Severil Sums against our names.

Dated at Plympton October 1731."

Georg Shaw	Peleg Barrows
Jonathan Shaw, Jun	Joseph Pratt, Jun
Abel Crocker	Benajah Pratt
Benj. Churchill	Jabez Eddy, Jun
John Murdock, Esq.	Timothy Tillson
John Witton	Moses Eddy
Isaiah Witton (?)	Benj. Wood

CHURCH MEMBERS

Jabez Nye
John Shurtleff
Nehemiah Benett
Capt. Hall,
   of Little Compton
Nathaniel Morton
Sam'l Wood
William Lucas
John Cole
John Doten, Jun
Jacob Doten
Moses Barrows
Ebenezer Bonum
John Murdock
Ichabod Shurtleff
David Shurtleff
Samuel Shurtleff
Jona'n Shaw
Samuel Barrows
Benj. Gurney
Joseph Cole
Benjamin Cole
Jabez Pratt
Ebenezer Ransom
Joseph Ransom
Elezer Jackson

Moses Shaw
John Robens
Sam'l Jackson
John Doten
Ransom Jackson
Thos. Pratt
Shubet Lewes
Joseph Lucas
George Barrows
Jonathan Shaw
Sam'l Lucas
Jabez Eddy
Sam'l Shaw
Isaac Waterman
Benoni Shaw
James Shaw
Richard Dwely
Elisha Lucas
John Shaw
Nath'l Atwood
Barnabas Shurtleff
Barnabas Atwood
Sam'l Ransom
Benj. Pratt
Theophilus Crocker

MEMBERS OF FIRST CHURCH

With date when admitted

1746 John Howland
     Anne Barns
1748 Joseph Rickard
1749 Rowland Hammond
1750 Richard Bowman

1751 Eleazer Crocker
1752 George Barrows
     Abigail Lucas
1754 David Hearvy
     (Pembroke)

- 1754 Elizabeth Hearvy
    (Pembroke)
  Capt. Joel Ellis (Mid)
- 1755 Elizabeth Wheton
    (Kingston)
  Mrs. Elizabeth
    Howland
  Rebecca Cobb
- 1757 Lucy Tillson
  Benjamin Lucas
- 1758 Wid. Hannah Fuller
- 1759 Lydia Lucas
  Joanna Bridgham
- 1761 Sarah Wattis
  Elizabeth Boardman
- 1762 Barnabas Lucas
  Mary Hammond
- 1763 David Wood
  Rebecca Wood
- 1764 Jemima Barrows
  Sabatha Bennett
  Deliverance Churchel
- 1765 George Barrow
  Rebecca Doten
  Jemima Shurtleff
  Abel Crocker
    (W. Barnstable)
  Mary Crocker
    (W. Barnstable)
  Issacher Fuller
    (Kingston)
  Elizabeth Fuller
    (Kingston)
  Wid. Elizabeth Shaw
- 1767 Hannah Perkins
- 1769 Eleazer Robens
- 1770 Isaiah Tillson
  Phebe Tillson
  Elizabeth Cole
  Samuel Cobb
  Daniel Faunce
  Capt. Nathaniel Shaw
  Isaac Nye
  Consider Chase
  Eunice Chase
  John Dunham
  Mary Dunham
  Ebenezer Doten
  Mary Doten
  Lydia Cobb
  Lucy Atwood
  Dea. Thomas Savery
  Daniel Vaughan
  Abigail Vaughan
  Elizabeth Vaughan
  Joshua Totman
  Elizabeth Totman
  Timothy Cobb
  Deborah Cobb
  Hannah Dunham
  Lemuel Crocker
  Lucy Shaw
  Ruth Witon
  Frances Shurtleff,
    Esq.
  Abigail Ransom
  Mary Cobb
  Priscilla Robens
  Mary Shaw
  Lydia Wood
- 1771 Lydia Lucas
  Deborah Shaw

CHURCH MEMBERS

1771 Joseph Crocker
    Margaret Crocker
    Sarah Faunce
      (Weymouth)
    Ruby Lucas
    Sarah Barrow
1772 Sarah Murdock
    John Maxim, Jr.
1773 Lydia Lucas
    John Lucas
1774 Elizabeth Atwood
1775 Ruth Wattins (?)
    Thankful Howland
1777 William Morse
    Lieut. Jonathan
      Tillson
    Abigail Ripley
1778 Abigail Lucas
1780 Benjamin Cobb
    Priscilla Witon
    Martha Maxim
    Hannah Shaw
    Elisha Lucas
    Rebecca Lucas
    Isaac Perkins
    Molly Perkins
1781 Joshua Benson
    Rebecca Shaw
1783 John King
1785 Abigail Crocker
1786 Dea. Nehemiah Cobb
1787 John Bennett
    Keziah Bennett
1789 Asaph Churchill
    Lydia Shaw
    Martha Lucas

1792 Patience Pratt
    Capt. Abijah Lucas
1795 Dea. Isaac S. Lucas
    Eleazer Dunham
    Rhoda Holmes
1796 Capt. John Sherman
    Abigail Howland
1800 Benjamin Shurtleff
    Benjamin Ransom
    Hazadia Ransom
1801 Abial Shurtleff
      (aged 67)
    Huldah Vaughan
    Sarah Barrow
1802 Betsey Cobb
1803 Barnabas Shurtleff
    Lemuel Cobb
      (to Plympton)
    Polly Cobb
      (to Plympton)
    Nathan Cobb
      (to Bath)
    Nehemiah Cobb 2nd
      (to Camden, N.Y.)
1806 Jemima Barrows
    Mary Barrows
      (to Barnstable)
    Deborah Washburn
    Jane Bisbee
1807 Ebenezer Doten
    Rebecca Doten
    Alvin Cobb
      (to Taunton)
    Mehetable Cobb
      (to Taunton)

1807 Hannah Vaughan
(to Taunton)
James Vaughan
Lydia Vaughan
Ebenezer Fuller
Lieut. Levi Vaughan
Perez Washburn
Mary Bumpus
Mary Maxim
Sophronia Maxim
John Maxim, Jr.
Asaph Washburn
Mary Washburn
Lieut. Isaiah Tillson, Jr.
Daniel Vaughan
Lewis Vaughan
Lothrop Barrows
George Barrows
Frederick Cobb
Lois Cobb
Nancy Faunce
Rebekah Ransom
Hannah Chase
Jemima Washburn
Sophia Washburn
Melissa Cobb
Susanna Vaughan
1808 Sarah Atwood
Azubah Murdock
Stephen Shurtleff
Lydia Shurtleff
Polly Atwood
Betsey Shurtleff
James Savery
Temperance Perkins
1809 James Savery
1811 Lois Lucas
1812 Hannah Hammond
1813 Hannah Doten
Deborah Doten
(to Plympton)
1814 Harriet Robins
Mary Lucas
Eleanor Lucas
1815 Wid. Zillah Bradford
1819 Hannah Waterman
1821 Sarah Cobb
Martha Cobb
Thomas Hammond
1822 Elizabeth Donham
Phebe Cobb
Ebenezer Cobb
1823 Lucy Shaw
Bennett Cobb
(Plympton)
Mary (his wife, Plympton)
John Adams
Lucy Cobb (Fred) (Plympton)
Wid. Susanna Cobb
Ruth Pratt (Isaiah)
Mary Sherman (Capt. Jabez)
Deborah Cobb (Nathan)
Wid. Sarah Parker
Jane Cole (Hezekiah)
Lydia Vaughan
John Doten
1824 Joseph Vaughan

CHURCH MEMBERS

1824 Samuel Lucas
Jemima Lucas
Phebe Vaughan (Dea. Levi)
Persis Hammond (Thos.)
Wid. Persis Lucas
Rebecca Vaughan
William Veal
Lucy Doten
Anna Winslow Hammond
Joann Waterman (Savery)
Thomas Cobb, Jr.
Timothy Cobb
Thomas Cobb
Charles Cobb
Jabez Sherman, Jr.
Thomas Hammond, Jr.
John Ransom (to Plympton)
Phebe Vaughan (James 2nd)
Eunice Vaughan (Brazilla)
Sarah Shurtleff Vaughan (Alvan)
Matilda Dunham (Lucas)
Sylvia Cobb (Chas.)
Mary Drew Cobb
Persis Cobb Hammond (Reed)
Mary Hammond (Cobb)
Polly Tillson
Andrew Sherman
Henry Dunham
John Chase
Sylvia Veal (William)
Patience Robbins
Hannah Nelson Crocker
Israel Dunham
Chandler Robbins

1828 Joseph Robbins, Jr.
Lucy Sherman (Rufus)

1829 Abigail Robbins

1830 Louisa L. B. Chase (Rev. P.)
Rebecca Robbins, Jr.
Jemima Lucas
Hannah Lucas
Mary A. Fuller
Hannah Shurtleff

1831 ?Mercy Sherman
Betsey Tillson
Mercy Bisbee

1831 Asa Humphrey (Weymouth)
Allen Pratt
Isaac Vaughan
Levi Ransom
Thomas Tillson
Phebe Ransom
Waitstill Vaughan
Hannah Cobb

1831 Eunice Vaughan
    Lucy Dunham
    Lydia Crocker
    Stephen Shurtleff
    Sarah B. Washburn
    Jemima D. Washburn
    Mrs. Mary W. Gibbs
    Phebe Shurtleff
    Lydia A. Shurtleff
    Ezra Lucas
      (3d Plymouth)
    Anna Lucas
      (3d Plymouth)
1832 Mary Ann Stetson
    Joseph Sherman
    Consider Robbins
      (to Middleboro)
    Asel Cole
    Winslow Pratt
    Priscilla Pratt
    Lucy Shurtleff
    Ichabod Sampson
    Hannah Morse
      (Sampson)
    Lydia Shaw
      (Hammond)
1833 Rebecca Shaw
    Wilson Shaw
    Otis Cobb
    Mercy Cobb
    Ephraim Harlow
    Hannah Harlow
    Rufus Sherman
    Alvan Vaughan
1834 Benjamin Ransom
    Lucy Ransom
    Levi Sherman
    Lydia Sherman
    William Hammond
    Calista Sherman
      (Andrew)
    Ruth Chandler
      (Zebadee)
1840 Barnibus Ellis
      (to Plymouth)
    Ruth Morse
1841 Benjamin Chase
    Keziah Chase
    James B. Tillson
    Anne Maria F. Tillson
    Betsey W. Sherman
    Lucinda Cobb
    Deborah Barrows
    Charles A. King
      (to Abington)
    Ruel Atwood
    James Waterman
    Lydia Sherman
    Nehemiah C. Hammond
    George W. Hammond
      (to Chelsea)
    Ezra Lucas
    Wilson Barrows
    Mercy Barrows
    Louisa Barrows
    Job C. Chandler
    Nancy S. Chandler
    Alvin C. Harlow
    Deborah Aplin

MRS. PRISCILLA JANE BARROWS

CHURCH MEMBERS

1841 Job Morton
Polly Vaughan
Jerusha C. Cushman
Samuel Vergin
Melissa C. Vergin
Stillman Ward
Mary B. Ward
Warren Lucas
Charlotte Lucas
Sally B. Pratt
Elizabeth Barrows
1842 Jane E. Cobb
(to Fall River)
1844 Thomas Cushman
Pheby Vaughan
Cordelia F. Harlow
Anne W. Shaw
(to Abington)
1846 Hannah Fuller
(Ebenezer)
Amanda Waterman
(James)
Dea. John Freeman
Polly C. Freeman
(Dea. John)
1850 Phebe D. Waterman
1851 Phebe A. Sherman
Hannah B. Pratt
(to Middleboro)
1853 Ebenezer Fuller, Jr.
Rosette B. Harlow

Deborah Cole
Charles H. Chase
Laura Ann Cole
Mary T. Cobb
Almira H. Cobb
Mary T. Savery
Maryett Sherman
Juliet W. Cobb
1855 William W. Atwood
Lydia M. Hammond
Solon Cobb
Ralph Copeland
Nancy Copeland
1857 Fanny D. Barrows
1858 Wid. Mary Thomas
Mary M. Eames
Mrs. Louisa Bent
1859 Miss Hannah
Waterman
Mrs. Nancy Bump
Rev. William C.
Whitcomb
Mrs. Hannah L.
Whitcomb
Sara L. Wheeler
1860 Ezra Vaughan
Abby F. Barrows
Rev. Jonathan King
(Abington)
Mrs. Sarah F. King
(Abington)

CONGREGATIONAL CHURCH

Members who have joined since 1860

Annie S. Atwood
Susan B. Atwood
Mary H. Barrows
Edward G. Bradford
Lois A. Bradford
Mary P. Bryant
Marion C. Brett
Rufus J. Brett
William L. Brett
Lucy A. Chandler
Nancy B. Chandler
William F. Chandler
Nellie Chase
Rev. Solon Cobb
Theron M. Cole
Laura Coombs
Charles F. Cornell
Hannah H. Dunham
Harriet A. Dunham
Andrew R. Eames
Flora I. Eames
Luther Eames
Mabel H. Eames
Eliza Faunce
Charles A. Forbes
Dorothy C. Forbes
Jennie A. Forbes
Rev. Washington H. Forbes
Adeline Gardner
Edgar E. Gardner
William Hammond
Fulmer A. Higgins
Josephine A. James
Hattie W. King
Lizzie C. King
Amelia A. Lincoln
Rev. Nehemiah Lincoln
William W. Livingston
Emma Lucas
Helen F. McKay
Cephas Morse
Mary A. Morse
Phebe M. Morse
Susannah Morse
John C. Owers
Elmer B. Perkins
Jonathan B. Perkins
Olive Perkins
Anna L. Pink
Leonard S. Powers
Lydia C. Powers
Nancy Pratt
Hiram L. Rickard
Lucy W. Rickard
Christy L. Riggs
Rev. Ezra J. Riggs
Ida L. Riggs
Annie H. Robbins
Benjamin W. Robbins
Ethel V. Robbins
Evelyn F. Robbins
Jane E. Robbins
John S. Robbins
Lizzie A. Robbins
Lloyd C. Robbins

Maurice F. Robbins
Susie A. Robbins
William S. Savery
Charles S. Shaw
Charles A. Sherman
Hannah C. Sherman
Hannah M. Sherman
Maria C. Sherman
Nellie W. Sherman
Sarah A. Sherman
Addie A. Shurtleff
Eliza G. Shurtleff
Lizzie G. Shurtleff
Micah G. Shurtleff

William Shurtleff
Lottie W. C. Stetson
Rev. Oscar F. Stetson
James Tillson
William Tillson
Ann Janette Ward
Clara E. Ward
Fred A. Ward
Emma G. Washburn
Joseph H. Washburn
Leah M. Whitehead
Almeda E. Winter
Cynthia M. Wrightington
Henry Wrightington

BAPTIST SOCIETY

The following, in addition to those otherwise named, were connected with the Baptist Society previous to 1854; dismissals and exclusions not being considered.

Seth Ames
Abigail C. Atwood
Betsey Atwood
Ebenezer Atwood
Lydia Lucas Atwood
Lydia Atwood
Margaret Atwood
Mary Atwood
Mary A. Atwood
Molly Atwood
Nathaniel Atwood
Patience Atwood
Peggy Atwood
Salmon Atwood
Sarah L. Atwood

Waity Atwood
Waitstill M. Atwood
Fanny Barrows
Phebe Barrows
Ruth Barrows
Seth Barrows
Asa Benson
Betsey Benson
Constant Benson
Deborah Benson
Drucilla Ward Benson
Ebenezer Benson
Elisabeth Benson
John Benson
John Benson, Jr.

Patience Benson
Rebecca Benson
Ebenezer Blossom
David Bursell
Elisabeth Bursell
Chloe Hooks Bumpus
Abigail Bryant
Jean Bryant
Thomas Bradford
Peter Bosworth
Sarah Bosworth
Philip Chamberlain
Dinah Churchill
Lydia Cobb
Mary Cole
Perez L. Cushing
Huldah Doten
Sarah Doten
John Douglass
Lydia Douglass
Barnabas M. Dunham
Benjamin Dunham
Betsey Dunham
Ebenezer Dunham
Ephraim Dunham
Ichabod Dunham
Lydia Dunham
Mary Dunham
Mary G. Dunham
Joseph Dunham
Priscilla Dunham
Rebecca Dunham
Susanna Dunham
Samuel Dunham
Alden Faunce
Daniel Faunce

Ruth Faunce
Jairus Gammons
Mary Gammons
Rainah Grady
Mary Griffith
Eliza A. Hall
Anne Hart
Sophe Hart
Swanzea Hart
Rowland Hammond
Benjamin Harlow
Benjamin Harlow, 2nd
Lavinia Harlow
Lydia D. Harlow
Noah Haskell
John B. Hatch
Charity Holmes
Church Holmes
Nathaniel Hooks
William Irwin
Miriam Keith
Caleb King
Nathaniel King
Abigail LeBaron
Lazarus LeBaron
Mary LeBaron
Sarah LeBaron
Temperance LeBaron
Abigail Lucas
Bethia Lucas
Ebenezer S. Lucas
Eleanor Lucas
Eliza H. Lucas
Hannah S. Lucas
Harvey Lucas
Horatio A. Lucas

CHURCH MEMBERS

Martin L. Lucas
Mary Lucas
Mary S. Lucas
Ruth Lucas
Salla Lucas
Zillah Lucas
Alden Manter
Pardon Manter
Polly Manter
Elisha Morton
Elisabeth Morton
Lucy Moss
Theodore Moss
Abijah Muxham or Maxim
Basheba Muxham or Maxim
Caleb Muxham or Maxim
Joseph Muxham or Maxim
Lydia Muxham or Maxim
Mehitable Muxham or Maxim
Patience Muxham or Maxim
Phebe Muxham or Maxim
Elisabeth J. Nicholls
James C. Nicholls
John B. Panis
Susan Panis
Anna Parsons
James Parsons
Alvin Perkins
Elisabeth Perkins
Priscilla (Dunham) Perkins
Ignatius Pierce
Jesse Pierce

Joseph Pierce
Keziah Pierce
Betsey T. Pratt
Noah Pratt
Tillson Pratt
Benjamin Ransom
Willis Ransom
Abigail Robbins
Consider Robbins
Joseph Robbins
Patience Robbins
Priscilla Robbins
Elisabeth Sears
Hannah Sears
Joseph Sears
Lucetta Sears
Ruby Sears
Abigail Shaw
Adeline B. Shaw
Jacob Shaw
Hannah Shaw
Hannah Shaw, 2nd
Harrison Shaw
Lydia Shaw
Molly Shaw
Nathaniel Shaw
Albert Shurtleff
Benjamin Shurtleff
Dr. Benjamin Shurtleff
Deborah Shurtleff
Deborah Shurtleff, 2nd
Ebenezer Shurtleff
Elisabeth Shurtleff
Levi Shurtleff
Lot Shurtleff
Lucy T. Shurtleff

318   HISTORY OF CARVER

Lydia Shurtleff
Marcy Shurtleff
Martha Shurtleff
Mary Shurtleff
Mary Shurtleff, 2nd
Priscilla Shurtleff
Rhoda Shurtleff
Ruth Shurtleff
Ruth B. Shurtleff
William Shurtleff
Mary A. Soule
Jonathan Stetson
Arad Thomas
Foxwell Thomas
Martha Thomas
Moses Thomas
Susan Thomas
Hazadiah Vail
Hannah Vail
David Vaughan

Huldah Vaughan
Olive S. Washburn
Mary Jane Watson
Robert Watson
Benjamin Ward
Eliab Ward
Molly Ward
Priscilla Ward
Sally Ward
Dinah Wood
Agatha Wright
Caleb Wright
James Wright
Mercy Wright
Molly Wright
Moses Wright
Winslow Wright
Benjamin Wrightington
David Wrightington

BAPTIST SOCIETY

A list of those who have joined since 1856

George Adams
Lillian M. Atwood
P. Jane Barrows
George E. Blair
Thomas E. Blanding
Augustus Boucher
Sarah E. Bumpus
Barnard O. Burbank
Esther A. Burbank
C. Frank Case
Mabel S. Cassidy

Abbie E. Cole
Orinna C. Covill
Anson F. Cornish
Bernice E. Cornish
Blanche E. Cornish
Ellis G. Cornish
Ellis H. Cornish, M. D.
Gertrude E. Cornish
Irene A. Cornish
Mary A. Cornish
Nancy L. Cornish

CHURCH MEMBERS

Paul D. Cornish
Virginia H. Cornish
William E. Cornish
Ada L. Dimond
Ira C. Dimond
Maria W. Dimond
Lottie Dowset
Annie Ellison
Joseph Ellison
Minnie D. Ford
Lizzie Gammons
Katherine Goetz
Betsey J. Gonsalves
Betsey N. Gould
Samuel W. Gould
A. Davis Graffam
Annie F. Graffam
James M. Jefferson
Abbie A. Johnson
Abby Leach
Albert Leach
L. Georgie Leaming
Marion W. Lewis
Jennie M. Lincoln
George E. Lockhart
George H. Lockhart
Lorena Lockhart
Herbert Lockhart
Margaret Lockhart
Wilfred B. Loring
E. Allen Lucas
Eleanor Lucas
Eleanor Lucas
Henry E. Lucas
Helen Lucas
Lot S. Lucas

Maria E. Lucas
Mary R. Lucas
Mabel McFarlin
Cordelia Metcalf
Lillian F. Moranville
Russell T. Morse
Ann E. Nye
Lucy Nye
Joshua F. Packard
Susie D. Packard
Abbie F. Pearson
Abbie J. Peckham
Annie G. Peckham
Annie H. Peckham
Henry M. Peckham
Mabel I. Peckham
Alma M. Pratt
Adelbert P. Robbins
Grace I. Robbins
Mary E. Robbins
Rebecca L. Robbins
Rosina F. Robbins
Susan Robbins
Eugene E. Shaw
E. Watson Shaw
Mary Shaw
Mary A. Shaw
Cordelia F. Shurtleff
Benjamin L. Shurtleff
Eliza B. Shurtleff
Geneva E. Shurtleff
Lula Shurtleff
Oliver L. Shurtleff
Perez T. Shurtleff
Lizzie Swan
Minnie D. Swan

Ponsonby M. Swan
Estella M. Sweezey
James J. Tobey
Mary A. Tobey
Mary E. Thomas
Bertha F. Vaughan
Christina C. Vaughan
Desire A. Vaughan
Edwin A. Vaughan
James A. Vaughan

Blanche E. Vinal
Cora E. Vinal
Mrs. E. Vinal
H. Y. Vinal
Simeon L. Whidden
Eva L. White
George E. White
Helen E. White
Lillian F. Wood

METHODIST CHURCH

Members under its different forms

Reformed Methodist

Mary Atwood*
Sumner Atwood *
Alice Bumpus
Edward P. Bumpus
Sullivan Gammons
Patience Maxim
Susan A. Maxim*

Thomas Maxim*
Thomas Maxim, Jr.*
Anna Ryder*
Charles Ryder
Ichabod Shurtleff*
Sylvia Shurtleff*

Methodist Protestant

Lucinda Andrews*
Clio Atwood*
Harriet Atwood
  (McFarlin)*
Joanna Atwood
Levi Atwood
Lydia Atwood*
Rebecca Atwood

Shadrach F. Atwood*
Fidelia Harlow (Bates)*
Margaret Bates*
James H. Bosworth
Susan Bosworth
Betsey Bumpus*
Daniel Bumpus
Daniel Bumpus, Jr.

---

*Transferred to M. E. Church Aug. 9, 1867.

ELLIS H. CORNISH, M. D.

CHURCH MEMBERS

Daniel Bumpus, 2nd
Dorcas Bumpus
Edward Bumpus
Edmund P. Bumpus
Marcus Bumpus
Moses Bumpus
Silas G. Bumpus
Susan Bumpus
Matthew H. Cushing
Polly Cushing
Susannah Cushman
Ebenezer Dunham*
Elisha M. Dunham*
Ruth F. Dunham*
Mary Ellis
Abigail Hathaway
Galen Humphrey
Benjamin Jefferson*
Aaron B. Knott
Sally Knott
Barney Lucas
Susan Look
Almira Maxim*
Ansel B. Maxim
Elisabeth Maxim
Ellis Maxim
Huldah McFarlin*

Jason B. McFarlin*
John Murray Maxim
Joseph T. McFarlin*
Mary Maxim
Patience Maxim
Rebecca McFarlin*
Sarah Maxim*
Seth S. Maxim*
Watson T. Maxim*
William S. McFarlin*
Wilson McFarlin
Clara Nixon*
Ichabod Shurtleff, 2nd
Lucy Shurtleff
Luther Shurtleff
Martha Shurtleff
Mercy Shurtleff
Cintia Tillson
Joanna Tillson
Louisa Tillson
Rebecca Tillson*
Henry C. Washburn*
Joanna Washburn
Louisa Washburn*
Marshall Washburn
Ephraim C. Westgate
Benjamin Wrightington

Methodist Episcopal Church

Ida F. Andrews
Sarah F. Andrews
Z. W. Andrews
Abbie F. Atwood

Angie F. Atwood
Charles H. Atwood
Eliza A. Atwood
Emma Atwood

---

*Transferred to M. E. Church Aug. 9, 1867.

Flora Atwood
Frances N. Atwood
George W. Atwood
Gilbert W. Atwood
Grace D. Atwood
Ida F. Atwood
Josephine Atwood
Lottie Atwood
Lucy Atwood
Mabel L. Atwood
Mercy J. Atwood
Susan Atwood
Carrie E. Babcock
Grace L. Babcock
Benoni T. Baker
Charles E. Baker
Edward E. Baker
Everett B. Baker
Lillian V. Baker
Minnie M. Baker
Irene Bates
Martha A. Bates
Henrietta Besse
Fannie S. Blanding
Jennie Burgess
Ella Bumpus
Mrs. H. W. Bumpus
Lucy H. Bumpus
Martha Bumpus
Moses Bumpus
Martha Douglass
Nancy Douglass
Ebenezer Dunham, Jr.
Irving Dunham
Julia A. Dunham
Mary Dunham

Silvester Dunlap
Nancy C. Fish
Dora F. Gammons
Henry H. Gammons
Minnie Garvin
Benjamin F. Harlow
Lydia D. Harlow
Herbert H. Hayden
Rosa C. Hayden
Sophronia Hobill
Patience Howard
James S. Hudson
Julia Hudson
Emily F. Hunt
William Hurd
Carrie Jefferson
Madison Jefferson
Ellen Long
Gustavus H. Long
Susie Lavender
Hattie Manter
Sylvia E. Manter
Sarah Maxim
Susan Maxim
Alberta M. McFarlin
Cora McFarlin
Elvira S. McFarlin
John B. McFarlin
Martha McFarlin
Medella McFarlin
Susan A. McFarlin
Veretta McFarlin
Nellie A. Miller
William Miller
John P. Morse
Clara Nixon

CHURCH MEMBERS 323

Sophia Penno
Charles C. Perkins
Flora Perkins
Grace Perkins
Rosa Ryder
Ella A. Sears
Orrin B. Sears
Adaleita Shaw
Melora Shaw
Charles L. Sherman
Mary E. Sherman
Chloe Shurtleff
Ichabod S. Shurtleff
Lizzie L. Smith
Emma H. Souther
Mary Stanly
W. Frank Stanly

Henry Storms
Adeline M. Tabor
Augusta C. Thomas
Herbert I. Thomas
Mary Thomas
Thompson P. Thomas
Mary E. Washburn
Nathan H. Washburn
Samuel D. Washburn
Sarah W. Washburn
Virginia H. Washburn
George H. Westgate
Charles Weddling
Hilma Williams
Mary A. Williams
Hattie T. Wright

UNION SOCIETY

Frederick Anderson
Albert F. Atwood
Delia Atwood
Isette G. Atwood
Josiah W. Atwood
Lucius Atwood
Marcus Atwood
Stephen D. Atwood
Susan F. Atwood
Laura A. Austin
Hugh R. Bailey
Mary Bailey
Eleanor Barrows
Elizabeth J. Barrows
Ellen B. Barrows
Olive M. Barrows

Thomas B. Barrows
William N. Barrows
John L. Benson
Kate A. Benson
Irene A. Bent
John Bent
Eliza A. Bowers
J. Myrick Bump
Laura H. Bump
Lucinda Bump
A. Freeman Cornish
Wilhelmina L. Cornish
Gamaliel Cushing
Betsey B. Gibbs
Thomas Gibbs
Thomas F. Gibbs

Sadie F. Gibbs
Alonzo D. Griffith
Henry S. Griffith
Helen A. Griffith
Orville K. Griffith
Mabel Griffith
Martha M. Griffith
Hannah C. Hawkes
Harry O. Hawkes
Donald Barrows Ingham
Katherine Barrows
   Ingham
Walter T. Jefferson
Mary P. S. Jowitt
George E. MacIlwain
Donald McFarlin
Anne R. McFarlin
Eldoretta T. McFarlin
Helena McFarlin
Isadore L. McFarlin
Sarah F. McFarlin
Veretta McFarlin
Rose Morris
E. Herman Murdock
Susan A. Murdock
Hannah P. Richards

Rufus L. Richards
Lawrence M. Rogers
Mary C. Rogers
James J. Ryan
Anna B. Savery
Ethel Savery
Harriet D. Savery
S. Louise Savery
Alfred M. Shaw
Alice G. Shaw
John F. Shaw
Nancy A. Shaw
Lulu Shurtleff
Lucy A. Southworth
Thomas M. Southworth
Lester W. Swift
Nehemiah G. Swift
Sarah J. Swift
Chester F. Tillson
Deborah Tillson
Reba B. Tillson
Wilfred A. Tillson
George W. Van Schaack
Daisy Vaughan
Elva H. Washburn
Harriet D. Winberg

ADVENT SOCIETY

Those who joined in 1870

Elial Benson
Harriett Benson
James Breach
Lucy Chase
Sally T. Dunham
Betsey S. Hammond

Sarah A. Hammond
Abigail S. Hatch
John B. Hatch
Lucy P. Hathaway
William E. Hathaway
I. I. Leslie

CHURCH MEMBERS

John Maxim
Lucinda E. Morse
Winslow Pratt
Levi Ransom
Louisa Ransom
Lucy Ransom
Nathaniel M. Ransom, M.D.
Atwood Shaw

Chloe S. Shaw
Mary A. Shaw
Lydia D. Sherman
Eunice Vaughan
Waitstill Vaughan
W. E. H. Vaughan
Abby W. Wade

Those who have joined since 1870

Sally Benson
Francelia F. Boynton
J. R. Boynton
Solon R. Boynton
W. Otis Boynton
William Breach
George Burnham
John A. Coad
Nancy L. Cornish
Jesse P. Douglass
Maria F. Douglass
Almira C. Dowsett
Harriett A. Dunham
Luella Dunham
Ruth Dunham
Rose Garnett
Burt J. Glazier
Elmer D. Glazier
I. Christine Glazier
Lettie L. Glazier
Benjamin Hammond
Julia F. Hammond
Anna G. Hatch
Sarah F. King
Emma L. Lewis
Katy H. Lewis

Mary Eva Lewis
Anna R. Loveland
Samuel McHenry
Emma F. Merritt
George F. Morse, M. D.
Daniel W. Nash
George Newhall
Jesse M. Northern
Lydia F. Northern
Arthur C. Perkins
Elmer B. Perkins
Catherine L. Pratt
Sarah L. Ransom
Polly Reed
Rebecca L. Robbins
Lorenzo N. Shaw
Percy W. Shurtleff
Austin N. Vaughan
Charles E. Vaughan
J. Erville Vaughan
Julia F. Vaughan
Minnie M. Vaughan
Webster E. C. Vaughan
William E. W. Vaughan
Esther A. Wade
Henry W. Wade

HISTORY OF CARVER

STATE AND COUNTY OFFICERS

A list of those who have served in a state or county office since the Town was incorporated.

In the Governor's Council

Hon. Jesse Murdock	1847, 48

In Constitutional Conventions

Benjamin Ellis	1820
Joseph Barrows	1853

County Commissioner

Thomas Southworth	1858—60

State Senate

Hon. Benjamin Ellis	1825, 32
Hon. Jesse Murdock	1844, 45
Hon. Matthias Ellis	1854
Hon. Peleg McFarlin	1882—84

Representatives in General Court

Frances Shurtleff	1791, 1802
Capt. Nathaniel Sherman	1800
Capt. William Atwood	1806
Benjamin Ellis	1810—12, 16, 20, 21, 29, 30
John Savery	1827, 28, 42, 47
Lewis Pratt	1831
Thomas Cobb	1832
Benjamin Ransom	1833
Jesse Murdock	1834—37, 47
Joseph Barrows	1838, 39
Timothy Cobb	1840, 48
Henry Sherman	1842
William S. Savery	1844
Matthias Ellis	1850, 51

Capt. Benjamin Ransom	1852
George P. Bowers	1854
James B. Tillson	1855
Rufus C. Freeman	1858
Ralph Copeland	1860
Elisha M. Dunham	1866
Thomas B. Griffith	1869
Horatio A. Lucas	1873
William Savery	1879
Peleg McFarlin	1881
Benjamin W. Robbins	1882
Gustavus Atwood	1896
Eugene E. Shaw	1908

TOWN OFFICERS

TOWN CLERKS

Nehemiah Cobb	1790
Samuel Lucas, 3d	1791
Samuel Lucas, Jr.	1792
Nehemiah Cobb	1793—98
Barnabas Cobb	1799—1801
Ephraim Pratt	1802—10
Stephen Shurtleff	1811—13
Samuel Shaw	1814—27
Dr. Samuel Shaw	1828
Samuel Shaw	1829
Isaac Vaughan	1829
Isaac Vaughan	1830—36
Isaac Vaughan	1837
John Savery	1837
Isaac Vaughan	1838—41
David Pratt	1842—45
Thomas Vaughan	1846—58
Ansel B. Maxim	1859—63
Ansel B. Maxim	1864
Thomas Vaughan	1864
Thomas M. Southworth	1865, 66
William Hammond	1867—69
Nelson Barrows	1870, 71
Peleg McFarlin	1872—78
Albert T. Shurtleff	1879—92
Henry S. Griffith	1893—

TOWN TREASURERS

Frances Shurtleff	1790—93
Frances Shurtleff	1794
Lothrop Shurtleff	1794
Samuel Lucas	1794

TOWN OFFICERS

Samuel Lucas	1795—1801
Benjamin Shurtleff	1802, 03
Samuel Lucas	1804—09
Thomas Hammond	1810
Lieut. Samuel Shaw	1811, 12
Samuel Shaw	1813
Lewis Vaughan	1814
Jonathan Atwood	1815
Thomas Hammond	1816—24
Ira Murdock	1825
Thomas Hammond	1826
Jonathan Atwood	1826
Jonathan Atwood	1827, 28
Isaac Vaughan	1829—33
Jonathan Atwood	1834, 35
Huit McFarlin	1836—41
David Pratt	1842—51
Isaac Vaughan	1852
John Bent	1853—61
Thomas Cobb	1862—82
Andrew Griffith	1883—91
Andrew Griffith	1892
James A. Vaughan	1892
James A. Vaughan	1893—1904
Henry S. Griffith	1905—

TAX COLLECTORS

Jonathan Tillson, Caleb Atwood	1790
Jonathan Tillson, Consider Chase	1791
Consider Chase, Abial Shurtleff	1792
Benjamin Cobb, Perez Washburn	1793
Nathaniel Atwood, Jr., Consider Chase	1794
Nathaniel Vaughan, Consider Chase	1795
Consider Chase, Nathaniel Atwood	1796, 97
Ebenezer Doten, Consider Chase	1798

330   HISTORY OF CARVER

Ebenezer Doten	1799
Lieut. Gideon Shurtleff, Consider Chase	1800
Ebenezer Doten, Levi Chase	1801
Ebenezer Doten	1802—07
Nehemiah Cobb, Seth Barrows	1808
Lieut. Isaiah Tillson, Asaph Washburn	1809
Barnabas Shurtleff, Nathaniel Atwood	1810
Levi Vaughan, Nathaniel Atwood	1811
Stephen Shurtleff	1812
Jabez Maxim	1813
Hezekiah Cole, Capt. Elisha Murdock	1814
Hezekiah Cole, Lieut. Luke Perkins	1815
Capt. Elisha Murdock	1816
John Sherman, Nathaniel Atwood	1817
Levi Vaughan, Samuel Shaw	1818
Joseph Robbins	1819
Hezekiah Cole, Jacob T. Perkins	1820
Capt. Gideon Shurtleff	1821
Jesse Murdock	1822
Ephraim Harlow, Ebenezer Dunham	1823
Samuel Shaw	1824, 25
Ephraim Harlow, Elisha Murdock	1826
Hezekiah Cole, Barnabas M. Dunham	1827
The Treasurer	1828—1912

SELECTMEN

Those who have served on the Board of Selectmen, with years of service

Asaph Atwood	1818—22
Ensign Caleb Atwood	1809
Gustavus Atwood	1879—81
Jonathan Atwood	1816, 17, 29, 30
S. Dexter Atwood	1907—10
Capt. William Atwood	1790—92, 97, 1803, 04
Charles Barrows	1841—44

TOWN OFFICERS

Joseph Barrows	1829, 30, 35—37, 45, 46, 52—54, 63
William Barrows	1834, 35, 46
John Bent	1835, 36
Fred Cobb	1852—54, 65—69, 79—81
Nehemiah Cobb	1799, 1800
Thomas Cobb	1817, 19, 20—27
Thomas Cobb	1851
Timothy Cobb	1836, 37, 40—42, 47—50
Elmer B. Cole	1888
Hezekiah Cole	1812—15, 18
Ellis G. Cornish	1911—13
Capt. Cornelius Dunham	1810, 11
Benjamin Ellis	1806, 07, 12
Seth C. C. Finney	1886, 87, 98—1905, 12, 13
Andrew Griffith	1864—79, 82—92
Thomas B. Griffith	1860—62
Thomas Hammond	1806, 07
Thomas Hammond	1838, 39
John A. Kenney	1906, 07
Capt. Abijah Lucas	1799—1809
Eben S. Lucas	1870, 71
Horatio A. Lucas	1855, 61, 72—81
Samuel Lucas, Jr.	1790, 93, 96, 98
Huit McFarlin	1820, 21
Bartlett Murdock, Jr.	1793, 94
Bartlett Murdock	1816
Capt. Elisha Murdock	1805
Jesse Murdock	1813—15, 18, 19
Alvin Perkins	1859—64, 68—74
Stewart H. Pink	1908
David Pratt	1831—34
Lewis Pratt	1827—29
Benjamin Ransom	1830, 31, 38, 39, 58—60
Charles Ryder	1840—42
John Savery	1826—28

Peleg Savery	1808
Dea. Thomas Savery	1790—92
William S. Savery	1843, 44
Daniel Shaw	1837, 45—51
David Shaw	1838
Eben D. Shaw	1875—78
Joseph Shaw	1823—25, 31—33
Capt. Samuel Shaw	1828
Henry Sherman	1839, 40, 45
Capt. John Sherman	1793, 94
Levi Sherman	1832—34
Capt. Nathaniel Sherman	1795—98, 1809
Nelson Sherman	1882—85
Albert T. Shurtleff	1882—89
Benjamin Shurtleff	1791, 92, 94—96, 99, 1800—02
Capt. Gideon Shurtleff	1805, 10—15
Samuel A. Shurtleff	1847, 48
Thomas Southworth	1849—51, 55—58
Herbert A. Stanley	1911—13
Edward Stephens	1803, 04
Truman B. Tillson	1859
Wilfred A. Tillson	1893—1906
James Vaughan	1808, 10, 11, 16, 17
Theodore T. Vaughan	1890—1910
Thomas Vaughan	1852—58, 62—67
Capt. Benjamin Ward	1797, 98
Benjamin Ward	1822—26
Eliab Ward	1843, 44
Fred A. Ward	1889—97, 1901, 09, 10, 11
Stillman Ward	1856, 57
Benjamin White	1801, 02

SCHOOL COMMITTEE

Those who have served, with years of service. Beginning with 1827 a board of three has been elected with the exception of 1872, when the number was increased to six.

Gustavus Atwood	1878, 84—86, 88—1901, 04
Mrs. Bernice E. Barrows	1897—99
Charles Barrows, Jr.	1840
E. W. Barrows	1865
Horatio Barrows	1849
James Barrows	1844
Joseph Barrows	1832, 33
Dr. William Barrows	1832—37, 45, 46
Mrs. Rebecca W. Benson	1888—94
Mrs. Irene A. Bent	1884—88
John Bent	1860
Ezra Brett	1853
Rufus J. Brett	1872
Dr. Charles S. Bumpus	1849, 51, 53, 54
Henry L. Chase	1864, 65
Rev. Plummer Chase	1829—31
Nathaniel Coggswell	1855, 56
Mrs. Nellie M. Cole	1879—81
Ellis G. Cornish	1910—
Dr. Ellis H. Cornish	1868, 82—84, 88—90
Nathaniel S. Cushing	1858—60
Robert M. Dempsey	1872
Elisha M. Dunham	1855. 56, 60—62
Matthias Ellis	1847, 48, 50, 51
Seth C. C. Finney	1900—04
Rufus C. Freeman	1867—69, 74, 75, 80—82
Ezra Fuller	1838, 44
Samuel Glover	1839
Henry S. Griffith	1887, 1901—03
Nehemiah C. Hammond	1842, 43

Thomas Hammond	1863
S. Freedom Jenkins	1858, 59
John A. Kenney	1902
Rev. Jonathan King	1839, 41—43
Rev. William Leach	1866—69
Rev. Nehemiah Lincoln	1889—91
Ebenezer S. Lucas	1853, 79, 81—83, 94—96
Ansel B. Maxim	1863, 64
Peleg McFarlin	1873—75
Solomon F. McFarlin	1855—57, 70—74
Ira Murdock	1827
Robert B. Pearson	1871, 72
Charles C. Perkins	1905—
Elmer B. Perkins	1896—1900
David Pratt	1827—31, 33, 36—39, 46, 47, 51, 52
Ephraim T. Pratt	1849, 50, 54
E. Tillson Pratt	1858, 59, 61—64, 70—73
Joseph Pratt	1836—38, 40
Miles Pratt	1848
Stillman Pratt	1852
Nathaniel M. Ransom	1854, 57, 65, 66
Charles Ryder	1852
John Savery	1831, 34, 35
William Savery	1857, 61, 62
Mrs. Alice G. Shaw	1905—
Eben D. Shaw	1872
Dr. Samuel Shaw	1827—29
William M. Shaw	1905—09
Benjamin Shurtleff	1844, 45, 47
Miss Flora M. Shurtleff	1885—87
George A. Shurtleff	1841—43
Samuel A. Shurtleff	1840, 41, 48
Thomas M. Southworth	1876—78
Ezra Thompson	1830
Charles Threshie	1869, 70

TOWN OFFICERS 335

Augustus F. Tillson	1875—77
Rev. J. J. Tobey	1891—93
Isaac Vaughan	1828, 32, 34, 35
James A. Vaughan	1878—80, 1903, 04
Thomas Vaughan	1850
Ansel B. Ward	1876, 77
Eliab Ward, Jr.	1845, 46
G. F. Wood	1866, 67

ASSESSORS

Those who have served on the board, with years of service. From 1845 to 1893 and from 1896 to 1910 the Selectmen were also chosen Assessors.

Ensign Caleb Atwood	1794, 96
John Atwood	1818, 19
Jonathan Atwood	1811—14, 16, 17, 20—24, 28, 29, 30
Lucius Atwood	1894, 95
S. Dexter Atwood	1911—
William Atwood	1836
Frank E. Barrows	1911—
Joseph Barrows	1828—30, 34, 35, 43, 44
John Bent	1894, 95
Barnabas Cobb	1790—95, 97, 99
Nehemiah Cobb	1791, 93, 94, 1800, 01, 09
Timothy Cobb	1839—42
Hezekiah Cole	1815
Ebenezer Doten	1802—07, 09, 10, 14, 16, 17
Edward Doten	1808
Benjamin Ellis	1805—07
Thomas Hammond	1802—07, 09
Thomas Hammond	1837, 38
Capt. Ichabod Leonard	1897, 98
Samuel Lucas, Jr.	1790, 92

Samuel Lucas   1795, 96, 98, 99, 1800—04, 17
Huit McFarlin   1808, 10—13, 18, 19, 33
Bartlett Murdock, Jr.   1792
Ira Murdock   1816, 25—27
Jesse Murdock   1815
Alvin Perkins   1837—43
Luke Perkins   1808
David Pratt   1820, 21, 31, 32
Lewis Pratt   1825—27
Benjamin Ransom   1831—38
Thomas Savery   1814
David Shaw   1835
Daniel Shaw   1836
Eugene E. Shaw   1894, 95
Anthony Sherman   1844
Levi Sherman   1825—27
Capt. Nathaniel Sherman   1796
Albert Shurtleff   1834
David Shurtleff   1833
Gideon Shurtleff   1815
Lot Shurtleff   1820, 21, 31, 32
Stephen Shurtleff   1810—13, 22—24
Isaac Vaughan   1839
Levi Vaughan   1818, 19, 22—24, 28, 30
Theodore T. Vaughan   1912—
Thomas Vaughan   1840—44
Fred A. Ward   1911
Benjamin White
       1790, 91, 93, 95, 97—99, 1800, 01

OVERSEERS OF POOR

1838

Samuel Shaw   Benjamin Ransom
            Thomas Hammond

TOWN OFFICERS

1845
Lot Shurtleff   John Bent
Ebenezer Atwood

1852
Benjamin Chase   Albert Shurtleff
Henry Sherman

1856
Thomas Cobb   Eliab Ward
Paine M. C. Jones

1857—1912
Selectmen.

TRUSTEES OF THE PUBLIC LIBRARY

J. Myrick Bump	1910—
Seth C. C. Finney	1896—
Henry S. Griffith	1895—
Eugene E. Shaw	1907—09
Nelson Sherman	1895
Albert T. Shurtleff	1895—1901
Rev. Oscar F. Stetson	1902—05

ROAD COMMISSIONERS

Following an early custom the roads were repaired and built by surveyors elected or appointed by Districts at the annual town meeting until 1889 when an optional law was accepted and the roads were placed under the management of a board of three Commissioners. In 1893 this system was abolished leaving the roads in the hands of the Selectmen with a superintendent as their agent. A change was made again in 1899 when the town returned to the Road Commissioner system.

ROAD COMMISSIONERS
With Years of Service

Zephaniah W. Andrews	1904—
John E. Atwood	1910—
Henry T. Hammond	1889—91
Levi F. Morse	1902—
E. Herman Murdock	1902—09
Benjamin Robbins	1892, 99, 1900, 01
Frederick W. Shaw	1892
Ichabod S. Shurtleff	1889—91
Oliver L. Shurtleff	1889—91, 99, 1900, 01
William F. Stanley	1892
Frank F. Tillson	1899—1903

SUPERINTENDENT OF STREETS

E. Herman Murdock	1893—99

INDEX OF NAMES

INDEX OF NAMES

With few exceptions simple names are indexed regardless of title or suffix

Atwood, Abbie F., 321
  Abigail C., 315
  Abner, 167
  Albert F., 162, 207, 323
  Allen S., 232, 236
  Angie F., 321
  Annie S., 314
  Arthur C., 262
  Asaph, 132, 146, 167, 330
  Barnabas, 294, 298, 307
  Betsey, 213, 315
  Caleb, 61, 103, 105, 138, 148, 167, 202, 330, 335
  Charles, 238
  Charles H., 321
  Clio, 320
  Delia, 263, 323
  Ebenezer, 173, 202, 315, 337
  Ebenezer E., 234
  Eli, 127, 131, 132
  Eli, Jr., 234
  Elisabeth, 309
  Eliza A., 321
  Emma, 321
  Flora, 322
  Frances N., 322
  Frederick, 238
  George W., 150, 189, 322
  Gilbert W., 322
  Grace D., 322
  Gustavus, 249, 327, 330, 333
  Hannah, 280
  Hannah W., 162
  Harriet, 161
  Herbert F., 262
  Ichabod, 108
  Ida F., 322
  Isaiah F., 235
  Isette G., 323
  Jason, 161

Atwood, Joanna, 320
  John, 22, 103, 131, 167, 168, 335
  John E., 262, 338
  Jonathan, 131, 145, 146, 158, 159, 167, 329, 330, 335
  Joseph, 102, 131, 167, 188, 228
  Josiah E., 236
  Josiah W., 189, 190, 234, 249, 323
  Josephine, 322
  Joshua, 132, 168
  Lazarus, 167
  Levi, 105, 167, 320
  Lillian M., 318
  Lottie, 322
  Lucius, 189, 190, 323, 335
  Luther, 132, 219
  Lucy, 308, 322
  Lydia, 161, 315, 320
  Lydia Lucas, 315
  Mabel L., 322
  Marcus, 188, 190, 249, 323
  Margaret, 315
  Mary, 175, 315, 320
  Mary A., 315
  Melissa, 161
  Mercy J., 322
  Miranda, 189, 281
  Molly, 315
  Nathaniel, 61, 102, 125, 131, 138, 164, 165, 168, 199, 200, 253, 257, 298, 300, 307, 315, 329, 330
  Oren, 189, 226
  Patience, 315
  Peggy, 315
  Polly, 279, 310

Atwood, Rebecca, 320
  Ruel, 303, 312
  Salmon, 213, 315
  Samuel, 131, 167
  Samuel, Jr., 167
  Samuel S., 228
  Sarah, 310
  Sarah L., 315
  Shadrach F., 320
  Stephen, 108, 167, 188
  S. Dexter, 190, 249, 323, 330, 335
  Stephen T., 234
  Sumner, 175, 176, 320
  Susan, 322
  Susan B., 314
  Susan F., 323
  Thomas, 236
  Tillson, 261
  Waitstill M., 315
  Waity, 315
  William, 100, 102, 137, 148, 163, 167, 168, 258, 326, 330, 335
  William W., 303, 313
Atwood Brook, 3
Atwood Rebellion, 258
Abbot, Elder Samuel, 166, 167
Adams, Amanda J. 162
  Amos, 243
  George, 318
  John, 310
  Thomas, 157
Advent chapel, 182
Agawam, 21
Agriculture, 251
Almshouse burned, 147
American Game P. & P. Assn., 264
Ames, Seth, 315
Andrews, Ida F., 321
  Lucinda, 320
  Robert W., 228, 260
  Sarah F., 321
  Z. W., 162, 207, 321, 338
Annasnapet, 17
Anthony, Hannah D., 288
Anderson, Frederick, 207, 263, 323
  Philip, 239
Appling, Deborah, 312
  John, 109, 168
Armory, 227

Austin, Laura A., 263, 323
Avery, Edward, 206
  Nathan, 176

Babcock, Carrie E., 322
  Rev. Edwin G., 179
  Grace L., 322
Bachus, Elder Isaac, 165
Bailey, Ellen, 276
  H. R., 323
  Mary, 323
Baker, Benoni T., 322
  Charles E., 322
  Edward E., 322
  Everett B., 322
  Lillian V., 322
  Minnie M., 322
Baptists, 75, 125, 163, 185
  Kingston, 259
  Meetings, 170
  Ministers, 171
  Plympton, 259
Barker, Rev. Joseph, 77
  Rev. Nathaniel, 120
Barnes, Anne, 307
  John, 22, 109
  Jonathan, 22
Barnes' Mill, 267
Barrows, Abby F., 313
  Abner, 105
  Andrew, 107, 297, 298
  Arad, 275
  Asa, 107, 225, 268
  Benjamin, 109, 199
  Bernice E., 333
  Carver, 108, 131, 139, 168
  Charles, 296, 298, 303, 330, 333
  Deborah, 312
  Eleanor, 263, 323
  Elisabeth, 313
  Elisabeth, J., 263, 323
  Ellen B., 323
  Ephraim, 108
  Rev. E. W., 177, 179, 187, 333
  Fanny, 315
  Fanny D., 313
  Frank E., iii, 243, 262, 263, 335
  Gideon, 295

INDEX OF NAMES

Barrows, George, 61, 131, 196, 248, 257, 293, 297, 298, 307, 308
  Horatio, 333
  James, 333
  Jemina, 308, 309
  John, 22
  Jonathan, 102, 104, 249
  Joseph, 97, 102, 104, 121, 131, 132, 158, 188, 189, 190, 199, 215, 258, 261, 326
  Lothrop, 80, 213, 226, 298, 300, 303, 310
  Louisa, 312
  Malachi, 108, 109
  Mary, 309
  Mary H., 314
  Mercy, 312
  Moses, 108, 295, 298, 307
  Nelson, 126, 132, 186, 189, 328
  Olive M., 323
  Peleg, 107, 121, 131, 199, 295, 298, 306
  Peleg, Jr., 131
  Pelham W., 228, 234, 285
  Phebe, 315
  Priscilla Jane, 145, 162, 249, 262, 285, 318
  Ruth, 315
  Samuel, 297, 307
  Samuel B., 236
  Sarah, 309
  Seth, 131, 165, 168, 315, 330
  Simeon, 104
  Simeon H., 228
  Simmons, 102, 131
  Thomas, 131, 201, 202, 296
  Thomas B., 323
  William, 105, 243, 302, 331, 333
  William H., 237, 281
  William N., 276, 323
  Wilson, 312
Barrows homestead, 62
Barter, 200
Bartlett, John, 108
  Joseph, 22
  Sylvanus, 97, 103
Bates, David, 176
  David M., 190, 228

Bates, Mrs. D. M., 162
  Fidelia, 320
  George E., 232, 236
  Irene, 322
  James H., 233
  John, 109
  Margaret, 320
  Martha A., 322
  N. Byron, 234
Bay State hall, 128, 160
Bay State Light Inf't'y, 227
Beavers, 5
Bemis, 285
Bennett, Charles H., 228
  John, 75, 309
  Keziah, 309
  Nehemiah, 307
  Sabatha, 308
  Stephen, 202
Benson, Asa, 315
  Benjamin, 102
  Betsey, 315
  Caleb, 171, 202
  Constant, 315
  Deborah, 315
  Drucilla Ward, 315
  Ebenezer, 315
  Elial, 324
  Elisabeth, 315
  Elnathan, 109
  Harriet, 324
  Ichabod, 125, 131
  Jephtha, 108
  John, 58, 315
  John, Jr., 315
  John L., 323
  Joshua, 60, 121, 131, 309
  Joshua, Jr., 131
  Kate A., 323
  Patience, 316
  Rebecca, 316
  Rebecca W., 333
  Sally, 325
Benson's bridge, 59
Benson Cemetery, 269
Benson forge, 267
Bent, Experience, 202
  Frances, 164
  George W., 255
  Ira C., 188
  Irene A., 323, 333
  Louisa, 313

Bent, John, 127, 132, 152, 189, 190, 223, 249, 331, 333, 335, 337
    John, Skipper, 156, 197, 200, 201, 202, 209
    Joseph, 213
    Joseph F., 232, 236
Bent, Griffith & Co., 255
Besse, Rev. A. B., 179
    Barzilla, 123
    Henrietta, 322
Bisbee, Abner, 105
    Asaph, 298
    George, 105
    Elijah, 101
    Isaac, 104
    Issacher, 103, 105
    Jane, 298, 309
    John, 105
    Jonah, 298
    Mercy, 311
    Noah, 105
    Reuben, 109
    Rev. Robert E., 179
Bishop, James, 103, 105
Blair, George E., 249, 318
Blake, Edson C., 238
    Emma, 161
    Henry S., 263
Blanding, Fanny S., 322
    Thomas E., 318
Blossom, Benjamin, 109
    Ebenezer, 316
Boardman, Elizabeth, 139, 143, 308
Bonney, David, 201
    Ebenezer, 103
    E. and Nathaniel, 201
    Isaac, 109
    James, 109
    Joseph, 201
    Nathaniel, Jr., 103
    Samuel, 105
    Seth, 201
    Simeon, 105
Bonum, Ebenezer, 307
    George, 22
Bosworth, Benjamin, 105
    James H., 320
    Noah, 103
    Peter, 316
    Sarah, 316
    Susan, 320

Boucher, Augustus, 318
Bounties, 46, 52
    Birds, 259
    Indians scalps, 13
    Soldiers, 231
Bourne, Sylvanus, 26
Bowers, Eliza A., 323
    George P., 142, 152, 188, 189, 190, 210, 220, 254, 268, 282, 327
Bowers & Jenkins, 189
Bowers & Pratt, 211
Bowman, Richard, 307
Boynton, Francelia, 325
    J. R., 182, 183, 325
    Solon R., 325
    W. Otis, 325
Bradford, Calvin, 108
    Edward G., 314
    Gideon, Jr., 105
    Capt. John, 93, 100, 136
    John, 104
    Lewis, 97
    Lois A., 314
    Oliver, 109
    Perez, 105
    Samuel, 104, 135
    Thomas, 316
    William, 108
    Winslow, 103
    Zillah, 310
Bradley, John, 189
Breach, James, 183, 324
    John, 237
    William, 325
Brett, Ezra, 333
    Hannah A., 162
    James E., 161
    Marion C., 314
    Elder Pliny, 175, 179
    Rufus J., 303, 314, 333
    Rufus L., 243
    Sylvanus L., 162
    William L., 314
Bodfish Bridge, 265
Bridgham, Joanna, 308
    John, 94, 100, 105, 131, 199, 295
    Joseph, 122, 293, 298, 300
    Dr. Joseph, 298
    Samuel, 108
Briggs, Abitha, 167
    Ebenezer, 167

INDEX OF NAMES 345

Briggs, M. Elvira, 162
  Samuel, 159, 197
  Samuel B., 207
Brimhall, Sylvanus, 109
Bryant, Abigail, 316
  Benjamin, 105, 108
  Billa, 164, 165, 173
  Consider, 105
  Ephraim, 103
  Ford, 109
  George, 93
  Jacob, 109
  Jean, 316
  John, 75
  Joseph, 103
  Joshua, 103, 108
  Lemuel, 72
  Levi, 105
  Luther, 109
  Mary P., 314
  Nathan, 108
  Patrick, 109
  Samuel, 109
  Zenas, 105
Buckles, Rev. H. W., 172
Bull Run, first, 233
  second, 232
Bump, J. Henry, 228
  John, 213
  J. Myrick, 323, 337
  Laura H., 323
  Lucinda, 323
  Nancy, 313
  P. W., 219, 228
  Seth, 108
Bumpus, Alice, 175, 320
  Andrew M., 189
  Betsey, 176, 320
  Dr. Charles S., 333
  Chloe Hooks, 316
  Daniel, 108, 320
  Daniel, Jr., 320
  Deborah, 161
  Dorcas, 321
  Edmund, 213, 265
  Edmund P., 321
  Edward, 321
  Edward P., 175, 320
  Ella, 322
  Mrs. H. W., 322
  Ira B., 161
  Capt. Jeremiah, 77
  John, 131, 132, 168, 210

Bumpus, Lucy H., 322
  Marcus, 321
  Martha, 322
  Mary, 310
  Moses, 321, 322
  Salathiel, 102, 131
  Sarah E., 318
  Silas, 215, 226
  Silas G., 321
  Susan, 321
Burbank, Arthur W., 262
  Bernard O., 318
  Esther A., 318
Burgess, Jennie, 322
Burnham, George, 325
Bursell, Rev. David, 166, 171, 316
  Elisabeth, 316
Butler, Paul, 263

Camp, Rev. Wellington, 172
Camp Meetings, Meth., 177
Campbell, Rev. Othniel, 69, 70, 71, 72, 120
Campello Foundry, 214
Caples, John, 239
Carnes, Edward S., 237
Cartee, Benjamin, 201
  John S., 190, 228
  Mrs. John S., 162
Carter, Rev. C., 179
Carver Green, 269
Carver, Gov. John, 137
Carver Light House, 130
Case, Frank, 161, 318
Casey, Augustus, 16, 267
  Augustus G., 16
  Frances Y., 240
  Frank, 16
  John, 16
  Joseph Y., 16, 240
  Thomas, 16
  William, 16
Casey Place, 17, 267
Cassidy, Mabel S., 318
Cedar Swamp, division, 24, 25, 26
  Doty's, 8, 26
  South Meadow, 8
Cemeteries, 245
  Centre Assn., 248
  Commissioners, 249

Cemetery, Cushings Field, 247
Chamberlain, John, 105, 136
    Joseph, 107, 109
    Philip, 316
Chandler, Job C., 237, 305, 312
    John B., 234
    Joseph S., 228
    Josiah, 106
    Lucy A., 314
    Nancy B., 314
    Nancy S., 312
    Repentance, 244
    Ruth, 312
    William B., 234
    William F., 314
    Zebedee, 108
Chandler Brothers, 252
Chapin, Rev. Seth, 120
Charlotte Furnace, 62, 198, 199, 261
Chase, Benjamin, 303, 312, 337
    Charles H., 228, 234, 302, 303, 313
    Consider, 84, 104, 148, 258, 295, 296, 308, 329
    Eunice, 308
    Hannah, 310
    Rev. Henry L., 120, 333
    John, 311
    Keziah, 312
    Levi, 330
    Louisa L. P., 115, 181, 311
    Lucy, 324
    Nellie, 314
    Rev. Plummer, 120, 243, 333
    Rev. Walter, 172
Cheever, Rev. Samuel, 172
Chris Springs, 267
Church, Meth. Epis., 178
Churchill, Asaph, 309
    Benjamin, 306
    Caleb, 105
    Daniel, 105
    David, 108
    Deliverance, 308
    Dinah, 316
    Ebenezer, 105, 108
    Elias, 105, 108
    Isaac, 94, 103, 196, 258
    Isaac, Jr., 103
    James, 103
    Jabez, 296
    John, 103, 104, 105, 108

Churchill, John W., 268
    Joseph, 23, 108
    Joshua, 105, 107
    Nathaniel, 103
    Stephen, 107, 109
    Timothy, 108
    William, 105
Clark, Barnabas, 166
    George B., 263
    Elisha, 166
    Nathan, 175, 179
    Thurston, 20
Clarks Coal House, 260
Clarks Island, 266
Cloth Making, 252
Coad, John A., 325
Coaling, 193
Cobb, Almira H., 313
    Alvin, 309
    Barnabas, 107, 138, 224, 225, 296, 300, 328, 335
    Benjamin, 105, 139, 214, 276, 295, 296, 297, 298, 299, 309, 329
    Bennett, 118, 310
    Betsey, 309
    Charles, 224, 311
    Deborah, 308, 310
    Ebenezer, 115, 146, 310
    Erastus W., 228
    Frederick, 152, 310, 331
    George, 213, 228, 229
    Hannah, 311
    Isaac, 139
    Jane E., 313
    John M., 232, 233
    Jonathan, 105
    Joseph, 143
    Joseph F., 234
    Juliet W., 313
    Lemuel, 309
    Levi, 240
    Lois, 310
    Lucinda, 312
    Lucy, 310
    Lydia, 308, 316
    Marcus E., 228
    Marstin, 210
    Marstin F., 228
    Martha, 310
    Mary, 308, 310
    Mary Drew, 311
    Mary T., 313

INDEX OF NAMES 347

Cobb, Mehitable, 309
  Melissa, 310
  Mercy, 312
  Nathan, 88, 105, 115, 295, 299, 305, 309
  Nathaniel, 295
  Nehemiah, 97, 101, 104, 137, 224, 225, 268, 293, 294, 296, 299, 300, 305, 309, 328, 331, 335
  Nehemiah, 2nd, 309
  Rev. Oliver, 114
  Otis, 312
  Phebe, 310
  Polly, 309
  Rebecca, 308
  Roland, 107
  Samuel, 105, 297, 298, 308
  Sarah, 310
  Sidney O., 234
  Solon (Rev.), 288, 313, 314
  Susanna, 310
  Sylvia, 311
  Thomas, 145, 152, 159, 224, 225, 281, 294, 296, 299, 302, 303, 305, 311, 326, 329, 331, 337
  Thomas, Jr., 311
  Timothy, 104, 138, 297, 299, 303, 308, 311, 326, 331, 335
  William, 105, 106
Cobb & Drew, 214, 276
Cobb Place, 268
Coggeshall, Josiah W., 232, 235
Coggswell, Rev. Nathaniel, 119, 120, 333
Cole, Abbie E., 318
  Asel, 312
  Benjamin, 307
  Charles H., 228
  Charlotte, 262
  Deborah, 313
  Gersham, 108
  Hezekiah, 107, 144, 296, 331, 335
  Hugh, 22
  Edmund, 105
  Elisabeth, 308
  Elmer B., 331
  Ephraim, 107
  James, 22
  Jane, 310

Cole, Job, 298
  John, 22, 293, 307
  Joseph, 101, 307
  Joshua, 88, 224, 225
  Laura Ann, 313
  Leander S., 276
  Lemuel, 225
  Mary, 316
  Nellie M., 333
  Rosa A., 247, 276, 277
  Susannah, 139
  Theron M., 303, 305, 314
  Thomas C., 228
Collins, Cuffy, 144
Committee, Safety, 96
  Alarm report, 93
  Correspondence, 258
Common lands, 24, 26
Conant, Rev. Gaines, 111
  Rev. Sylvester, 244
Continental money, 140
Coombs, Rev. Henry C., 171
  Laura, 314
  Elder Simeon, 166
Cooper, John, 196
  Richard, 22
Cooperage, 252
Copeland, Nancy, 313
  Ralph, 260, 302, 303, 313, 327
Corban, Lucien B., 239
Cornell, Charles F. 314
Cornish, A. Freeman, 318, 323
  Bernice E., 318
  Blanche E., 318
  Ellis G., 318, 331, 333
  Ellis H., M. D., 289, 318, 333
  Gertrude E., 318
  Irene A., 318
  Mary A., 318
  Nancy L., 318, 325
  Paul D., 319
  Virginia H., 319
  Wilhelmina L., 263, 323
  William E., 319
Costello, Catherine, 263
  Julia, 263
Counterfeit money, 84
Courts, 37
Covil, Alfred C., 161
  Orinna, 318

Cranberries, 218, 220, 221, 222, 260
Cranberry road, 269
Crocker, Abel, 196, 294, 297, 299, 306, 308
    Abigail, 309
    Benjamin, 108, 136, 148, 294
    Eleazer, 96, 97, 103, 295, 299, 300, 307
    Elijah, 201
    Heman, 103
    Hannah Nelson, 311
    Joseph, 105, 309
    Lemuel, 308
    Lemuel N., 207
    Lydia, 312
    Margaret, 309
    Mary, 308
    Theophilus, 307
Cross Paths, 87
Crowell, Eben, 161
Cummings, Rev. Abraham, 171
Curry, Rev. John M., 183
Curtice, Benjamin, 199
Curtis, Rev. David, 171
Cushing, Gamaliel, 323
    Matthew, 176
    Matthew H., 219, 321
    Nathaniel S., 199, 219, 228, 333
    Rev. Perez L., 172, 316
    Polly, 321
    Seth, 257, 258
Cushman, Ann, 244
    Andrew, 109
    Benjamin, 97, 105
    Caleb, 61, 109, 258
    Ebenezer, 106
    Elkanah, Jr., 103
    Isaac, 43, 103, 168, 258
    Isaiah, 94, 96, 97, 103, 108, 109, 257, 258
    Jacob, 105
    Jerusha C., 313
    Josiah, 105
    Samuel, 103
    Stephen, 132, 133, 188
    Susannah, 321
    Thomas, 103, 109, 116, 303, 305, 313
    William, 108
    Zachariah, 105

Cushman, Zebedee, 109
Cushman farm, 61

Darby road, 58
David Place, 62
Davis, William T., viii
Deacons, Baptist, 173
    Congregationalist, 305
    Advents, 183
Declaration of Independence, 96
Dempsey, Robert M., 333
Derby, John, 20
Dexter, Rev. Elijah, 115
Dimmick, Charles W., 263, 264
Dimond, Maria W., 319
    Ira C., 319
    Ada L., 319
Donham, Marcy, 47
Dorr, Rev. R. M., 179
Doten, Amaziah, 105
    Deborah, 310
    Ebenezer, 294, 296, 300, 308, 309, 329, 335
    Edward, 335
    Hannah, 310
    Huldah, 316
    Jacob, 307
    James, 103
    John, 307, 310
    Lucy, 311
    Mary, 308
    Rebecca, 308, 309
    Sarah, 316
    Seth, 108
    Thomas, 107
Doty, Edward, 20
    Samuel, 22
    Thomas, 107, 300
Douglass, Jesse P., 325
    John, 316
    Lydia, 316
    Nancy, 322
    Nannie, 161
    Maria F., 325
    Martha, 322
Dowsett, Almira C., 325
    Lottie, 319
Drew, Atwood R., 240
    Edwin O., 240
    John, 172
    Lieut. Thomas, 16, 199
    William R., 276

INDEX OF NAMES

Dunham, Asa, 108
  Barnabas M., 316, 330
  Benjamin, 316
  Benjamin W., 235
  Betsey, 316
  Charles O., 262
  Consider, 253
  Cornelius, 168, 295, 331
  Daniel, 22
  Daniel B., 235
  Ebenezer, 106, 131, 159, 168, 173, 228, 316, 321, 322, 330
  Eleazer, 309
  Elijah, 109
  Elisabeth, 310
  Elisha M., 161, 179, 228, 321, 327, 333
  Ellis D., 234
  Ephraim, 173, 316
  Hannah, 308
  Hannah H., 314
  Harriet A., 314, 325
  Henry, 311
  Henry A., 228, 234
  Hervey, 210
  Ichabod, 132, 316
  Irving, 322
  Israel, 108, 224, 225, 296, 299, 311
  Isaac, 159
  Isaac L., 213
  James, Jr., 109
  John, 22, 58, 105, 219, 229, 232, 261, 308
  Joseph, 22, 23, 316
  Julia A., 322
  Luella, 325
  Lucy, 312
  Lydia, 316
  Mary, 308, 316, 322
  Mary G., 316
  Matilda, 311
  Micager, 23
  Moses, 296
  Nathaniel, 22
  Priscilla, 316
  Rebecca, 316
  Ruth, 325
  Ruth F., 321
  Sally T., 324
  Samuel, 131, 316
  Silas, 105

Dunham, Simeon, 106
  Susannah, 316
  Sylvanus, 103, 299
  Thomas S., 235
Dunlap, Sylvester, 322
Duxbury, Rev. J. E., 179
Dwelly, Richard, 68, 86, 299, 300, 307

Eames, Andrew R., 314
  Charlotte E., 305
  Flora I., 314
  Luther, 314
  Mabel H., 314
  Mary M., 313
East Head, 3, 4
East Head bog, 220, 283
Eaton, Noah, 109
Eddy, Jabez, 257, 307
  Jabez, Jr., 294, 306
  Joshua, 197, 199, 208
  Moses, 306
Edson, David, 77
Egypt, 266
Eldredge, Zelotus K., 161
Ellis, Barnabas, 312
  Benjamin, 16, 126, 131, 156, 159, 202, 203, 209, 224, 225, 226, 271, 299, 301, 326, 331, 335
  Eliza, 161
  Freeman, 105
  Hannah, 133
  James, 132, 243
  Joel, 103, 104, 308
  Joseph, 132, 168, 202, 203, 205
  Mary, 133, 321
  Matthias, 188, 199, 205, 227, 243, 255, 272, 326, 333
  Stephen, 105
Ellis, Benj. & Co., 203
Ellis, Matthias & Co., 205
Ellis Foundry Co., 205, 206
Ellison, Annie, 319
  Rev. Joseph, 171, 319
Everett, Rev. Noble, 77

Faulkner, Belle, 161
Faunce, Alden, 316

Faunce, Daniel, 104, 308, 316
    Eliza, 314
    Nancy, 310
    Ruth, 165, 316
    Sarah, 309
Farmers Boilers, 207
Finney Bros., 57
Finney, Abbot G., 263
    Benjamin D., 217, 219
    Laura L., 262
    Harvey, 236
    Seth, C. C., 331, 333, 337
Fire, Railroad, 261
First Swamp, 268
Fish, Rev. John S., 179
    Nancy C., 322
Fisher, Rev. T. P., 179
Fflallowel, John, 22
Forbes, Charles A., 314
    Dorothy C., 314
    Jennie A., 314
    Rev. Washington H., 314
Ford, Minnie D., 319
Foundry, Charlotte burned, 203
    E. D. Shaw & Sons, 262
Fox Island, 266
France School house, 175
Freelove, John, 202
Freeman, Rev. Frederick, 115
    John, 313
    Polly C., 313
    Rufus C., 128, 189, 190, 327, 333
Fresh Meadows, 51, 269
Fresh Meadow Village, 59
Fuller, Andrew A., 239
    Benjamin, 107
    Benjamin F., 237
    Bridget, 22
    Ebenezer, 296, 297, 298, 299, 303, 310
    Ebenezer, Jr., 313
    Elisabeth, 308
    Ezra, 333
    Hannah, 308, 313
    Isaac, 299
    Issacher, 106, 139, 143, 294, 297, 308
    John, 105
    Mary, 116
    Mary A., 311
    Nathaniel, 105
    Noah, 107

Fuller, Samuel, 105
Fullerton, Rev. Noah, 171
Furnaces, blast, 192
    Federal, 207
    Fresh Meadows, 215
    Slug, 213
    Wenham, 213, 214
    Pratt & Ward, 213
Furnace Village, 199

Game Preserve, 263
Gammons, Dora F., 322
    Henry H., 322
    Jairus, 316
    Lizzie, 319
    Mary, 316
    Sullivan, 175, 320
Gannett, Benjamin, 99
    Thomas, 136
Gardner, Adeline, 314
    Edgar E., 266, 305, 314
    William, 109
Garnett, Rose, 325
Garvin, Minnie, 322
Gay, Rev. E., 120
Gibbs pond, 258
Gibbs, Betsey B., 323
    Caroline, 263
    Mary W., 312
    Sadie F., 263, 324
    Thomas, 323
    Thomas F., 323
    William B., 189, 190.
Gill, Lucie H., 161
Glazier, Rev. Burt J., 183, 325
    Elmer D., 325
    I. Christine, 325
    Lettie L., 325
Glover, Rev. Samuel, 171, 333
Goetz, Katherine, 319
Goldsmith, Rev. Charles F., 120
Goodwin, Nathaniel, 209
Gonsalves, Betsey J., 319
Goulds Bottom, 266
Gould, Betsey N., 319
    Samuel W., 173, 319
Grady, Martin, 63
    Rainah, 316
Gradys pond, 63
Graffam, Rev. A. Davis, 171, 319
    Annie F., 319
Grassy Island, 61

INDEX OF NAMES

Gray, John, 26
Great Line, first, 28
Great Lots, cedar swamp, 25
   P. and P. Commons, 27, 28
Greenwood, Rev. ——, 120
Griffith, Alonzo D. 324
   Andrew, 152, 161, 190, 228, 329, 331
   Carrie B., 161
   Charles W., 228, 233, 260
   Ellis, 104, 109, 132, 141, 188
   Ephraim, 61, 103, 131, 161, 168, 219
   E. Lloyd, 207
   Helen, 161
   Helen A., 324
   Henry S., 190, 249, 324, 328, 329, 333, 337
   John W., 210
   Lucius E., 236
   Mabel, 263, 324
   Martha M., 324
   Mary, 316
   Obed, 132, 202
   Orlando P., 207
   Orville K., 207, 324
   Silvanus, 132, 213
   Stephen, 132, 226
   Thomas B., 227, 229, 233, 249, 255, 283, 327, 331
   Wilson, 132
Gurney, Benjamin, 307
Gutterman, 192

Halfway ponds, 62
Hall, Abner, 103
   Eliza A., 316
   Ferdinand, 109
   Jabez, 202
   Lydia, 132
   Rev. T. M., 179
   Capt. of Little Compton, 307
Ham, Samuel, Jr., 239
Hamblin, Rev. H. W., 179
   Rev. J. B., 179
Hammond, Anna W., 311
   Benjamin, 132, 325
   Betsey S., 324
   George, 100, 301
   George W., 312

Hammond, Hannah, 310
   Henry T., 338
   Julia F., 183, 325
   Lucien T., 161, 236
   Lydia M., 313
   Mary, 308, 311
   Nehemiah C., 312, 333
   Persis, 311
   Persis Cobb, 311
   Rowland, 102, 131, 164, 165, 173, 293, 294, 301, 307
   Sarah A., 324
   Thomas, 79, 113, 132, 144, 146, 158, 241, 260, 261, 296, 299, 301, 303, 305, 310, 329, 331, 334, 335
   William, 161, 312, 314, 328
Harlow, Abner, 109
   Alvin C., 228, 243, 303, 312
   Barnabas, 106
   Benjamin, 161, 316
   Benjamin, 2nd, 316
   Benjamin F., 322
   Maj. Branch, 197
   Cordelia F., 313
   Elijah, 109
   Ephraim, 293, 296, 297, 298, 301, 303, 312, 330
   Ephraim T., 228
   George, 107
   Hannah, 312
   Isaac, 161
   James, 94, 109
   Lavina, 316
   Lazarus, 106
   Lydia D., 316, 322
   Nathaniel, 106, 258
   Robert, 108,
   Rosette B., 313
   Samuel, 22
   Simeon, 161
   Thomas, 103
   William, 22, 105, 109
Hart, Annie, 316
   Sophe, 316
   Swanzea, 168, 202, 316
Haskell, Noah, 316
Haskins, William, 22
Hatch, Abigail S., 324
   Anna G., 325
   Ichabod, 105
   John B., 228, 237, 316, 324
   William C., 262

Hatfield, Rev. E., 172
Hathaway, Abigail, 321
  Lucy P., 324
  Rufus, 228
  William E., 182, 183, 324
Haverty, Thomas, 239
Hawkes, Hannah, 263, 324
  Harry O., 324
Hayden, Herbert H., 322
  Joseph, 207
  Rosa C., 322
  William, 207
Haywood, Dr. Nathan, 209
Hearse, 142
Hearvy, David, 307
  Elisabeth, 308
Hemlock Island, 265
Herring Brook, 267
Higgins, Fulmer A., 314
Highland Foundry Co., 212
Highways, 52
Hoar, Peter, 166
Hobill, Sophronia, 322
Hogreaves, 141
Holiday, first general, 70
Holmes, Charity, 316
  Charles H., 240
  Church, 316
  Eleazer, 107, 109
  Jacob, 189
  Jesse A., 262
  Job, 103
  Job, Jr., 103
  John, 26
  Jonathan, 107, 109
  Capt. Joseph, 146
  Lewis, 225
  Philander J., 240
  Mrs. P. J., 249
  Rhoda, 309
  Simeon, 103
  Rev. Sylvester, 114
Hooks, Nathaniel, 316
Hooper, Asa, 109
Hopkins, Stephen, 20
Hovey, James, 199
Howard, Patience, 322
Howland, Abigail, 309
  Calvin, 298
  Elisabeth, 308
  Rev. John, 72, 73, 74, 76, 120, 137, 259, 307
  Thankful, 309

Huckleberry Corner, 61
Hudson, James S., 322
  Julia, 322
Hunt, Rev. E. A., 178, 179
  Emily F., 322
Hunting, Henry A., 239
Huntinghouse Brook, 2, 268
Humphrey, Asa, 311
  Galen, 321
Hurd, Manoah, 238
  William D., 322

I. O. G. T. lodges, 161
Indians, 13, 14, 16, 17, 267
Inflation, 74, 84
Ingham, Donald B., 323
  Katherine B., 276, 323
Inspector of nails, 141
Intemperance, 155, 159, 171, 193
Inquisition, 159
Irwin, William, 234, 316
Island Farm, 62

Jackson, Abraham, 22
  Barnabas, 109
  Eleazer, 297, 299, 307
  Ransom, 307
  Samuel, 293, 299, 307
  Sarah, 16
Jacksons Point, 266
James, Josephine A., 314
Jefferson, Benjamin, 321
  Carrie, 322
  James M., 319
  Madison, 322
  Walter T., 324
Jenkins, S. Freedom, 128, 189, 190, 254, 334
  William F., 254
Jenney, John, 20, 267
Jewett, Rev. Paul, 120
Johnson, Abbie A., 319
  Rev. Charles G., 179
  Ezekiel, 108
  Rev. Lorenzo D., 175
  Seth, 108
Joel Field, 265
Jones, Paine M. C., 337
Jourdan, John, 22
Jowett, Mary P. S., 261, 263, 324

INDEX OF NAMES 353

Judson, Rev. Adoniram, 77

Keith, Miriam, 316
    Union, 201
Kelley, Charles, 207
    John, 239
Kendall, Rev. Ezra, 166, 171, 259
    Rev. James, 77
Kenney, A. R., 190
    Della G., 263
    John A., 331, 334
Kennedy, James P., 145
Kentucky Furnace, 199
Kidds Island, 269
Kilroy, John, 238
King, Amaziah, 143
    Caleb, 316
    Charles A., 312
    Hattie W., 314
    Isaac, 143
    John, 107, 309
    Jonathan, 132
    Rev. Jonathan, 120, 313, 334
    Joseph, 132
    Lizzie C., 314
    Lydia, 144
    Nathaniel, 316
    Sarah F., 313, 325
King Philip hall, 141, 267
    Spring, 267
    War, 14, 23, 267
Knights of Labor, 261
Knott, Aaron B., 321
    Sally, 321

Lakenham, 14, 21, 57, 58, 267
Lalor, Thomas, 239
Langly, Samuel, 239
Land, 19, 20, 22, 23
Lavender, Susie, 322
Law, Alexander, 279
Lawrence, Susan A., 285
Lawson, Thomas W., 263
Lazell, Gen. Sylvanus, 208
Leach, Abbie, 319
    Rev. Albert, 171, 319
    Lizzie, 161
    Rev. William, 171, 334
Leach's forge, 267
Leaming, L. Georgie, 319
Lebaron, Abigail, 316

Lebaron, Lazarus, 196, 316
    Mary, 316
    Sarah, 316
    Temperance, 316
Leonard, Benjamin F., 128
    Rev. H. P., 120
    Ichabod, 225, 335
    Rowland, 131
    Rowland & Co., 200
Leslie, Elder I. I., 182, 183, 324
Lettuce, Thomas, 22
Lewis, Eleazer, 131
    Emma L., 325
Lewis, Katy H., 325
    Marion W., 319
    Mary Eva, 325
    Shubet, 307
Lincoln, Amelia A., 314
    George P., 249
    Jennie M., 319
    Mary, 263
    Rev. Nehemiah, 120, 314, 334
Linfield, William, 77
Liquor Agents, 160, 260
Livingstone, William W., 314
Lobdell, Ebenezer, 106
    Isaac, 108
Lockhart, George E., 319
    Rev. George H., 171, 319
    Herbert, 319
    Lorena, 319
    Margaret, 319
Lodging House, 204
Long, Gustavus H., 322
    Ellen, 322
Look, Susan, 321
Loring, Caleb, 106, 244
    Ignatius, 103, 106
    Isaac, 104
    Jabez, 201
    Jacob, 109
    Joshua, 101, 103
    Simeon, 108
    Thomas, 96, 103
Loring, Wilfred B., 319
Lothrop, Isaac, 196
    Isaac, Jr., 196
Lothrops forge, 267
Loveland, Anna R., 325
Lovell, Ella, 161
Loyal Temp. Union, 162

Lucas, Abigail, 164, 307, 309, 316
  Abijah, 108, 224, 225, 258, 299, 309, 331
  Anna, 312
  Barnabas, 88, 106, 107, 295, 308
  Barney, 321
  Benjamin, 107, 109, 225, 308
  Lieut. Benjamin, 225
  Benoni, 22, 58
  Bethia, 316
  Calvin, 168
  Charlotte, 313
  Consider, 109
  Eben S., 316, 331, 334
  E. Allan, 173, 319
  Eleanor, 310, 316
  Elijah, 106
  Elisha, 103, 109, 196, 257, 294, 301, 307, 309
  Eliza H., 316
  Elkanah, 131, 163, 295
  Emma, 314
  Ephraim, 109
  Ezra, 303, 312
  Hannah, 311
  Hannah S., 316
  Harvey, 316
  Helen, 319
  Henry E., 319
  Horatio A., 152, 172, 173, 219, 249, 316, 327, 331
  Hosea, 168
  Isaac, 107
  Isaac Shaw, 107, 225, 296, 305, 309
  Jesse F., 237
  Jemina, 311
  John, 22, 107, 225, 301, 309
  Lieut. John, 225
  John S., 159
  Joseph, 68, 103, 196, 293, 299, 301, 307
  Lois, 310
  Lot S., 319
  Lydia, 308, 309
  Martha, 309
  Martin L., 317
  Maria E., 319
  Mary, 310, 317

Lucas, Mary R., 319
  Mary S., 317
  Nehemiah, 104
  Persis, 181, 311
  Rebecca, 309
  Ruby, 309
  Ruth, 317
  Salla, 317
  Samuel, 68, 106, 131, 144, 168, 172, 196, 258, 293, 294, 299, 301, 307, 311, 329, 336
  Samuel, Jr., 137, 138, 294, 301, 328, 331
  Samuel, 3d, 109, 148, 294, 299, 301, 328
  Lieut. Samuel, 299, 301
  Dea. Samuel, 93, 95, 294, 301
  Warren, 313
  William, 294, 307
  Zillah, 317
Lumber trade, 251
Lyon, Asahel, 108
  Obadiah, 131
  Zebedee, 109

Macadam Road, 262
Mace, Rev. J. M., 171
MacIlwain, Geo. E., 324
Magoon, James, 104
Makepeace, Abel D., 220
Mann, Isaac, Jr., 75
Manter, Alden, 317
  Ella F., 162
  Emma F., 162
  Everett T., 240
  Hattie, 322
  Nelson F., 161, 207
  Pardon, 317
  Polly, 317
  Sylvia E., 322
  Thomas P., **161**
Manly, Rev. W. E., 179
Marshfield, **98**
May training, 226
Mayhew, Thomas, 87
Maxim, Abijah, 317
  Almira, 321
  Ansel B., 238, 321, **328**, 334
  Basheba, 317

INDEX OF NAMES

Maxim, Caleb, 317
   Elisabeth, 161, 321
   Ellis, 189, 321
   Jabez, 107, 123, 168, 330
   Jabez, Jr., 168
   John, 106, 131, 139, 176, 258, 325
   John, Jr., 117, 285, 309, 310
   John M., 228, 235, 321
   Joseph, 317
   Lydia, 317
   Martha, 309
   Mary, 310, 321
   Mehitable, 317
   Nathan, 238
   Patience, 175, 317, 320, 321
   Phebe, 317
   Sarah, 321, 322
   Seth S., 176, 177, 321
   Sophronia, 310
   Susan, 322
   Susan A., 175, 320
   Thomas, 102, 131, 159, 168, 175, 176, 177, 190, 320
   Thomas, Jr., 175, 176, 320
   Watson T., 321
McCabe, Thomas, 239
McFarlin, Alberta M., 322
   Anne R., 263, 324
   Charles D., 219, 220
   Cora, 322
   David, 109
   Donald, iii, 207, 324
   Eldoretta, 249, 263, 324
   Elijah, 106, 109
   Elvira S., 322
   Harriet, 320
   Helena, viii, 263, 324
   Huit, 126, 131, 168, 329, 331, 336
   Huldah, 321
   Isadore L., 324
   Jason B., 162, 321
   Joseph, 108
   Joseph T., 161, 321
   John B., 162, 207, 235, 322
   Lucretia, 161
   Mabel M., 162, 319
   Martha, 322
   Madella, 322
   Mercy J., 161

McFarlin, Peleg, 189, 190, 199, 206, 243, 289, 326, 327, 328, 334
   Rebecca, 321
   Sampson, 188, 219, 227
   Sarah F., 263, 324
   Solomon F., 161, 227, 228
   Susan A., 322
   Thomas H., 219
   Veretta, 263, 322, 324
   Capt. William S., 161, 227, 229, 232, 234, 321
   Wilson, 228, 232, 234, 321
McHenry, Samuel, 325
McKay, Helen F., 262, 314
   James S., 59
McMahon, Thomas, 239
McSheary, James, 237
Mead, Rev. Asa, 77
Meade, Rev. Alfred F., 183
Meeting House, 85, 86, 89, 169, 305
Megone, David, 94
Melish, Rev. John, 177
Merritt, Andrew D., 233
   Emma F., 325
Metcalf, Cordelia, 319
Methodism, 81, 115, 175
Middleton, William R., 238
Miller, Edward, 239
   Nellie A., 322
   William, 161, 322
Millerites, 116, 181
Military duty, 36, 223
Minute Men of 1861, 232
Molly Holmes Place, 267
Moore, Emma F., 263
   George, 20
   Jane L., 263
   Rev. John, 120
Moranville, Lillian F., 319
Morris, John, 109
   Rose, 324
Morrison, William, 108, 131, 269
Morse, Cephas, 314
   Ephraim, 108
   Dr. George F., 325
   Hannah, 312
   Hosea B., 238
   John P., 322
   Levi F., 338
   Lucinda E., 325
   Mary A., 314

Morse, Phebe M., 314
    Robert P., 232
    Russell T., 319
    Simeon, 202
    Susannah, 314
    William, 309
Moss, Lucy, 317
    Theodore, 317
Morton, Elisabeth, 317
    Elisha, 109, 317
    George, 23
    Job, 296, 313
    Nathaniel, 22, 307
    Seth, 197
Mt. Misery, 266
Mt. Washington Iron Co., 280
Mulford, Sarah P., 285
Murder, Pero, 109
Murdock, Azubah, 310
    Bartlett, 15, 62, 102, 103, 104, 121, 131, 198, 202
    Bartlett, Jr., 131, 200, 201, 202, 331, 336
    Col. Bartlett, 205, 209, 224, 226, 242, 280, 331
    Deborah, 203, 272
    Edward, 110
    Elisha, 131, 132, 202, 225, 228, 330, 331
    Elisha, Jr., 132
    E. Herman, 324, 338
    Fanny, 247
    Henry C., 189, 190
    Ira, iv, 126, 132, 226, 334, 336
    James, 107, 131, 199
    Jesse, 110, 126, 132, 152, 159, 186, 188, 189, 190, 203, 205, 247, 255, 261, 272, 326, 331, 336
    John, 61, 68, 161, 189, 190, 202, 228, 233, 301, 306
    Mary A., 161
    Sarah, 309
    Seabury, 210
    Susan A., 263, 324
    Swanzea, vii, 110
    William, 168, 226
Murdock Homestead, 62
Murdock Parlor Grate Co., 256

Nash, Daniel W., 183, 325

Nelson, Elder Ebenezer, 165, 166
    Elder Samuel, 166
    Stephen, 165
    William, 22
Newhall, George, 325
Newport, Prince, 110
New Bridge, 269
N. E. Town meeting, 35
New Meadows, 3, 219
Nicholls, Elisabeth J., 317
    James C., 317
Nicol, Adam, Jr., 240
Niles, Rev. Asa, 172
    Rev. Samuel, 77
Nixon, Clara, 321, 322
Northern, Jesse M., 325
    Lydia F., 325
Nott, Aaron, 133, 176
Nova Scotia, 255
Nye, Ann E., 319
    Bonum, 295
    Elias, 295
    Jabez, 294, 307
    Isaac, 295, 308
    Lucy, 319

O'Connell, William H., 233
Ocean house, 267
Old Gate road, 265
Old Home Week ins., 262
Onset Bay, 283
Ore, bog, 198
    Jersey, 200
    Pond, 198
Overseers of Poor, 146
Owers, John C., 314

Packard, Rev. Joshua F., **171**, 319
    Susie D., 319
    Rev. Willard F., 171
Paine, Rev. Emerson, 115
Palmer, Joshua, 105
Panis, John B., 317
    Susan, 317
Paper money, 91
Park Commission, 263
Parker, Rev. C. A., 171
    Rev. Jonathan, 66
    Jonathan, 244

INDEX OF NAMES

Parker, Samuel, 240
    Sarah, 310
Paro, Edward, 207
Parris, Rev. John B., 171
Parrish, Josiah, 105
Parish, abolished, 83
Parsons, Anna, 317
    James, 317
    Rev. James, 171
Parting Ways, 58
Pawtuxets, 13
Pearson, Abbie F., 319
    Ezra F., viii, 233
    Robert B., 238, 334
    William W., 236
Peckham, Abbie J., 319
    Annie G., 319
    Annie H., 319
    Henry M., 319
    Mabel I., 319
Penno, Sophia, 323
Perkins, Albert W., 234
    Alvin, 210, 317, 331, 336
    Alvin S., 228
    Arthur C., 325
    Charles C., 323, 334
    Calvin, 105
    Ebenezer, 110
    Elisabeth, 317
    Elmer B., 314, 325, 334
    Flora, 323
    Gideon, 102, 168
    Grace I., 323
    Hannah, 308
    Isaac, 309
    Jacob T., 330
    John, 110
    Jonathan B., 314
    Joseph, 93, 106
    Joshua, 75, 96, 101, 195, 295, 299
    Josiah, 103, 106, 110
    Luke, 103, 226, 301, 330, 336
    Molly, 309
    Nancy B., 161
    Olive, 314
    Priscilla, 317
    Temperance, 310
    Zephaniah, 101
Perras, Moses, 166
Perry, Abisha S., 228
    Ezra, 107

Perry, Salathial, 202
Phenix Iron Works, 279
Phillips, Betsey, 16
Plympton, settlement with, 139, 140
Plymouth, bounds of, 21
Plymouth Foundry Co., 284
Plymouth and Plympton Com., 26, 27
Pierce, Ignatius, 317
    Jesse, 317
    Joseph, 317
    Keziah, 317
Piercon, John, 207
Pink, Anna L., 314
    Stewart H., 243, 331
Pokanet, 17
    Field, 17, 269
Polypody cove, 266
Pool, Jacob, 77
Poor, 142, 143, 144
Poor farm, 145, 146
Ponds, Atwood, 61
    Bates, 3, 61
    Barretts, 4
    Beaver Dam, 3
    Bowers Trout, 268
    Cedar, 4
    Clear, 4
    Coopers, 4
    Cranebrook, 15
    Derby or Darby, 20
    Dotys, 4, 57
    Dunhams, 3
    Furnace, 62
    Goulds Bottom, 4
    Johns, 4, 22
    Sampsons, 3, 198
    Tihonet, 4
    Triangle, 4, 267
    Wenham, 57, 269
Pope, Thomas, 22, 58, 194
Popes Point, 58, 194
Popes Point furnace, 59, 195
Population, 250
Post Offices, 243
Powers, Leonard S., 314
    Lydia C., 314
Pratt, Allen, 311
    Alma M., 319
    Benijah, 22, 306
    Benjamin, 110, 307
    Betsey T., 317

Pratt, Catherine L., 325
  Charles F., 235
  Consider, 110
  Daniel, 103
  David, 214, 301, 328, 329, 331, 334, 336
  Eleazer, 23
  Ellen, 285
  Ephraim, 107, 213, 293, 296, 328
  Ephraim T., 334
  E. Tillson, 284, 334
  Enoch, 228
  George H., 237
  Hannah B., 313
  I. and J. C., 260
  Jabez, 307
  John, 22, 57
  Joseph, 23, 210, 272, 294, 306, 334
  Joseph 2nd, 214
  Lemuel, 293, 301
  Lewis, viii, 159, 168, 213, 214, 215, 272, 274, 326, 331, 336
  Matthias, 214
  Miles, 273, 334
  Nancy, 289, 314
  Nathaniel, 103, 110
  Noah, 109, 164, 165, 317
  Patience, 139, 309
  Priscilla, 312
  Ruth, 310
  Sally B., 313
  Stillman, 334
  Rev. Stillman, 116, 119, 120
  Susannah, 285
  Tillson, 317
  Tillson & Son, 260
  Thomas, 307
  Winslow, 181, 312, 325
Precinct, 65, 67, 68, 69, 75, 77, 78, 80
Precinct records, iv
Province Rock, 265
Province tax, 95
Putnam, Rev. Israel W., 119

Quieting of possessions, 38
Quinby, Byron C., 277
Quitticus, 17, 269

Ramsden, Daniel, 22
Ransom, Abigail, 308
  Capt. Benjamin, 224, 225
  Benjamin, 104, 159, 165, 181, 183, 243, 299, 301, 303, 309, 312, 317, 326, 331, 336
  David, 104, 295
  Ebenezer, 105, 106, 297, 299, 307
  Elijah, 106
  Hazadiah, 309
  John, 311
  Joseph, 106, 307
  Levi, 181, 183, 237, 311, 325
  Louisa, 325
  Lucy, 181, 312, 325
  Nathaniel M., M. D., 183, 325, 334
  Phebe, 181, 311
  Rebecca, 181, 310
  Robert, 22
  Samuel, 307
  Sarah L., 325
  Willis, 317
Rardon, John, 239
Rates abated, 124
Ray, John, 239
Raymond, Stephen, 108
Recall of decision, 72
Reed, John, 209
  Polly, 325
Revival, 113, 169, 177
Richards, Elijah, 108
  Hannah P., 324
  Rufus L., 195, 324
Richmond, Rev. Abel, 77, 114
  Henry, 202
Rickard, Abner, 108
  Eleazer, 103, 108
  Elijah, 107, 110
  Gyles, Jr., 22
  Hiram L., 314
  Isaac, 106
  John, 22, 104
  Jonathan, 103
  Joseph, 307
  Josiah, 26
  Lemuel, 106
  Lucy W., 314
  Samuel, 26
  Theodore, 106

INDEX OF NAMES

Ridge, the, 2, 151
Riggs, Christy L., 314
    Rev. Ezra J., 314
    Ida L., 314
Ring, Andrew, 22
    William, 22
Ripley, Abigail, 309
    Eleazer, 108
    Frances, 105, 110
    Isaiah, 106
    Joseph, 103
    Josiah, 103
    Samuel, 106
    Timothy, 97, 103
    William, 93, 109
Risse, Peter, 22
Robbins, Abigail, 311, 317
    Adelbert P., 319
    Annie H., 314
    Benjamin W., 219, 303, 314, 327, 338
    Consider, 312, 317
    Chandler, 303, 311
    Eleazer, 103, 107, 295
    Ephraim, 243
    Ethel V., 314
    Evelyn F., 314
    Grace I., 319
    Harriet, 310
    Mrs. Horace C., 59
    James, 301
    Jane E., 314
    Jeduthen, 23
    John S., 232, 237, 314
    Joseph, 132, 139, 143, 168, 173, 181, 219, 299, 304, 311, 317, 330
    Joseph S., 237
    Josiah, 228
    Lizzie A., 314
    Lloyd C., 314
    Mary E., 319
    Maurice F., 315
    Patience, 181, 311, 317
    Priscilla, 317
    Rebecca, 311
    Rebecca L., 319, 325
    Rosina, F., 319
    Susan, 319
    Susie A., 315
Robens, Eleazer, 308
    John, 307
    Priscilla, 308

Robinson, Rev. E. W., 120
    Elder George, 165
Robinson swamp, 266
Rochester road, 62, 57
Rogers, Lawrence M., 324
    Mary C., 324
Roy, Ethel V., 263
Ruggles, Jacob Loring, 110
Rum shops, 122, 155, 156
Runnells, Samuel B., 240
Ryan, James J., 263, 324
Ryder, Anna, 175, 320
    Charles, 175, 176, 177, 320, 331, 334
    Nathan, 219
    Nathaniel, 103
    Rosa, 323

Sampson, Deborah, 99
    Gideon, 106, 295
    Henry, 103
    Ichabod, 304, 312
    John, 75, 201
    Peleg, 106
    Capt. Thomas, 100
    William, 110
    Zabdiah, 106
Sanborn, John D., 232, 237
Sandwich, 21
Savery, Anna R., 263, 324
    Benjamin H., 237
    Ethel, 263, 324
    Harriett D., 261, 263, 324
    James, 117, 141, 298, 310
    John, 126, 132, 151, 159, 176, 202, 203, 278, 279, 326, 328, 331, 334
    Mary, 272
    Mary T., 313
    Peleg, 332
    Peleg Barrows, 275
    Polly, 189
    Samuel, 22
    S. Louise, 263, 324
    Thomas, 93, 96, 107, 136, 137, 146, 163, 258, 297, 305, 308, 332, 336
    Hon. Thomas, 279
    Timothy, 210
    Waitstill A., 283

Savery, William, 142, 152, 185, 186, 187, 189, 190, 260, 261, 273, 327, 334
   William E., 190, 233
   William S., 304, 315, 326, 332
Savery's Avenue, 261
Savery Place, James, 267
Saw mills, 54, 60
Schools, 47, 147, 148, 149, 150, 151, 152, 257, 260
   Endowments, 153
   Masters, 35, 147
Schouler, Lizzie M., 162
Sears, Elisabeth, 317
   Ella, 161, 323
   Hannah, 317
   Joseph, 317
   Lucetta, 317
   Orrin B., 323
   Ruby, 317
Seipets, 15, 62
Seipet, Desire, 16
   Launa, 16, 267
   Moses, 257
Selectmen, care of Indians, 16
   Qualifications, 35
Sextons, 142
Shattuck, Rev. Frank, 183
Shaky Bottom bridge, 265
Shaw, Abigail, 168, 317
   Adaleita, 323
   Adeline B., 317
   Alfred M., 189, 190, 219, 249, 324
   Alice G., 324
   Alonzo D., 161, 233
   Alvan, 132
   Ambrose, 106
   Anna K., 263
   Anne W., 313
   Atwood, 176, 219, 325
   Bartlett, 228, 232, 234
   Benjamin, Jr., 104
   Benoni, 248, 299, 307
   Cephas, 228, 275
   Charles S., 304, 315
   Chloe S., 325
   Crispus, 132, 267
   Daniel, 188, 189, 226, 243, 332, 336
   David, 332, 336
   Deborah, 308

Shaw, Eben D., 284, 332, 334
   Edward C., 162, 262
   E. Watson, 243, 319
   Elbridge A., 235, 262
   Elisabeth, 161, 308
   Eliza A., 161, 283
   Ellis, 168, 213
   Elmer, 161
   Eugene E., 145, 249, 269, 319, 327, 336, 337
   Frederick W., 338
   George, 165, 306
   George H., 232, 233
   Gertrude F., 263
   Gilbert, 228
   Hannah, 309, 317
   Hannah, 2nd, 317
   Harrison, 213, 317
   Ira B., 228
   Isaac, 235, 296
   Isaac W., 262
   Jacob, 172, 173, 317
   James, 165, 307
   Jesse M., 234
   John, 94, 103, 120, 122, 131, 152, 168, 189, 196, 243, 294, 299, 307
   Rev. John, 77, 111, 120
   Maj. John, 224
   Capt. John, 225
   Lieut. John, 101, 159, 258
   John, 3d, 228
   John, Jr., 258, 295
   John, of Middleboro, 168
   John F., 128, 190, 228, 249, 324
   Jonathan, 22, 23, 57, 104, 194, 196, 248, 297, 307
   Jonathan, Jr., 306
   Jonathan W., 232, 233, 237
   Joseph, 139, 166, 225, 226, 299, 332
   Laura, 161
   Levi, 168
   Linas A., 232, 234
   Lorenzo N., 234, 325
   Lucy, 308, 310
   Lydia, 161, 309, 312, 317
   Mary, 308, 319
   Mary A., 319, 325
   Mary E., 161
   Melora, 323
   Mercy, 311

INDEX OF NAMES

Shaw, Molly, 317
  Moses, 294, 307
  Nancy A., 263, 324
  Nathaniel, 197, 224, 234, 294, 299, 308, 317
  Nellie W., 162
  Oliver, 280
  Oliver, 2nd, 228
  Perez, 132, 189
  Rebecca, 309, 312
  Samuel, 70, 144, 148, 157, 168, 190, 226, 297, 300, 307, 328, 330, 332
  Capt. Samuel, 132, 159, 188, 226
  Dr. Samuel, 272, 328, 334
  Silas, 132, 189
  Silvanus, 132, 168
  Silvanus, Jr., 168
  Maj. Stillman, 224, 226
  Thomas, 63
  William M., 262, 334
  Wilson, 312
Shaws Island, 266
Sheep marks, 253
Sherman, Amelia, 161
  Andrew, 311
  Anthony, 224, 225, 336
  Betsey W., 312
  Calista, 312
  Charles, 161
  Charles A., 315
  Charles L., 323
  Earl, 219
  Eben, 219
  Hannah C., 315
  Hannah M., 315
  Henry, 146, 301, 304, 326, 332, 337
  Jabez, 80, 311
  John, 59, 224, 297, 300, 309, 330, 332
  Joseph, 312
  Joseph W., 227
  Levi, 159, 300, 301, 304, 312, 332, 336
  Lucy, 311
  Lydia, 312
  Lydia D., 325
  Maria C., 315
  Mary, 310
  Mary E., 323
  Maryette, 313

Sherman, Nathaniel, 104, 300, 301, 326, 332, 336
  Nellie W., 315
  Nelson, 304, 332, 337
  Phebe A., 313
  Rufus, 159, 294, 304, 312
  Sarah A., 315
Sherman hall, 59
Shoemaking, 252
Shoestring Factory, 254
Shurtleff, Abial, 23, 107, 167, 228, 293, 295, 300, 301, 309, 329
  Addie A., 315
  Albert, 117, 243, 317, 337
  Albert T., viii, 233, 328, 332, 337
  Allerton L., 58, 243
  Andrew G., 228
  Barnabas, 68, 148, 196, 300, 301, 307, 309, 330
  Benjamin, 93, 112, 167, 199, 203, 269, 277, 293, 294, 296, 300, 301, 309, 317, 329, 332, 334
  Benjamin L., 319
  Betsey, 310
  Carlton, 262
  Chloe, 323
  Cordelia F., 319
  David, 62, 108, 257, 301, 307, 336
  Deborah, 317
  Deborah, 2nd, 317
  Ebenezer, 131, 167, 172, 173, 317
  Elisabeth, 317
  Eliza B., 319
  Eliza G., 315
  Geneva E., 319
  Flavel, 167
  Flora M., 334
  Francis, 102, 137, 167, 224, 225, 293, 301, 308, 326, 328
  George, 219, 239
  George A., 334
  Gideon, 108, 131, 167, 225, 242, 330, 332, 336
  Gideon, Jr., 167
  Hannah, 311
  Henry F., 235

Shurtleff, Ichabod, 110, 175, 176, 177, 190, 294, 307, 320
   Ichabod, Jr., 321, 338
   James, 132
   James F., 235
   Jemina, 308
   Joel, 61
   John, 104, 295, 307
   Joseph F., 228
   Joseph T., 161
   Levi, 165, 228, 234, 317
   Lizzie G., 315
   Lot, 132, 159, 167, 317, 336
   Lothrop, 300, 328
   Lucy, 312, 321
   Lucy T., 317
   Lula, 319, 324
   Lydia, 310, 312, 318
   Marcy, 318
   Maria Y., 150, 249
   Martha, 318, 321
   Mary, 318
   Mary, 2nd, 318
   Mercy, 165, 321
   Micah G., 235, 315
   Nathaniel, 132, 167, 176, 202
   Nathaniel, of Middleboro, 168
   Oliver L., 262, 319, 338
   Percy W., 262, 325
   Perez T., 228, 237, 249, 319
   Peter, 123, 131, 167
   Phebe, 115, 312
   Priscilla, 165, 318
   Rhoda, 318
   Robert, 131
   Ruth, 318
   Ruth B., 318
   Samuel, 307
   Samuel A., 279, 332, 334
   Stephen, 296, 310, 312, 328, 330, 336
   Sylvia, 175, 320
   Thomas, 131, 167, 202
   William, 14, 164, 165, 295, 315, 318
   William F., 228
Shurtleff Park, 269
Six-Mile brook, 20, 268
Skipper, 192
Skipper Edmund Place, 265
Slug furnace, 275

Small pox, 182, 244, 245
Smith, Caesar, 106
   Rev. Charles, 179
   Rev. George L., 187
   Hannah, 161
   Lizzie L., 323
   Lois, 161
   Perez, 190
   Elder T., 172
   Rev. W., 183
Snappit, 269
Snell, Capt. Josiah, 87
Soldiers Monument, 262
Sons of Temperance, 160
Sons of Veterans, 262
Sonnett, Dorothy, 14
   Samuel, 14
Soule, Asa, 105
   Asaph, 104
   Daniel, 106
   Ebenezer, 106
   Ephraim, 108
   James, 108
   Mary A., 318
   Zephaniah, 105
South Carver, 16, 61
South Meadows, 20
South Meeting House, 121, 123, 151, 165
South Middleboro, 170, 177
Souther, Emma, 161, 323
Southworth, Carl Z., 207
   Eli, 189, 261
   Lucy A., 324
   Thomas, 133, 188, 326, 332
   Thomas M., 189, 190, 243, 324, 328, 334
Sparrow, Richard, 22
Spaulding, George L., 262
Spruce Church, 167
Stamp Act, 92
Standish, Ebenezer, 107
   Moses, 107
   Nathaniel, 132, 201
   Peleg, 110
   Shadrach, 104
   Zachariah, 106
Standish Guards, 229
Stanley, Herbert A., 332
   Mary, 323
   William F., 323, 338
Stetson, Edward, 143
   Jonathan, 318

INDEX OF NAMES

Stetson, Lottie W. C., 315
    Mary Ann, 312
    Rev. Oscar F., 120, 315, 337
Stevens, Edward, 104, 106, 300, 332
    John, 104
    Lemuel, 106
    Sylvanus, 108
    William, 106
Storms, Henry, 323
Storrs, Rev. Richard S., 114
Stringer, Ephraim E., 207
    Horace D., 262
    James H., 232, 234
    John A., 234
    Joseph F., 232, 235
Strong, Rev. Jonathan, 77
Sturtevant, Asa, 107
    Caleb, 105
    Cornelius, 106
    David, 110
    Frances, 101, 102, 104, 106, 110, 131, 199
    Jesse, 102
    Nehemiah, 108
    Noah, 103
    Robert, 102, 199, 201
    Silas, 102, 106
    William, 106, 107
Sturtevant house, 58
Sullivan, Thomas, 239
Swan, Lizzie, 319
    Minnie, 319
    Ponsonby M., 320
Swan Hold, 3, 17, 266
Swedenborg, Emanuel, 115
Sweezy, Estelle, 320
Sweet, Rev. Charles H., 183
Swift, Lester W., 324
    Nehemiah G., 249, 324
    Sarah J., 162, 324

Taber, Adeline M., 323
Tarbox, George F., 239
Tariff, 93
Tarr, Rev. J. J. G., 120
Taylor, John, 110
Tea Kettle, first, 197
Thatcher, Dr. James, 209
Thayer, Isaac, 110
    Peter, 106

Thomas, Abial, 195
    Arad, 318
    Augusta C., 323
    Eli, 61, 168
    Foxwell, 318
    George P., 262
    Herbert I., 323
    Isaiah, 106
    Israel, 127, 132
    John, 87, 176
    Joseph, 135
    Martha, 318
    Mary, 313, 323
    Mary E., 320
    Moses, 318
    Perez, 77
    Seneca R., 227, 229
    Susan, 318
    Thompson P., 189, 229, 323
    William, 199
Thompson, Rev. C. S., 171
    Ezra, 151, 157, 159, 334
    Jacob, 24, 77
    Lothrop, 111
Threshie, Charles, 205, 334
Tibbetts, Andrew S., 229
Tiger Field, 265
Tihonet, 48, 123
Tillson, Ann M. F., 312
    Augustus F., 190, 228, 243, 335
    Bethnel, 168
    Betsey, 311
    Chester F., 161, 324
    Cintia, 321
    Deborah, 324
    Dora F., 263
    Ephraim, 22
    Edmund, 23
    Frank F., 338
    George W., 234
    Hannah, 161
    Harriett, 161
    Hiram, 133, 228
    Hiram B., 232
    Hiram O., 161, 228, 232, 236
    Hope, 213
    Ichabod, 106, 131, 201
    Ida M., 162
    Isaiah, 103, 163, 225, 294, 296, 298, 300, 308, 330
    James, 315

Tillson, James B., 303, 304, 312, 327
  Joanna, 321
  John, 106, 132
  Jonathan, 138, 258, 294, 296, 297, 300, 301, 309, 329
  Louisa, 321
  Lucy, 308
  Luther, 132
  Marcus M., 228
  Phebe, 308
  Polly, 311
  Reba B., 263, 324
  Rebecca, 321
  Samuel, 295
  Stephen, 132
  Thomas, 132, 311
  Timothy, 306
  Truman B., 332
  Wilfred A., 324, 332
  William, 315
  Zenas, 133, 189
Tillson Farm, 62
Tinkham, Ephraim, 14, 22, 108
  Isaac, 107
  Joseph, 110
Tirrell, Rev. Eben, 179
Tisdale, Samuel, 272
Tories, 96, 258
Tory lands, 95, 96, 258
Town, division of, 47, 48, 67
  fined, 259
  hall, 141
  meeting places, 140
  officers, 35
  pound, 142
  records, iv
Totman, Elisabeth, 308
  Joshua, 107, 308
Tobey, Gerard, 206
  Rev. James J., 171, 320, 335
  Mary, 162
  Mary A., 320
Tozer, Rev. William, 179
Tounsend, Rev. Paul, 179
Training field, 258, 269
Tripp, John, 164, 165, 171, 172
Trudo, Nelson, 239
Tubbs, Benjamin, 106
Turner Place, 268
Turner, Hannah, 16

Turner, Job A., 268
Tithingmen, 46, 141

Undesirable citizens, 47
Union meetings, decline of, 81
Union Cemetery, 249
Union Society, 188
United Fruit Co., 283
Universalism, 116
Universalists, 185, 186

Vail, Adoniram W., 229
  Hannah, 318
  Hazadiah, 318
  Isaac B., 232, 235
Valley Forge, 107
Van Schaack, George W., 324
  Mary Page, 273
Vaughan, Abigail, 308
  Alvin, 159, 294, 297, 303, 304
  Austin N., 183, 325
  Bertha F., 320
  Charles E., 325
  Christina C., 320
  Daisey, 263, 324
  Daniel, 104, 107, 300, 304, 308, 310
  David, 168, 318
  Desire, 162, 320
  Edward, 161
  Edwin A., 320
  Elisabeth, 308
  Eunice, 181, 311, 325
  Ezra, 304, 313
  Hannah, 310
  Huldah, 309, 318
  Isaac, 183, 304, 311, 328, 329, 335, 336
  Isaac C., 229
  James, 79, 139, 143, 300, 310, 332
  James A., 161, 172, 173, 243, 249, 320, 329, 335
  J. Erville, 325
  Joseph, 104, 258, 300, 310
  Julia F., 325
  Levi, 115, 158, 159, 224, 225, 293, 296, 297, 300, 301, 303, 304, 305, 310, 330, 336

INDEX OF NAMES

Vaughan, Levi C., 237
  Lewis, 310, 329
  Lydia, 310
  Mrs. L. C., 162
  Minnie M., 325
  Nathaniel, 225, 296, 329
  Phebe, 181, 311, 313
  Polly, 313
  Rebecca, 311
  Samuel, 107, 190
  Sarah S., 311
  Susannah, 310
  Theodore T., 161, 249, 332, 336
  Thomas, 248, 328, 332, 335, 336
  Waitstill, 181, 311, 325
  Webster E. C., 325
  William E. H., 325
  William E. W., 183, 325
Veal, Sylvia, 311
  William, 311
Vinal, Blanche E., 320
  Cora E., 320
  Mrs. E., 320
  Rev. H. Y., 171, 320
Virgin, Melissa C., 313
  Samuel, 313
Voters of Plympton 1708-9, 44, 45

Wade, Abbie W., 325
  Esther A., 325
  Henry W., 325
  William, 239
Walker & Pratt Co., 215, 274
Wallace, Rev. S. Y., 179
Wallis, James, 297
Wankinquoah, 2, 4, 17
Wankinco bog, 220
War of 1812, vii, 241
Ward, Ann Janette, 315
  Ansel, 228
  Ansel B., 234, 335
  Austin, 237
  Benjamin, 96, 97, 106, 121, 122, 131, 168, 226, 227, 318, 332
  Col. Benjamin, 132, 213, 224, 225
  Capt. Benj., 139, 226, 332

Ward, Benjamin, Jr., 168
  Clara E., 315
  Eliab, 141, 146, 243, 318, 332, 335, 337
  Ephraim, 131, 132, 168
  Fred A., 249, 315, 332, 336
  Henry T., 238
  Mary B., 313
  Molly, 318
  Priscilla, 318
  Sally, 318
  Stillman, 313, 332
  Stillman W., 240
  Rev. William I., 179
Warren Association, 165
Warren, Benjamin, 77
Washburn, Asaph, 61, 80, 132, 296, 310, 330
  Charles F., 207
  Deborah, 309
  Elva H., 263, 324
  Emma G., 315
  Henry C., 321
  Jemima, 310
  Jemima D., 312
  Joanna, 321
  John, 106
  Joseph G., 234
  Joseph H., 315
  Louisa, 321
  Marshall A., 235, 321
  Mary, 310
  Mary E., 323
  Nathan H., 323
  Olive S., 318
  Peleg B., 235
  Perez, 133, 310, 329
  Salmon, 202
  Samuel D., 323
  Sarah B., 312
  Sarah W., 323
  Sophia, 310
  Virginia H., 323
  William, 61, 107, 131
Waterman, Amanda, 313
  Benjamin, 202
  Eliphalet, 105
  Hannah, 310
  Ichabod, 202
  Isaac, 86, 196, 297, 307
  James, 229, 312
  John, 22, 296
  Joanna, 311

Waterman, Phebe D., 313
   Robert, 110
   T. Rogers, 202
Wattins, Ruth, 309
Wattis, Sarah, 308
Watson, George, 22, 194
   Goodman, 22
   Mary Jane, 318
   Robert, 318
Watsons Cove Brook, 194
Wenham, 266
Weddling, Charles, 323
West, Samuel, 110
Westgate, Ephraim C., 321
   George H., 207, 323
   Howard G., 207
   Rufus S., 207
Weston, Daniel, 272
   Frank F., 262
   Hannah, 189
   Jabez, 106
   Job, 102
   Seneca T., 262
   Thomas, 197
   Zadock, 103
Wheeler, Sarah L., 313
Wheton, Elisabeth, 308
Whidden, Simeon L., 320
White, Benjamin, 131, 138, 168, 200, 332, 336
   Eva L., 320
   Friend, 209
   George E., 243, 320
   Helen E., 320
   Henry, 232, 234
   Samuel, 202
Whites Mill, 254
Whitehead, James C., 243
   Leah M., 315
Whitcomb, Hannah L., 313
   Dr. Jonah, 245
   Rev. William C., 120, 313
Whiting, Benjamin, 77
   William, 107, 110
Whitton, Azariah, 295
   Joseph, 108
   Elisha, 103
Wild game, 264
Williams, Rev. Edward, 179
   Hilma, 323
   Mary A., 323
Winatuxet, 2, 17

Winberg, Hattie D., 263, 324
   John A., 207
Winter, Almeda E., 315
Witham, John, 229
Witon, Ruth, 308
   Priscilla, 309
   Isaiah, 306
   John, 306
Wolf Island, 266
Woman's Alliance, 263
Woman's C. T. Union, 162
Wood, Benjamin, 306
   David, 103, 104, 295, 308
   Dinah, 318
   G. F., 335
   Lillian F., 320
   Lydia, 308
   Nathaniel, 22
   Noah, 202
   Rebecca, 308
   Samuel, 307
Wright, Adam, 103
   Agatha, 318
   Benjamin, 103
   Caleb, 210, 318
   Ebenezer, 110
   Edmund, 110
   Hattie, 323
   Isaac, 106
   Jacob, 106
   James, 132, 213, 318
   Joseph, 104, 106, 108, 110, 257
   Joshua, 108
   Levi, 106
   Rev. Luther, 113, 120
   Mercy, 318
   Molly, 318
   Moses, 166, 318
   Nathan, 110
   Samuel, 104, 106
   Stephen, 210
   Winslow, 318
   Zadock, 108, 132
   Zoath, 132, 213
Wrightington, Benjamin, 131, 207, 318, 321
   Cynthia M., 315
   David, 318
   Henry, 210, 315
   Thomas, 188
   Thomas W., 228

www.ingramcontent.com/pod-product-compliance
Lightning Source LLC
Chambersburg PA
CBHW060314230426
43663CB00009B/1695